REVIEWS

"Mario Peshev's 'MBA Disrupted' is a masterclass in modern entrepreneurship, blending deep industry insights with actionable strategies to empower any growth exec or tech CEO to take their digital business to new heights."

– Blake Hutchison, CEO, Flippa

"MBA Disrupted: Your Step-by-Step Guide to Bootstrapping $1M+ Digital Businesses" is a deeply masterful compendium of digital entrepreneurship. Mario's understanding of the digital landscape is rare and elite. After reading MBA Disrupted, I sent the book to my son as a must-read.

– James Schramko, JamesSchramko.com

"The proverbial saying goes, 'Those who can't do, teach'. In this book Mario Peshev goes beyond disrupting the business impact of an MBA degree. He disrupts the meaning of this saying by transforming access for aspirational MBA candidates across the globe who need the knowledge and guidance from someone who can not only teach them, but who has also walked in the shoes of the entrepreneurs who he is teaching."

– Eric Siu, CEO Single Grain

"The world does not need more mental models. It needs more hands-on guidance on establishing and growing businesses from entrepreneurs such as Mario, who have been in the trenches and succeeded "against the odds." Most of us do not have Ivy League degrees, years of runway to burn, and hundreds of people to manage. We must secure our business models in the next 3-6 months. Marios's book covers what a small business owner should know about running a business and provides actionable advice on building a business. My favorite part of the book is about processes. It is evident that the author has built and grown multiple businesses and shares proven frameworks with us, readers. I will recommend this book to my mentees who are scaling service and digital businesses."

– Maja Voje, GTM Advisor & Mentor, Best-selling Author of GTM Strategist

CONTENTS

MBA DISRUPTED:

YOUR STEP-BY-STEP GUIDE TO BOOTSTRAPPING $1M+ DIGITAL BUSINESSES

PREFACE

This isn't a book written by a veteran professor at your Ivy League university. My background is different – and so is MBA Disrupted.

As a kid, I built my first website in 1999, creating a Pokédex for the popular TV show Pokémon. Fast-forward a few years and several jobs assembling PCs, writing technical news, and managing websites and Internet forums, I took on my own entrepreneurial journey.

In 2008, in the midst of the Great Recession, I left my job as a software engineer and co-founded a seven-figure product startup on a marketplace in 2009, launched my mid-seven-figure agency in 2010, and went on bootstrapping and selling several businesses since. At the moment of writing this book, I'm running six different companies across various segments, with a heavy focus on my martech agency DevriX and my business advisory Growth Shuttle consulting 400+ clients.

Being an operator has been an integral part of my life. As a "learnaholic," I've picked the agency/consulting route as the best and most efficient way to study hundreds of businesses simultaneously, find out what works and what doesn't, capture trends before they get publicly recognized (and announced), and leverage that as a growth mechanism to pivot into new areas, channels, and directions.

I've used this experience to document my journey by blogging – authoring nearly 1,000 articles across my blogs, my columns in Entrepreneur and Forbes, guest contributions on Inc., Huffington Post, Business 2 Community, Thrive Global, Small Biz Trends, AllBusiness, and many more. Earlier in 2006, my professional path led to creating over 150 courses and presenting 300 conference sessions on technical, business, and marketing topics for organizations such as VMware, SAP, Saudi Aramco, Software AG, and CERN; various universities and colleges, private academies, and schools.

Lastly, I've been involved in the global startup ecosystem as an angel investor for 20+ startups, a business advisor for hundreds of fast-growing businesses and established enterprises, and a brand ambassador for some incredible global companies.

This book is my read on entrepreneurship after 25 years in digital, being personally involved in launching, managing, and growing over a hundred projects in different verticals.

Unlike traditional education, this is a practical workbook; instead of theoretical exercises based on outdated management models from the 1920s, I will cover what works today – a mix of proven management models infused with practical strategies for founding companies, hiring teams, managing financial models, selling, building marketing funnels, designing technical solutions, competing in a global market, and replicating these successful models continuously to isolate the "luck factor."

No matter what type of digital product or solution you want to build and get your hands dirty with, I have the underlying model covered in this book. If you consider yourself an experienced founder or manager who wants to dive into a specific chapter, go ahead. Otherwise, read the book cover-to-cover to uncover the fine details that make the system work, including relevant tools I personally use, resources I recommend, and other entrepreneurs worth following in the process.

This interactive book also includes access to my personal community, where you can connect with other students on the journey, new and experienced founders, and practitioners in building digital businesses. This is my gift to you to maximize the journey and transition the book into an ongoing workshop with success stories and meaningful launches once you're ready to roll your sleeves and go live.

Make sure you head to **mbadisrupted.com** for additional resources and ongoing lessons for your alternative MBA education.

Good luck,

Mario

INTRODUCTION

When it comes to professional education, MBA programs are one of the key indicators used to gauge whether an international college is reputable. After all, universities are supposed to provide practical value and open the doors to a successful career.

Students around the world pursue different passions, but the leading educational institutions see the highest demand for professions with a high forecasted return on investment: technology and engineering, consulting, law, medicine, economy, and politics. Universities like Yale and Harvard have been nurturing Supreme Court judges and CIA agents. MIT is where Buzz Aldrin gained a doctorate in astronautics before taking a step on the moon after Richard Feynman laid the foundations of modern physics earlier. Many Fortune 500 executives or global tech corporation leaders like Larry Page, Peter Thiel, or Sundar Pichai came from Stanford.

Colleges have long been perceived as the launchpad for successful career growth. The more lucrative the opportunity to grow in a professional capacity, the harder it is to enroll and the more it costs to stay on track for the full course of education.

The Master of Business Administration (MBA) has been one of the most esteemed professional paths, providing a broad blueprint for running a professional organization: finance, leadership, marketing, operations management, business analytics, and international economy. Regarding career opportunities, job satisfaction, minimum pay, and the number of positions available in that bracket, MBA is among the top. Why?

- Tens of millions of professional opportunities in a management capacity for white-collar jobs
- High reward and professional recognition for entrepreneurial roles (taking over or growing successful companies)
- High starting base pay
- Extremely high pay ranges at Fortune 500 and other global corporations
- Providing the high-level skills required to run the largest organizations in the world (in theory).

You can compare MBAs with any other industry and point to a number of wealthy individuals in each category (sports, art, healthcare), but not every actor ends up starring in a Hollywood film. A similar destiny follows musicians, athletes, economists, and politicians. The disparity is too high, with one success story for a thousand graduates and insufficient return for full-time roles available for everyone else.

However, traditional MBA programs are also flawed when we zoom out and consider the broader macroeconomic ecosystem.

1. Some colleges are better than others

Studying for an MBA at Harvard or Yale may be rewarding and impactful, but that doesn't translate to every single university on the planet. Students often get lost in interpreting the marketing lingo for university and college campaigns pitching their own programs. The actual quality varies - and errs on the lower side of efficiency.

2. Outdated curriculum

Even in more traditional programs that require foundational knowledge and high-level principles of economics, leadership, or management, innovation is bound to happen - new leadership principles, progressive entrepreneurs establishing new models, and organizational principles like EOS or OKRs that take years before they are even considered for the syllabus. It's not uncommon for university programs to be dragging behind with a decade or more compared to practical principles used on the field.

3. Highly dependent on individual professors

A university program depends on the full curriculum and its relevance, the quality level of materials, time spent on every business category, and of course, the professor teaching the class.

The best professors are highly skilled and experienced, motivating the auditorium, great public speakers, actively engaged, should go through an application process to take on a role, and often face different limitations preventing them from other professional occupancies. Also, a teacher's salary is a fraction of what an experienced executive earns to lead an organization, further limiting the number of qualified or motivated people taking on this role.

4. Theoretical vs. practical education

Traditional education has a bias in placing students into a predefined bracket of roles and positions. The current way of learning relies heavily on reading, quoting sources, and memorizing dates or events. However, in practice, executives have to face day-to-day programs, have access to reference sources (and the Internet), and navigate interpersonal conflicts or negotiate with stakeholders on matters that aren't covered in every textbook.

5. Contradicting goals between students and universities

Most reputable universities partner with established corporations and organizations locally and nationally, supporting the teaching process through resources, donations, equipment, access to internship programs, and additional exclusivity (hiring from a specific university). This can shape a program into something that serves the local market and a group of partners, but not necessarily applicable to aspirational CEOs of global organizations (or entrepreneurship in the first place).

6. Rigid curriculum

This same theoretical program is evaluated based on prejudice or a specific set of instructions and requirements assessed by the professor. This "inside the box" thinking shapes a cohort of graduates following the same mental and organizational models everywhere.

Most successful startups exist because they are unique, creative, and disruptive—they do not stick to the old ways and norms. An executive's value is finding niche opportunities and flaws in global processes and exploiting them with a radical solution. This is the exact opposite of what a high GPA is about.

7. Financial burden and lack of access

Accessing the top programs in top colleges is not just nearly impossible but also extremely expensive and hardly achievable. If you don't live anywhere near these schools and can't afford to relocate and pay tuition fees, this turns into a grueling effort compared to kids of other alumni who may get special treatment and a shortcut into the process, plus additional support from wealthier relatives.

In essence, while traditional education definitely has some pros, it's made available to a small number of individuals, requires complete devotion for several years (compared to gaining actual work experience), costs a ton ($230,280 for a 4-year private university, according to CollegeData.com). Of course, that's if you are able to get in at all.

When it comes to entrepreneurship, MBA - or college for that matter - has not been the traditional path forward for a long list of notable figures, including Oprah Winfrey, Steve Jobs, Mark Zuckerberg, Dick Cheney, Bill Gates, Tiger Woods, Ashton Kutcher, Ralph Lauren, Steven Spielberg, Vin Diesel, Travis Kalanick, Michael Dell, Dustin Moskovitz, Matt Mullenweg, John and Patrick Collison, Larry Ellison, and Richard Branson. This stems from a combination of luck, starting their journey at a very early age (often at school), creativity, experimentation, building hobby projects late at night, or pairing with other future entrepreneurs to sell door-to-door or uncover problems that haven't been solved yet.

They picked up the essential skills of building a business on the go: pitching ideas and products to early adopters, selling the vision to co-founders and early hires, building marketing funnels, developing operational models that scale, leveraging the latest digital channels and solutions as a launchpad to their own ideas.

This led to the creation and evolution of some of the most influential products, tools, services, marketplaces, e-commerce stores, communities, and networks on the planet.

"MBA Disrupted" compiles the most integral skills and principles you need as you prepare to start a digital business. We will review bootstrapped businesses and the opportunities to fund as needed, what the leading CEOs have in common, how to conduct market validation and assess ideas early on, what business models exist in the digital world (and which one to pick), how to put each of them in action (with practical steps, strategies, and tools), other successful examples you can follow, what go-to-market motions are most practical for founders, different pricing models and reinvestment strategies, the leading business challenges that executives face over time, and other best practices I've picked up after 25 years in tech and 16 years of building and advising companies.

This self-guided book won't cost the hundreds of thousands of dollars for a professional Ivy League degree and could be studied alongside your internship or a day job. You don't need to apply for the opportunity to learn the ropes. Knowledge is free. It's the ambition, hard work, determination, and perseverance that makes the difference. "MBA Disrupted" is focused on digital businesses and provides the necessary skills to start from zero without funding and grow to seven figures or higher in revenue. Whether you need additional capital to start and explore funding opportunities or not, these skills will carry you in both cases.

Overview of Funding Models for Businesses

Almost all companies I've founded were bootstrapped, but I have dealt with VC-funded businesses and acquisitions, too. I managed and sold a VC-backed company in early 2024. Also, as an angel investor, I have supported dozens of scaling businesses in exchange for equity.

In certain cases, launching a company without external funding is practically impossible. However, almost all of these cases are outside the digital realm: think of healthcare, logistics, and manufacturing. I have a health tech investment that would be impossible without external funding. The hardware device startups I invest in and advise require millions in R&D and manufacturing power to distribute and deploy until the model makes sense.

When it comes to venture capital and other sources of funding, the key is time to market and achieving high adoption levels as fast as possible. In competitive spaces, even if you launch an idea quickly, you may be unable to scale and acquire a significant portion of the market before a large corporation decides to invest $20M to build this in-house or acquire a vendor that catches up in six months and runs 10 times faster thanks to funding. So, making the right choices early on requires understanding the current funding landscape.

1. Bootstrapping

Bootstrapping involves financing a business using personal savings, revenue generated by the business itself, or assistance from friends and family. This funding model allows founders to retain full control over their venture, avoiding external pressures and obligations.

However, bootstrapping comes with its set of challenges. The availability of funds may be limited, constraining the scale and speed of growth. Entrepreneurs might need to make sacrifices and prioritize frugal spending to make every dollar count. Recruiting top talent may be impacted by limited budgets compared to better funded organizations. Yet, bootstrapping develops a strong sense of discipline and resourcefulness, instilling a lean and agile mindset within the organization.

2. Venture Capital (VC)

Venture capital funding is the lifeblood of many high-growth startups. It involves investors providing capital in exchange for equity ownership, typically targeting businesses with disruptive innovations and exponential growth potential. Venture capitalists are willing to take on higher risks in anticipation of substantial returns on their investments.

For startups, VC funding offers more than just financial resources. It often includes mentorship, extending connections to key players, and additional brand and PR exposure. However, pursuing rapid growth and profitability may lead to intense pressure and scrutiny from investors, requiring founders to navigate a delicate balance between vision and investor expectations.

3. Angel Investors

Angel investors play a pivotal role in supporting early-stage startups, providing capital, expertise, and mentorship to entrepreneurs. These affluent individuals often invest their funds in exchange for equity ownership or convertible debt, believing in the potential of promising ventures.

I have been personally involved with 20+ startups as an angel investor myself, along with esteemed VC funds, private equities, investment bankers, and other institutional investors.

Unlike venture capitalists, angel investors are typically more hands-on and involved in the day-to-day operations of the businesses they support. They offer strategic guidance, valuable industry insights, and access to their extensive networks, empowering entrepreneurs to navigate challenges and capitalize on opportunities.

4. Bank Loans

Bank loans are a traditional source of funding for businesses, providing access to capital in exchange for repayment with interest over a specified period. These loans may be secured by collateral or based on the borrower's creditworthiness and business viability.

For entrepreneurs, bank loans offer flexibility and autonomy in managing their businesses. They can use the funds for various purposes, such as launching new products, expanding operations, or covering operational expenses. However, securing a bank loan may require a solid business plan, collateral, and a favorable credit history, posing challenges for startups and small businesses with limited assets.

5. Crowdfunding

Crowdfunding has been popularized thanks to online platforms such as Kickstarter, Indiegogo, and GoFundMe where entrepreneurs can showcase their projects and ask for contributions from supporters worldwide.

One of the key advantages of crowdfunding is its ability to validate product concepts and engage with potential customers directly.

Entrepreneurs can gauge market demand, gather feedback, and refine their offerings before bringing them to market. However, running a successful crowdfunding campaign requires effective marketing, compelling storytelling, and transparent communication with backers.

6. Grants

Grants are non-repayable funds designed to support specific projects or initiatives, from scientific research (R&D) to community development programs. These funds are typically awarded by governments, foundations, or organizations based on eligibility criteria and alignment with the funder's objectives. The SBA in the United States and the European Union both offer a long list of relevant programs worth applying to.

For entrepreneurs and innovators, grants offer a valuable source of funding to pursue innovative ideas and address pressing challenges. They provide financial support without the burden of repayment, allowing recipients to focus on advancing their projects and achieving impact.

However, competition for grants can be fierce, requiring applicants to demonstrate creativity, feasibility, and potential for societal benefit.

7. Initial Public Offering (IPO)

The ultimate goal for many startups is to go public, retain partial ownership of their business, unlock liquidity opportunities by selling and buying shares on the open market, and invite other global investors to trade and manage the equity pool five days a week. An IPO represents a significant milestone in an executive's business journey, providing access to additional capital for expansion, funding acquisitions, and securing liquidity to early investors and employees.

While IPOs may be deemed nearly impossible for day-to-day entrepreneurs, there are workarounds that could unlock unmatched opportunities over time. Smaller (local) stock exchanges can be dramatically easier to list on, assuming you want to pursue that path and reach a certain profitability level in some local markets. I've worked closely with entrepreneurs listing on national exchanges in Europe (and some in Asia) that capitalize on liquidity, additional exposure in regional markets, additional support through individual and institutional investors, and incredible PR opportunities featuring local success stories.

Understanding the different funding tiers for digital startups is critical to building a successful business. Some businesses keep growing continuously by raising every year or two for a decade. Others never take on external funding. Hybrid options are also available - growing a sustainable business to a certain point and raising a larger round for massive expansion or acquisitions or raising once and holding off any additional rounds after.

During periods of uncertainty, investors may become more selective in their investment decisions, focusing on **businesses with strong fundamentals**, proven traction, and robust growth potential. Startups seeking funding at this time must demonstrate resilience, adaptability, and a compelling value proposition to keep attracting venture capital over time.

This is why prioritizing profitability and a healthy business model that can sustain itself over time is more important than ever. This book will provide the right foundations for building a business designed to withstand the test of time.

PART ONE

FOUNDATIONS FOR SUCCESS

CHAPTER ONE

THE DIGITAL CEO MINDSET

"Whatever the mind can conceive and believe, it can achieve."

– Napoleon Hill

Back in my early entrepreneurship days – as a teenager – I was obsessed with tactics and strategies.

The initial effort of launching a business is about brute force. It's about continuous efforts and iterations, incremental improvements, and a series of hit-or-miss events on the way.

If you study the greatest world leaders, you will quickly discover that they all work "on" the business, not "in" it. They've elevated their role into visionaries, delegating the day-to-day decision-making to their C-suite.

While it's dramatically harder to achieve that in the early days as a bootstrap founder, the concept remains the same: you need to build a business model that is not directly dependent on you.

Michael E. Gerber succinctly summarized this in his book, *The E-Myth Revisited: Why Most Small Businesses Don't Work and What to Do About It*, writing, "If your business depends on you, you don't own a business—you have a job. And it's the worst job in the world because you're working for a lunatic!"

Veteran entrepreneurs know that growing a business takes years, and legacy businesses grow in decades. It's not a sprint. **It's a marathon.**

This demands developing a resilient mindset that lasts through ups and downs, one that caters to your family, your mental and physical health, and your personal journey alongside your professional career.

If you haven't reached that stage yet and are busy in the trenches, you may decide to skip this chapter and jump straight to the operational topics. And that's fine. However, in the long run, lacking a 5, 10, and 20-year vision for the future will be an obstacle to creating a sustainable strategy that compounds with time.

Pick wisely, and in the meantime, here's what the digital CEO mindset looks like.

Building Mental Strength as a Digital CEO

The glory of successful founders is attractive on the outside, but the grueling day-to-day work during the first months or even years is a painful journey no rational human wants to go through. It demands a mindset capable of weathering storms, embracing challenges, and driving innovation. It's borderline paranoia and always looking around for the next problem to solve and fire to put out.

My first book, *126 Steps to Becoming a Successful Entrepreneur: The Entrepreneurship Fad and the Dark Side of Going Solo*, aimed to reveal the true challenges entrepreneurs face in their first months (or years) on the job: the feast and famine, grinding to close their first sales, wearing multiple hats 80+ hours a week, scraping to manage product quality alongside marketing while following regulations.

The German philosopher Friedrich Nietzsche once said, "That which does not kill us makes us stronger."

In other words - **CEOs grow a thick skin over time.**

When a major problem occurs, you have two options: overcome the obstacles and find a solution, or give up. Most CEOs would go through fire and ice before resorting to a regular 9-to-5 job with mundane processes and repetitive work.

In 1519, a Spanish explorer and conquistador, Hernán Cortés, pursued the treasures of the Aztecs with 11 ships and a crew of 100 sailors and 500 soldiers. His army was vastly outnumbered and some soldiers tried to escape. Cortés gave an order to burn the ships and left no choice but to fight until their last breath.

That wasn't the end for everyone. Part of the army survived, and they got a hold of the treasure.

Plenty of problems appear to be critical, but at the end, they should be solved.

- **Lost a client?** Go out there and start pitching again.
- **Broken feature in the product?** Get the tech team on it and release a fix as soon as possible.
- **Constant regressions from the core team?** Talk to your CTO and figure out what the long-term sustainable strategy is.
- **Have to work late at night on a proposal?** Dive in, make it happen, look for future options to offload this standard procedure or brainstorm on how to mitigate last-minute changes later on.

The role of a CEO isn't easy in the first place. Constant changes and surprises are not abnormal and at some point, they become a daily routine.

If being a CEO is among your highest priorities, work hard and make it work. If you are constantly complaining about lack of sleep, no time for family or friends, or are failing to see the future ahead, figure out a long-term solution within the business, find a replacement for you, or simply go back to a regular 9-to-5 and disregard all responsibilities.

Fixed vs. Growth Mindset

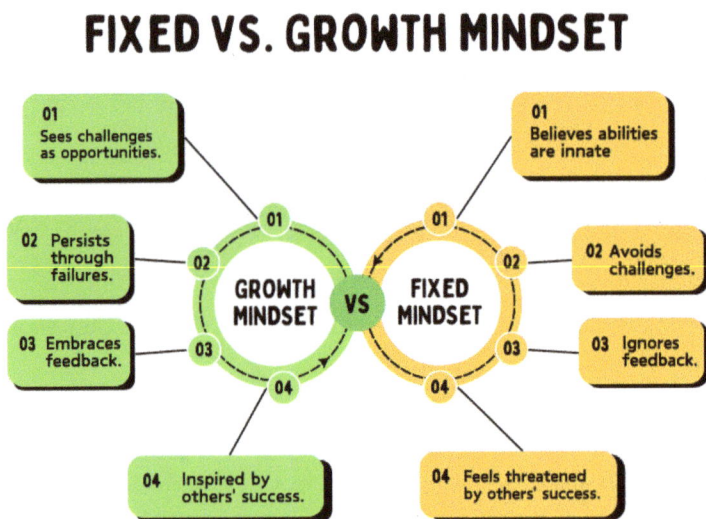

FIXED VS. GROWTH MINDSET

01 Sees challenges as opportunities.

02 Persists through failures.

03 Embraces feedback.

04 Inspired by others' success.

01

02

03

04

GROWTH MINDSET

VS

FIXED MINDSET

01

02

03

04

01 Believes abilities are innate

02 Avoids challenges.

03 Ignores feedback.

04 Feels threatened by others' success.

There are two primary types of mindsets: **fixed and growth**. Carol Dweck, a prominent psychologist renowned for her groundbreaking work on mindset theory research, has shed light on the differences between these two mindsets and their impact on success and achievement.

Fixed Mindset

Individuals with a fixed mindset believe that their basic qualities, such as intelligence or talent, are innate and unchangeable.

28

Consequently, they tend to avoid challenges, give up easily when faced with obstacles, view effort as fruitless, ignore constructive criticism, and feel threatened by the success of others. As a result, they often fall short of reaching their full potential.

Growth Mindset

People with a growth mindset believe that their abilities can be developed through hard work, dedication, and perseverance.

They see challenges as opportunities for growth, persist in the face of failure, view effort as the path to mastery, embrace constructive criticism as a means of improvement, and find inspiration in the success of others. Logically, they tend to achieve higher levels of success and fulfillment.

As the CEO on top of a business, it is essential to develop, nurture, and incentivize a growth mindset.

Nobody else would care as much about the company as you.

If you want to drive innovation and stay ahead of the competition, you are the first person on the battlefield leading everyone else and hoping for some backup in the process. In a rapidly changing digital landscape, where innovation is the key to staying ahead of the competition, **having a growth mindset can mean the difference between success and failure**. It's about being open to new ideas, embracing change, and continually striving for improvement.

This is what every successful leader has gone through in the early days. No matter if you're a proponent of Zuckerberg, Musk, Bezos,

Gates, Jobs or not, isolate emotions from hard facts and study the recurring patterns of what makes a successful business:

- Athletes watch games with other athletes
- Artists study international art
- Musicians attend concerts and draw inspiration from singing, dancing, stage arrangements
- Actors watch other movies and take notes.

Even the best out there study their environment closely and work with professional coaches and advisors who help them elevate higher.

In short, the digital CEO mindset is not just about technical skills or business acumen; it's about having the right mindset—the mindset of a resilient, adaptable, and growth-oriented leader.

How the 2020s Changed Entrepreneurship Forever

The past few years have been a great learning opportunity for us. The COVID-19 era has changed a lot of our working habits, and the concept of onsite work has transitioned from a "work from home" camp to a "return to office" corporate policy. Employees have bounced back and forth, between lockdowns and going back to the office, dealing with their own scheduled changes or major life updates, like relocating to a different city, state, or country.

2018 and 2019 were years of rapid growth and evolution - investment in research and development, pioneering changes in the metaverse, in-depth blockchain development, innovations in robotics and other areas. Then, the 2020 pandemic turned the world around, with corporations learning how to communicate and interact remotely and schools adopting online teaching in a few days. Governments kept pumping up stimulus checks to keep the economy afloat as best as possible, forgiving student loans, and printing money wherever possible. This unprecedented shift led to future consequences a year later.

2021 marked a new period called **"The Great Resignation,"** with a record number of employees voluntarily quitting their jobs. The mental shift of everything happening around the globe, the overwhelming fear of the virus, and remote work opening up opportunities to relocating or transitioning one's career entirely, led to a major macro shift as well. Investments in cryptocurrencies or other alternative assets grew dramatically, and popular exchanges like FTX amassed fortunes practically overnight.

Then, in 2022, these same exchanges were shut down and founders were attacked by the **Federal Trade Commission.** The US inflation rate in June of 2022 reached 9.1%, and the Federal Reserve went on an aggressive journey of raising its interest rate to the highest point since the global financial recession of 2008.

Several banks went under, global corporations conducted their first layoffs in 15 years (or ever), mortgage rates skyrocketed to record-high numbers, broad AI adoption kicked in, and replacing people with robots became a realistic possibility for the first time ever. This, and a myriad of additional factors, contributed to rapid and unexpected changes happening overnight, existing strategies failing to deliver, long-lasting brands filing for bankruptcy, venture funding capital withdrawing with over 80%, unicorn startups failing to raise follow-on rounds and trimming up to 90% of their staff unexpectedly.

Just five years ago, all of that would have been unthinkable, resembling the plot of an apocalyptic dystopian movie. And yet, here we are.

These global changes affected every single individual. But founders and executives faced significant challenges - many for the first time ever - and younger leaders who haven't felt the **Great Recession of 2008 or the dot com boom of 2000** were not prepared to face the backlash of a massive down market.

This walk down memory lane aims to illustrate the unpredictable challenges a founding executive faced in the past few years. As the economy goes through ups and downs, the reality is that, ever since World War II, the US has been facing a new recession every 6.5 years on average. We were lucky to nearly double this timeframe since 2008. Many millennial founders and Gen Z never considered the cyclical market trends in motion. But resilient leaders building a business that lasts understand that every growth trend has an equally opposing force, and certain skills are mandatory for survival - both individually (as a leader) and for the business.

Must-Have Leadership Skills for CEOs

If you are still determined to take the high road of launching a successful business, you have to be ready for the ups and downs of the market. Here are several critical leadership skills you need to keep top of mind at all times and continuously develop to stay on top of the market.

INTEGRITY
- Self-Aware
- Accountable

DIRECTION
- Communicative
- Empowering

INNOVATION
- Curious
- Experimental

THE AGILE LEADER

ENGAGEMENT
- Inclusive
- Collaborative

URGENCY
- Focused
- Decisive

1. Developing Focus

Developing focus involves mastering the art of prioritization, allocating resources efficiently, and maintaining clarity of mind and clear directions and processes for your team. It requires discipline and clear understanding of core objectives, dismissing and ignoring hundreds of small escalations and surprises popping up on a daily basis.

As a digital CEO, you have to be able to tell a small wave from a tsunami and only act on the destructive forces coming your way. Working in the business, it is tempting to hop on every single problem

- from a product bug through a customer ticket to a typo on your website.

First things first - prioritize what matters and focus on high-impact objectives that you, as a founder, are uniquely positioned and can execute for the best of the business.

Continuously improve your strategic, operational, and personal focus skills across the organization. Build repetitive processes and develop **standard operating procedures (SOPs)** for your team. Design an effective and repetitive feedback loop process through weekly meetings or reports and KPI dashboards and scorecards. Study organizational and operational methodologies like **EOS (the Entrepreneur Operating System), OKRs, 4DX** for goal setting and distribution of responsibilities internally.

2. Resilience

CEOs are facing an aggregated amount of stress compared to full-time employees in virtually every organization. Multiple studies reported mental illnesses, shortened life duration, critical physical condition in executives and founders unable to cope with the levels of stress on the job. There is an old joke in the funding circles: "Entrepreneurs sleep like babies; they wake up crying every two hours."

This is only natural - you are solely responsible for every step of the process:

- Recruiting your leadership and executive team
- Determining the corporate data protection and legal policies
- Approving budget allocations and accounting, the high-level business model value proposition, pricing, go-to-market model.

Every step of the process goes through you. Even at a later stage, organizations with thousands or tens of thousands of employees making critical mistakes can still be tracked down to the CEO. For example, a worker who makes a critical mistake is hired by a supervisor who has a manager reporting to a director, bubbling up to a VP who reports to a C-level hired by the CEO.

Every single business is bound to make mistakes. As a leader, you have to understand this is inevitable and do your best to minimize these, keep your customers happy, provide a product quality that's as high as possible, and avoid burning out or going crazy in the process.

I always recommend studying other great leaders and founders going through life challenges and still making it possible. Being a CEO is a lonely job. Surround yourself with other executives, join mastermind groups or entrepreneurship organizations, and normalize your levels of tolerance and stress as best as possible.

You will find different references and stories by founders and executives I've studied over the years or developed connections within the process. Also, I will include additional resources on the book's website, mbadisrupted.com.

3. Empathy

If you take the emotional detachment of being a resilient leader too literally and extract yourself from the day-to-day of the business, the risk is going out of touch with your peers who make your business possible: your customers and your team.

As a leader, you are not just responsible for making strategic decisions and driving results; you are also responsible for leading and inspiring a team of individuals. Empathetic leaders are not only great communicators, but they also possess a deep understanding of their team members' needs, concerns, and aspirations.

Gary Vaynerchuk, one of the most inspiring entrepreneurs of this generation with a net worth of over $220M, said., "When you realize you work for your employees and not the other way around, things start to change." Understanding the symbiosis between the founding team and the early members entrusting your company – not just any other firm or corporation out there – builds a strong empathetic connection that great leaders possess.

In my early days as an executive, I maintained a list of the top three goals and priorities for each of my team members. Everyone had a top three among a list of aspirations: aiming for a leadership role, frequent salary bumps, working on interesting projects, taking on notable brand roles, mentoring people, flexible hours or more time off for family duties, bringing their pets to the office, attending more events or mastering public speaking, and getting corporate support for their charity project.

People are driven by different needs and passions. The closer you get to your core team, the more respect and support you earn back from them.

4. Adaptability

Going through the turbulent market dynamics of the past years, successful businesses had to adapt or disappear. Being flexible and agile in a market that keeps mutating is a core skill that executive leaders have to master as early as possible.

Adaptability is a double-edged sword. You are either too slow to adapt to market shifts or rebuild processes under every indication that your radar intercepts. What tells a good decision from a bad one is a **matter of experience** - and often, trial and error.

Stephen McCranie once said, "The master has failed more times than the beginner has even tried." If you fail to experiment, you may end up like Kodak - the once leading photo giant that fell behind due to its reluctance to embrace the new opportunities in digital photography.

We will review some practical topics in this book - a handful of business models and monetization opportunities, different market groups and personas **(ICPs)**, along with go-to-market strategies to bring your product to market. Adaptable leaders are always ready to refine and switch their offers to test out new markets and categories and integrate different motions for revenue generation or customer retention.

5. Forecasting

Forecasting is about projecting different scenarios and strategies for the future based on current trends, market conditions, and business dynamics.

We've seen dramatic shifts throughout macroeconomic history over the past several years, then back to the **Great Recession of 2008 or the Dot-com bubble in 2000**. History repeats itself and has been studied extensively by economists, investors, executives, and consultants. Ray Dalio takes this a step further in his book *Principles for Dealing with the Changing World Order*, studying 500 years of global disruptions of wealth and power among the leading nations of the time. Relying on these global patterns will make you a better digital CEO – one who excels at forecasting, business plan development, pivoting, and iterating whenever needed.

Forecasting enables you to make informed decisions about resource allocation, budgeting, and strategic planning. Mapping out future revenues, expenses, and cash flows helps you ensure that your organization remains financially viable and stable in the face of uncertainty.

When forecasting becomes integral in your own workflow, if you anticipate a downturn in sales due to economic factors, you can implement cost-saving measures or diversify your revenue streams to mitigate the impact on your bottom line. Predictive models can be your main competitive edge in business.

6. Risk Management

As a CEO, you must always be prepared for whatever challenges or uncertainties may lie ahead. This means anticipating potential risks, developing contingency plans, and mitigating their impact on your organization's operations and objectives.

One anecdotal example of self-imposed risk management is a product called "Chaos Monkey" that Netflix designed. The premise of this service is to randomly terminate production servers and instances, mimicking failovers, outages, and server faults. Instead of waiting for a nightmare to happen, their engineering team has proactively created a simulated failover environment to better prepare for replication scenarios, backups, and multiple parallel plans for streaming continuously in the event of unexpected surprises.

Risk management also involves being able to adapt to changing market conditions and business environments. For example, if you're the CEO of a manufacturing company facing supply chain disruptions due to geopolitical tensions, you can mitigate the risk by diversifying your supplier base, establishing strategic partnerships, and investing in alternative sourcing channels.

This book will cover a number of business strategies to design offers, structure pricing plans, reach customers, develop a strong brand, manage consistent workflows. Understanding the major shifts in the market or hard dependencies for your business will help you focus better on areas you need to diversify on and safety buffers to keep handy if it comes to that.

7. Communication Skills

Your ability to effectively communicate plays a pivotal role in your leadership and the success of your organization.

Communication translates to all mediums: text, voice, video, creatives, and more. It's equally valid internally – with your staff and partners – and externally – with prospects, clients, and investors. It relates to company broadcasts, team messaging, public speaking, creating presentation decks, organizing meetings, collectively making it a critical business skill.

The compounding efforts of becoming a strong communicator pay off over time. You will learn how to vet, hire, and onboard talent, convey your product offer to prospects and partners, organize effective meetings, structure internal communication processes, handle conflict resolution cases, amplify the mission externally, and build a strong culture by following core communication principles.

A great primer on clear and effective communication is Amazon's guide, "Write like an Amazonian." I will link it in the resource section of the book's website, mbadisrupted.com.

Now that we have covered the core philosophy of leadership and executive management, let's move closer to startup viability and how to validate your idea.

CHAPTER TWO

DEFINING YOUR MARKET, NICHE, AND PERSONA

CB Insights is a reputable research organization that studies failing startups over the past year. In their 2021 analysis, 38% of all failing startups went under due to running out of cash, and 35% closed due to no market need.

We can safely attribute the majority of the first group to limited market need as well: after all, high-demand startups with great product-market fit would have been able to grow fast and stay afloat even without additional funding.

Validating your idea helps you avoid wasting time, effort, and money on something that might not work out.

So, how do you validate your idea as a digital CEO? It starts with a few key steps:

- Doing thorough research
- Finding your niche
- Understanding the problem your idea solves
- Evaluating your potential product market
- Identifying your ideal customers

Let's start with the niche definition and take it from there.

Defining Your Niche

In a competitive digital landscape, the only way to launch a successful business is by providing effective solutions to existing problems. But if you try to sell everything to everyone, this won't resonate with your prospective buyers, and you will never close business this way.

It's tempting to follow the industry giants and market leaders in consumer goods or companies like Apple or Samsung, which sell a handful of devices to half the planet. First, not every business is **business-to-consumer (B2C).**

For self-exploratory topics, I often refer to Eastern cultures in different parts of Asia. Niche exploration can be derived from the principles of **Ikigai** - a Japanese concept first traced back to the Heian period in Japan, somewhere between 794 and 1185 AD. In Japanese, "iki" means "alive" and "gai" means "worth". Simply put, this model, studied more thoroughly over the past 60 years, has been looking for a clear definition of what makes us worthwhile and what keeps us moving. This framework can be determined with four simple questions:

IKIGAI

- What I love?
- What I am good at?
- What the world needs?
- What I can be rewarded for?

Finding the cross-section between these four questions will reveal an overlap between your passions, skills, market needs, and problems worth paying for.

Let's break down how to get there step by step.

DEFINING YOUR NICHE: 4 STEPS

01 Evaluating your passion and skills

02 Establishing niche brackets

03 Ensuring a strong market presence

04 Narrowing down your niche

1. Evaluating Your Passion and Skills

Start by exploring thoroughly your passions and skills.

Ask yourself some pointed questions:

- What topics or areas truly ignite your passion?
- What are you naturally talented at or have a deep expertise in?
- Do you have any hobbies or interests that you're particularly enthusiastic about?

These are all important factors to consider when trying to identify your unique niche.

2. Establishing Niche Brackets

When defining the potential niche, you can consider various criteria such as:

- **Price Point:** Do you aim to serve the luxury market, the moderate-income segment, or more budget-conscious consumers?
- **Level of Quality:** Will you focus on premium, handmade, or more economical products and services?
- **Geographic:** Are you targeting prospects in a specific country, city, or even a particular neighborhood?
- **Demographics:** Is your niche defined by gender, age, income level, or educational background?
- **Psychographics:** Do your customers share specific values, interests, or attitudes?
- **Firmographics:** Are you focusing on businesses of a certain size, industry, or revenue range?
- **Technographics:** Does your target market prefer using specific types of technologies or platforms?
- **Behavioral:** Are there particular purchasing behaviors or usage patterns that define your customer base?

While working on the brand messaging and the value proposition of DevriX back in 2012-2013, our slogan was "bridging WordPress and the enterprise." While outsourced vendors and BPOs were charging $15 - $30 per hour, we billed $60 - $80 at the time as a niche consultancy providing specialized boutique services in a specific technical stack.

Back then, WordPress represented under 15% of all websites online (it now powers over 43% or nearly half of all websites). Most service providers were not professional engineers but rather self-taught site builders and designers creating simple sites. We brought in the big guns thanks to our experience with telecoms and banks in the enterprise space, and we worked with this higher tier segment when WordPress scalability was at the top of our minds.

This further established specific segments that work better for us - industries, locations (New York, California, Massachusetts), company size (50-200 and 200-500 employees), and specific personas.

3. Ensuring a Strong Market presence for Your Niche

One of the most crucial steps in finding your niche is determining whether there is a large enough market to support it. 99% of the time, you don't want to serve a market with a total of 100 potential clients worldwide. This limits your expansion opportunities significantly - unless your deal size is $500K or higher or the market is expected to grow exponentially due to a groundbreaking discovery or an innovative technology introduced recently.

When evaluating the viability of your potential niches, there are a few key metrics you'll want to explore:

- **Total Addressable Market (TAM):** The total potential revenue that your business could generate if you were to capture 100% of your target market. For example, if you're considering an entrepreneurial digital magazine for UK males aged 18-35, your TAM would be the total revenue generated by all businesses serving that demographic.

- **Size of the Niche Market:** The portion of the overall TAM that represents your specific target market. In our case, this would be the portion of 18-35 males in the UK subscribing to digital magazines in business-related topics. Not all individuals in a demographic are potential customers of the niche idea.
- **Growth Rate of the Niche Market:** The rate at which your target niche market is growing over time. Seek niches that are expected to grow with time, not stalled or shrinking ones. If you are to pick between an AI-driven startup or serving billboard or newspaper businesses, they will run in opposing directions.

The basic equation for calculating TAM is quite straightforward:

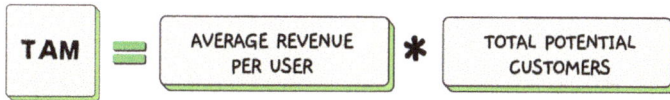

$$\text{TAM} = \text{AVERAGE REVENUE PER USER} * \text{TOTAL POTENTIAL CUSTOMERS}$$

Let's break this down step-by-step:

1. **Average Revenue Per User (ARPU):** This is the average amount of revenue you expect to generate from each customer or user of your product or service. This can be calculated by looking at your current pricing and projected sales. For example, if your product costs $10 per month, your ARPU would be $10.
2. **Total Potential Customers:** This is the total number of people or businesses that could potentially use your product or service. This is where it gets a bit more complex, as you need to define your target market and estimate the size of that market.

You can take a "top-down" approach, starting with broad market data and then narrowing it down based on factors like geography, demographics, industry, etc

To gather this information, you'll need to do some market research - and we will expand on the full suite of market research strategies in the next chapter, "Market Research."

4. Narrowing Down Your Niche

With the high-level considerations of the TAM, pricing bracket, demographics, and psychographics, we can apply the Ikigai principles and the market research to explore specific areas of interest that are underserved in the market or that you are uniquely positioned to deliver better than others.

- **Personal and Professional Experience:** Do you have any prior experience or expertise in this particular niche? Having relevant knowledge and connections can give you a significant advantage.
- **Passion and Enthusiasm:** Is this a niche that truly excites you and aligns with your interests? Your passion will be a driving force in building a successful business.
- **Competitive Landscape:** Is the niche you're considering overly saturated, or is there room for you to join and acquire market share? Look for opportunities where you can offer a unique value proposition.
- **Realistic Growth Potential:** Can you realistically see yourself building a thriving online business within this niche? Consider the size of the target market and your ability to reach and serve them effectively.

- **A Closer Look at the USPs:** Compare the unique selling points of each niche more closely. What are the distinct advantages you can offer that might set you apart from the competition?
- **Combine Complementary Niches:** If you're passionate about two or more areas, see if you can combine them into a single, more focused niche. For instance, software engineering services for financial firms or a niche newsletter about professional real estate opportunities in Florida for international investors.

If your initial niche feels a bit too broad, consider breaking it down into more specific sub-niches. Being laser-focused is easier to sell, and you can always expand later.

The more we narrow down your niche, the closer we get to refining the problem we solve and the actual solution we have. Having listed everything down, the only part left in our value proposition exercise is building a powerful offer that converts.

Once you've settled on an idea, run some validation experiments. Speak with former colleagues and friends. Attend a couple of events and meet prospective customers. Browse online communities, forums, and social networks for relevant questions or problems that others may face (that you are about to solve).

Effective products target specific corporate profiles or individuals. We will review one popular framework to align your niche and solution with the ideal customers you want to target.

Defining Your Ideal Customer Profile

The process of customer profiling is designed to narrow down the definition of your ideal clients. The better you understand what your perfect customers look like, the easier it is to reference them in your messaging, use the right channels and platforms, design strategic and personalized campaigns, and speak their language.

IDEAL CUSTOMER PROFILE EXAMPLES

INDUSTRY	LOCATION	COMPANY SIZE
BUDGET	BUYING PROCESS	DECISION MAKERS
PAIN POINTS	BUSINESS OBJECTIVES	TECHNOLOGIES

ATTRIBUTES

MARIO PESHEV

mariopeshev.com

Lack of clarity would otherwise result in bland, generic messages that don't resonate with your clients.

This type of positioning is more common in the business-to-business (B2B) world when working with high-ticket accounts, but the same premise can be applied to smaller accounts and other business segments. You can adapt the model to your niche definition and evolve the segmentation over time.

Also, these terms are often used interchangeably, and you may see varying definitions. I'll provide my read on account segmentation with the three core categories:

1. **Target Account:** The ideal company profile that fits your value proposition. Also known as firmographics, this determines company qualities such as industry, company size, location, and revenue.

2. **Buyer Persona:** The individual definition of the direct point of contact you will reference directly with their demographics and psychographics: gender, age, role in the organization, annual income, marital status, hobbies and interests, fears and desires, opinions, and clubs.

3. **Ideal Customer Profile:** A high-level cross-section between the ideal buyer persona working in your target account.

You may end up using all three in the process of growing your business - discussing the target accounts you serve as a whole, your overarching ICP profile, and a highly personalized and individualized card of Tom, a fictional persona representing the recipient of your paid campaign or cold email.

Here's how to refine your process and several actionable steps to creating your ICP:

1. **Describe Your Target Market:** Now that the niche has been defined, describe the industry, company size, location, and other relevant attributes of the customers you want to target.

2. **Identify Your Customer's Pain Points and Challenges:** Understand the specific problems, frustrations, fears, and needs that your products or services can solve for your ideal customers. This will help you position your offerings in a way that resonates closely with them.

3. **Determine Your Customer's Goals and Objectives:** Understand what your ideal customers are trying to achieve and how your products or services can help them reach their goals. Do they seek to generate more revenue? Save time? Reduce headcount? Increase efficiency?

4. **Create a Detailed Customer Profile:** Compile all the information you have gathered into a comprehensive customer profile. This should include demographic details (age, income, location), behavioral characteristics (buying habits, decision-making process), psychographic traits (values, interests, pain points), firmographics (industry, company size, revenue), and even technographics (digital solutions they use, contract sizes, renewal dates).

5. **Analyze Existing Customers:** If you have previously worked with individuals satisfying your ICP criteria, interview them and fill in the blanks. Alternatively, speak to users of competitive solutions to discover what keeps them around and any flaws you may be able to fill in.

6. **Validate and Refine Your ICP:** ICPs may evolve over time. Continuously gather feedback from your sales team, customer service, and existing customers to validate the profile and make

any necessary adjustments. As your business evolves, the ICP may evolve.

We have the niche cleared out and your ICP defined. The only thing left is finalizing the solution and running some experiments before investing in a fully fledged prototype.

Defining Your Solution

Once the niche has been cleared out, take it a step further and define the actual solution.

In chapter four, we will go through a list of 12 different business types you can base your solution on - but first, let's discover the problems your ICPs face in this niche.

You can brainstorm through different lenses and ask a series of questions to get to the bottom of this:

- What are some problems you face that don't have a great solution yet?
- Are there any products or services that solve a part of the problem but not the key challenges you want taken care of?
- Is there a product/solution that works well but isn't adapted or available for that niche/segment?
- Are there available solutions structured differently to what you are able to serve? For instance, books that could be video courses or real-time workshops or service vendors that could be automated with a SaaS solution?
- Are there any gaps missing in the space that leave some room for a new service, content site, or product?

- What questions keep hovering in the space from ICPs you've interviewed and online questions in forums/social media?
- Are there popular solutions that aren't utilizing the right medium for your audience? For instance, Instagram accounts delivering value but your ICP reading emails, opening an opportunity for a newsletter.
- Is there an available solution that's documented but too complex to deliver? This may open up opportunities for implementation of calculators, tools, mobile apps, and SaaS solutions.
- What are some complex problems where enterprise solutions exist, but the core premise can be simplified and delivered to your segment at a fraction of the cost?

Going through a series of similar questions and utilizing forums, social networks, ICP interviews, and additional market research, write down several ideas that seem plausible. Take some time to sleep on them and limit the two or three most promising ones. Picking the right solution will be the core of your business. The last thing you want to do is rush it and enter a saturated market that's hard to navigate.

Defining Your Offer

We have all the right pieces of the puzzle:

- The niche we want to serve with the corresponding traits of the market (size, price range, and level of solution)
- The ideal customer profile - who we want to sell to and their characteristics
- The definition of our solution - what we'll offer.

The next chapter will dive deeper into market research and we'll get a chance to dive deeper into market analysis and competitor research in order to check all the boxes. And chapter four will reveal the available business types we can implement our solution on.

Meanwhile, let's prepare a quick offer and run some tests while we're testing the waters. Being a digital CEO is about being agile, moving fast, running continuous experimentation, and launching pilot versions before you settle on a complete product.

There are two specific offer frameworks I recommend in my advisory firm Growth Shuttle and my team at DevriX implements for go-to-market initiatives.

The Godfather Offer

This framework was coined by Sabri Suby, the founder of KingKong agency in Australia and author of the bestseller *Sell Like Crazy*. In his book, Sabri breaks down the ideal offer into nine different chapters:

- Value
- Specificity
- Novelty
- Risk-Reward
- Scarcity
- Rationale
- Clarity
- Pricing
- Bonuses.

Sabri and his team are relentless when it comes to pitching their services, using a handful of fear of missing out (FOMO) approaches, featuring case studies and success stories with time-limited offers, promising groundbreaking revelations in the market with strategies that nobody else uses, and bundling with different bonuses in a sequence of sales journeys through videos, emails, and texts.

Iterating on these nine pillars and defining a value proposition that resonates will take you closer to the promise of the irresistible offer that Sabri coaches.

The Grand Slam Offer

Alex Hormozi is the co-founder of Acquisition.com, an Internet entrepreneur and creator who has been dominating the social space over the past couple of years. He authored two bestselling books, *$100M Offers* and *$100M Leads*. The former uncovers the equation that makes an offer a true winner:

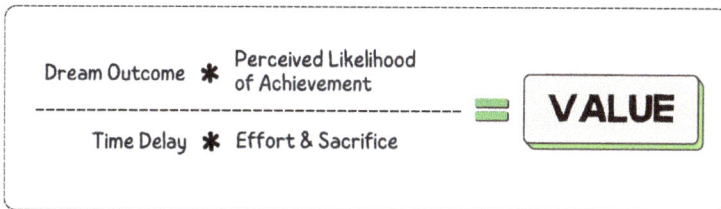

$$\frac{\text{Dream Outcome} * \text{Perceived Likelihood of Achievement}}{\text{Time Delay} * \text{Effort \& Sacrifice}} = \boxed{\textbf{VALUE}}$$

The best offers have a powerful dream outcome with a very high likelihood of achievement. They are possible with limited effort and in a short period of time.

This is why weight loss pills often convert better than gym workout memberships. They require lower effort and sacrifice and faster-perceived results for the same dream outcome.

Implementing safety measures like "money back guarantee" or "free license until promised ROI is achieved" immediately increases the value of the proposition.

While designing your offers, always strive for a perfect ratio following both frameworks.

Running a Live Test

Once everything else is in place, it's time to run light tests of the value proposition and your new offers. This doesn't mean you must have the entire model sorted out. During this phase, you still have the opportunity to fine-tune messaging, value proposition, pricing tiers, and communication mediums for the solution.

1. **Start a Blog, Newsletter, YouTube Channel:** One of the best ways to gauge interest in your niche is through a public social or communication channel that gathers your ideal audience. You can launch a blog, social profile, newsletter, or podcast – whatever medium works best for you and your audience. Producing regular content over the course of a few weeks or months, you can monitor key metrics like views, engagement, followers, likes, and subscriber growth. These insights can provide invaluable feedback on the viability of your niche.

2. **Set up a Landing Page:** Develop a simple, focused landing page that showcases the product or service you designed earlier. This could be a lead magnet, a digital offering, or even a physical product. Promote the landing page through social, paid ads, or direct messages to some of your prospects. If you're able to

generate significant interest and conversions, it's a clear sign that your offer has real market demand.

3. **Pre-Sell Your Offering:** Take the concept one step further by actually trying to pre-sell your product or service. This could involve running a crowdfunding campaign, taking pre-orders, or offering a limited-time early access opportunity. If you're able to generate revenue before the product is ready, it's a strong validation of your niche idea.

4. **Engage with Your Audience:** As you test your niche, actively engage with your potential customers. Respond to comments, join social discussions, and gather direct feedback in the process. It's the best form of market research meeting your prospective clients.

5. **Iterate and Adjust:** The testing phase is all about learning and refining your approach. Don't be afraid to adapt and pivot based on the ongoing feedback sessions. The more you learn from your initial experiments, the stronger your upcoming solution will be.

I founded my digital agency, DevriX, in late 2010, but the iterative journey of refining the niche and value proposition started two years earlier and concluded in 2012. I switched to full-time freelance and consulting in 2008 and worked closely with my target market through development projects and training solutions for a year, registering the company domain in 2009. Over time, I cleared out what was required to get this going and founded the company a year later.

The first two years were still experimental, working on various projects in different technical stacks. It was until 2012 when I finally managed to niche down, specialize in WordPress, and build a series of playbooks and operating procedures that helped us establish the agency as one of the top 20 global agencies in the space.

We have pivoted multiple times since - positioning ourselves as a SaaS vendor, inventing the WordPress retainers as a business model in the market, becoming the leading publishing expert for digital magazines over 100 million monthly views, introducing inbound marketing services, and growing the go-to-market consultancy on top of the martech suite we already had.

So don't be afraid to test offers fast and iterate actively until you get a working prototype. And if you do, you can still niche down, diversify, pivot, build on top of your current offer. Transitioning to a new market or segment may take anywhere from 6 to 18 months, but you can still keep the revenue generating portion of the business while moving to the new market segments or designing additional service lines.

The next chapter will dive deep into market research. This will provide a number of valuable frameworks for continuous offer refinement, interviewing your ideal customers, collecting market data, studying your competitors. This process may take weeks, months or even years - pace it out based on your current goals. You can also jump to chapter four, the definition of business models, and revisit the market research portion regularly as you reassess your niche and ICP every three to six months.

CHAPTER THREE

MARKET RESEARCH

Market research is all about understanding your potential customers and the market you want to enter. When you conduct market research, you're gathering and analyzing data to learn more about your target audience, their needs, preferences, and buying habits.

Working with hundreds of founders in my advisory firm Growth Shuttle and my agency DevriX, I know how easy it is to get wrapped in a bubble of like-minded individuals, colleagues, and partners - failing to identify and act upon market shifts and industry trends moving into different directions. AI is a recent example of how traditional businesses ignore the changing shift and digitalization of services and solutions, while progressive startups effectively utilize AI and corporations cut down their teams by implementing automation and AI-driven processes with comparable output but limited expenses.

The history of market research goes back quite a while. It got its start in Germany during the 1920s and took off in the United States during the Golden Age of Radio in the mid-20th century. Back then, companies that advertised on the radio wanted to know who was listening to their ads so they could target their messages more effectively. They started looking at things like demographics and sales numbers to see which ads were working and which ones weren't.

Let's take a closer look at some of the different types of market research that businesses can use to gain valuable insights.

THE THOROUGH MARKET RESEARCH PROCESS

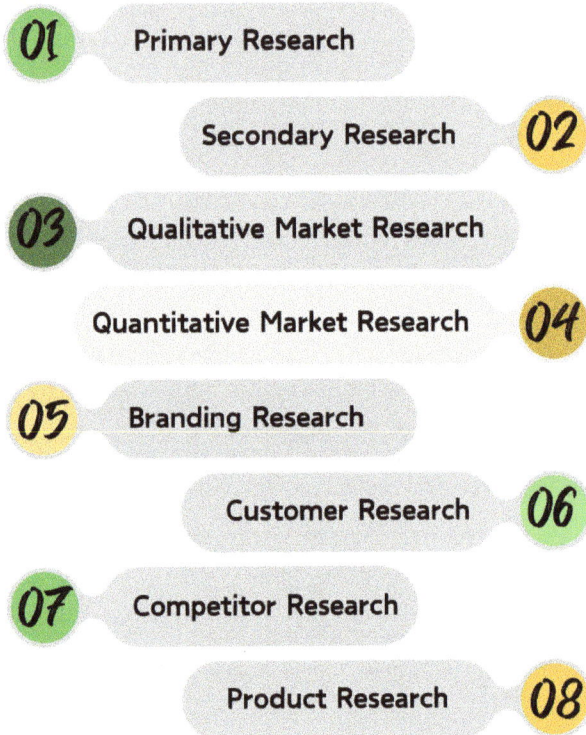

01 Primary Research

Secondary Research **02**

03 Qualitative Market Research

Quantitative Market Research **04**

05 Branding Research

Customer Research **06**

07 Competitor Research

Product Research **08**

1. Primary Research

Primary research is all about gathering data directly from your target market through various methods. This approach has the advantage of owning the data and having first-hand insights into what your potential customers think, feel, and need. There are two main types of results you can gather from primary research: exploratory information and conclusive information.

Exploratory primary research helps you determine the nature of a problem or opportunity that hasn't been clearly defined yet. This might involve doing some initial interviews or focus groups to get a sense of the market and uncover potential pain points or needs that your business could address.

Now, let's look at a few of the primary research methods in more detail.

Focus Groups

With focus groups, you bring together a sample group of people who represent your target market. A skilled moderator then leads a discussion, asking questions about a product, service, or concept. This allows you to gather rich, qualitative feedback and observe how people respond in a group setting.

The benefit of focus groups is that you can get a lot of input from multiple participants at once. However, you do have to be mindful of potential biases, like participants feeling pressure to go along with the group or the moderator inadvertently influencing the responses.

One-on-One Interviews

In this approach, you have an in-depth conversation with individual participants. CEOs of early-stage startups are directly involved in early research and ask open-ended questions with a closer look at a person's thoughts, feelings, and experiences. This can provide incredibly valuable, nuanced insights that might not come up in a survey or group setting.

This is by far the most effective strategy in the early days of a digital startup. Great founders and B2B leaders go through research of their ideal customers, invite them for quick calls, incentivize them if possible (Amazon coupons or paid sessions), dive into the industry and role pain points, and design their solution around the specific needs.

In the global business realm, discussing "**Return on Investment**" as a North Star is a common practice. But one crucial metric often left behind is the "**Cost of Inaction**" – or what are the consequences of not completing an initiative. When it comes to one-on-one interviews, the possible cost of inaction can be your entire business model – a product with no market need, investing time, capital, effort, and mental power into a potential "nice to have" solution that's not monetizable.

The main downside of interviews is that they are very time-consuming to conduct and analyze the data afterward. But the detailed, first-hand information you gather can be well worth the effort.

Surveys

Surveys allow you to collect data from a wider pool of participants. You can distribute surveys digitally, making it easy for people to complete them on their own time. Surveys work well for gathering more quantifiable data, like customer preferences, behaviors, and demographics.

The key to effective surveys is crafting the right questions that gather valuable information you can act upon. When implemented well, surveys can provide statistically significant insights to inform your business decisions.

For example, if you were launching a new digital fitness app, you could organize a virtual focus group of health-conscious individuals to discuss their current exercise routines, tracking preferences, and desired features in a fitness app. Alternatively, you could conduct one-on-one interviews with frequent users of similar fitness apps to understand their usage patterns, pain points, and ideas for improvement. You could also create an online survey to present mock-ups of your fitness app and have a wider audience rate different workout programs, tracking capabilities, and social features to help refine the product before launch.

Advisory Boards

Advisory boards consist of a group of experienced individuals who can provide strategic advice and insights about your market and product. By regularly meeting with an advisory board that understands your industry, you can receive ongoing, in-depth feedback that is both strategic and tactical.

This method is particularly useful for aligning your product development with industry expectations and customer needs.

Online Panels

Online panels involve assembling a large group of people online who fit your target demographic and are willing to participate in market research over a period of time. Participants can be engaged through various digital methods, such as web-based surveys, online forums, or even interactive webinars, to provide ongoing feedback on a range of topics.

This method is great for testing changes quickly and understanding trends over time.

2. Secondary Research

Secondary research is all about utilizing data that has already been collected, analyzed, and published by other sources. This can include a wide range of publicly available information, from government statistics and industry reports to academic studies and media articles.

One of the main benefits of secondary research is its cost-effectiveness. Since you're not conducting the research yourself, significantly fewer expenses are involved. This makes it a great starting point for your market exploration efforts.

This strategy can provide a solid knowledge base upon which to build. Studying the broader context and trends, you can then use primary research methods to dive deeper and fill in any gaps. I use government data and external platforms like Statista, to keep track of annual industry reports, market trends, and the global technology market to influence strategic decisions in my own companies and with executives I advise.

Of course, there are some potential drawbacks to relying solely on secondary data. The information may not be tailored to your specific business needs, and you have to be cautious about the reliability and validity of the sources. That's why it's best to use secondary and primary research together for a well-rounded, data-driven view of your market. As a digital CEO, you want to make sure you have a comprehensive understanding of your market before making any major decisions.

My weekly newsletter, Growth Blueprint, revolves entirely around the cross-section of primary and secondary research. I pull industry data for the stock market, inflation and unemployment rates, any macro analysis and research available from industry sources. And I infuse this with our own data set of agency clients, advisory contracts, startups I've invested in, growth experiments we conduct weekly, and conversations I have with other founders and business leaders. This acts as a complete 360 overview of the landscape, helping me make better decisions on investments or pivots based on hard data.

3. Qualitative Market Research

Qualitative market research is all about collecting non-numerical data that provides rich, in-depth insights into your target market. Rather than just focusing on the "what" and "how much," this approach helps you uncover the "why" behind consumer behaviors, attitudes, and preferences.

Using methods like in-depth interviews, focus groups, and observational studies, you can observe natural reactions, ask probing questions, and translate those insights into actionable business strategies.

Qualitative research is less about pinpointing exact truths and more about summarizing and inferring broader trends and patterns. While the data may not be as easily quantifiable, the depth of understanding it provides can reveal non-obvious challenges for businesses looking to develop innovative solutions and connect with their customers on a deeper level.

4. Quantitative Market Research

The other side of the coin, quantitative market research, is focused on collecting numerical data that can be measured and analyzed. This type of research is great for providing historical benchmarks, identifying trends, and establishing a solid foundation of facts and figures to inform your business decisions.

Quantitative data can be sourced in various ways, including surveys, polls, web analytics, and financial records. Aggregating enough data will help you to identify patterns, test hypotheses, and make more data-driven decisions about your products, pricing, marketing, and overall strategy.

For instance, if you wanted to understand the purchasing habits of your target customers, you could conduct a comprehensive survey to gather information on things like how often they shop, how much they typically spend, and what factors influence their buying decisions. This numerical data could then inform your pricing strategies, marketing campaigns, and product development roadmaps.

5. Branding Research

As a CEO, one of your most valuable assets is your company's brand. It's the unique identity that sets you apart from your competitors and resonates with your target customers. But building and sustaining a strong brand doesn't happen by accident – it requires a deep understanding of your market, your customers, and how your competitors' brands are perceived.

I'm a big proponent of branding when it comes to building legacy brands. Great companies don't waste their executive and leadership time on the feast and famine cycle, always afraid of market shifts and going out of business. Aside from incredible operational processes and management strategies deployed internally, developing a well-known brand is a revenue driver on autopilot, a customer retention mechanism, a free sales channel through loyal customers and advocates, and a strong employer branding strategy (helping recruit top talent). Investing in corporate and executive branding is often neglected by new businesses but often a missed opportunity compared to methodical founders who continuously invest in branding.

That's where branding market research comes into play. This specialized form of research is all about uncovering insights that can help you shape and refine your brand's tone, imagery, values, and overall identity.

Branding research measures awareness, brand loyalty, brand perception, brand positioning, brand value, and brand identity. By understanding how your customers feel about different brands in the space both positively and negatively, you can identify opportunities to enhance and amplify your brand's image and appeal.

6. Customer Research

As a business leader, one of your top priorities should be understanding your customers inside and out. After all, they are the lifeblood of your company, the ones who ultimately decide whether your products and services are worth their time and money. That's where customer market research comes into play.

In the business world, customer research is tied to defining a "buyer persona" or an ICP (ideal customer profile). I will expand on ICPs later in this book.

The goal of customer research is to provide you with a comprehensive understanding of your target audience – their behaviors, preferences, pain points, and the factors that influence their purchasing decisions. As a result, you will learn to attract, engage, and retain your most valuable customers.

One key area of customer research is customer satisfaction. Things like post-purchase surveys, customer support call feedback, and net promoter score (NPS) analysis can all provide valuable insights into customer satisfaction. Additional mediums to explore in the same category are customer loyalty research, the customer lifecycle, customer segmentation, and the overarching customer intelligence to wrap this up in a complete client profile.

7. Competitor Research

Competitor research allows you to understand your competitive landscape, identify your unique advantages, and uncover opportunities to outshine your rivals.

The goal of competitor research is to give you a clear, comprehensive view of who you're up against and how your business stacks up. This involves analyzing your competitors' strengths, weaknesses, market share, pricing, product offerings, and overall strategies. After a thorough analysis, you can pinpoint areas where you can differentiate yourself and deliver more value to your customers.

One powerful tool for competitor analysis is the SWOT (Strengths, Weaknesses, Opportunities, Threats) framework. This matrix provides four different areas you can fill out for each of your competitors - and align it to one copy for your own business.

HELPFUL
to achieving the objectives

INTERNAL
attributes of the organization

STRENGTHS

WEAKNESSES

SWOT ANALYSIS

OPPORTUNITIES

THREATS

EXTERNAL
attributes of the environment

HARMFUL
to achieving the objectives

Each quadrant lists traits that represents a company's:

- **Strengths**: Unique value proposition and competitive advantage for the business (capital, brand, connections)
- **Weaknesses**: Shortcomings that the company has to deal with (headquartered in a desolated region, poor user experience, late to market)
- **Opportunities**: Areas that the business is likely to invest in and generate substantial returns in a short period of time
- **Threats**: Risks, dependencies, legal hurdles, tax complications, or anything that would jeopardize the business.

Aside from the popular SWOT framework, different solutions and benchmark strategies exist that could outline and compare competitors side by side for qualitative or quantitative metrics: business size, revenue, staff, market size, product portfolio, pricing, and many more.

Two popular applications that can be used for conducting keyword research and competitor analysis are Semrush and Ubersuggest.

Semrush is an American public company profiling in keyword research, competitive analysis, site audits, backlink tracking, and a holistic overview of your own digital presence and how a digital estate compares to your competitors. Originally, it was founded as a solution for organic search and SEO, further evolving into search engine marketing (paid ads), and now presenting a large suite of tools for content creation, social posting, ad creative monitoring, and more.

I use Semrush extensively with my digital agency DevriX (which is a Semrush agency partner) and at Growth Shuttle, and this enabled me to scale my blog past 40,000 monthly views, ranking among the first results for competitive keywords like "business advisor," "small business advisors," "business consultant rates," "business challenges," "hiring consultants," and hundreds of other high profile keywords bringing traffic and revenue.

Ubersuggest is owned by renowned digital marketing expert Neil Patel – one of the leading global digital influencers and founder of NP Digital. Ubersuggest started as a simple tool that scraped Google's autocomplete suggestions but has since been expanded and improved by Patel.

Neil Patel is a prominent figure in the digital marketing industry, known for his expertise in SEO, content marketing, and growth hacking. He has built several successful online businesses and is the co-founder of companies like Crazy Egg, Hello Bar, and KISSmetrics. Patel acquired Ubersuggest in 2018 and has since transformed it into a comprehensive SEO tool that can help entrepreneurs and marketers research keywords, analyze competitors, and conduct site audits.

Ubersuggest's keyword research capabilities allow you to find new keyword ideas, see search volume and competition data, and understand the content that's ranking for specific keywords. This information can be invaluable when you're trying to identify the most promising market opportunities and create content that resonates with your target audience.

Additionally, Ubersuggest's competitor analysis features enable you to see the top-performing pages and content for your competitors, as well as the keywords they are targeting. This can give you valuable insights into the strategies and tactics that are working in your industry, allowing you to develop a more informed and effective marketing plan.

Including SEO tools like Semrush and Ubersuggest in your research stack, you can gain a deeper understanding of your target market, identify promising opportunities, and outmaneuver your competitors.

8. Product Research

Product market research takes it a step further and assesses the longevity of your products and services. This is an effective strategy for established businesses (surveying existing customers and prospective ones) and can be applied in the same way for competitive products (surveying against existing market solutions before you build yours.)

The goal of product research is to give you the insights you need to develop products and services that not only attract customers but also provide genuine value and solve real problems. This can involve exploring everything from product branding and design to feature testing and marketing messaging.

Let's take a closer look at some of the key areas of product research:

- **Product Branding**: Does the product's brand and design resonate with your target customers positively or negatively? Through surveys, focus groups, and other research methods, you can gauge how your product's visual identity, messaging, and overall positioning are perceived. It may turn out that the "dark mode" variant of your product and website is perceived better by your target group.

- **Product Feature Testing**: At various stages of development - from early prototypes to post-launch enhancements, you can gather feedback from your customers on new features or improvements. This allows you to refine your offerings and ensure you're delivering the functionality and value that your audience craves.

- **Product Marketing**: Are your marketing messages and campaign strategies related to how your buyers perceive products in the category? Product research can reveal opportunities to sharpen your value proposition, refine your positioning, and create more compelling content that resonates with your target audience.

- **Product/Market Fit (P/M Fit):** How well does your product satisfy the demand in the market? This is crucial to determine early in the development process. Regularly testing the market's response to your product can help you adjust features, pricing, or marketing strategies to better align with what your customers truly want and need.

- **Elasticity:** Understanding how sensitive your customers are to changes in price can significantly affect how you market and modify your products. By evaluating price elasticity, you can make informed decisions about pricing strategies that will either increase demand or maximize profit margins without alienating your customer base.

When it comes to conducting this kind of product research, primary methods like surveys, interviews, and in-person observation tend to perform best. These approaches give you direct, first-hand feedback from your customers, and you can dive deeper and schedule follow-up conversations as needed.

CHAPTER FOUR

BUSINESS MODELS 101

A business model is a comprehensive plan that outlines how a company will operate, make money, and achieve its objectives. It encompasses everything from the products or services you offer to the target market you serve, the pricing strategies you employ, and the distribution channels you utilize. Essentially, your business model is the DNA of your company – it's what sets you apart and determines your path to success.

Over the past 17 years, I have launched and run businesses in products in each and every one of the following categories - some more successful than others. As a business advisor, investor, and a serial entrepreneur obsessed with learning, experimentation is integral to uncovering new verticals and lines of business that work, intertwining them with other ventures I run with my teams. This led to a series of acquisitions and mergers into existing companies of mine, exits to cross-functional partners, and staying on top of the market waves during turbulent conditions or times of recession.

So take this breakdown as a personal overview from a practitioner who's been there and had to launch new ventures from zero - more than once.

Before we move to the actual types of business models to develop, there's one popular framework studied in traditional MBA programs called the "**Business Model Canvas.**" As you keep evolving your business and refining your value proposition, the canvas represents a one-pager that lists down the core initiatives and relationships that your business represents. It looks like this:

BUSINESS MODEL CANVAS

THE BUSINESS 1-PAGER

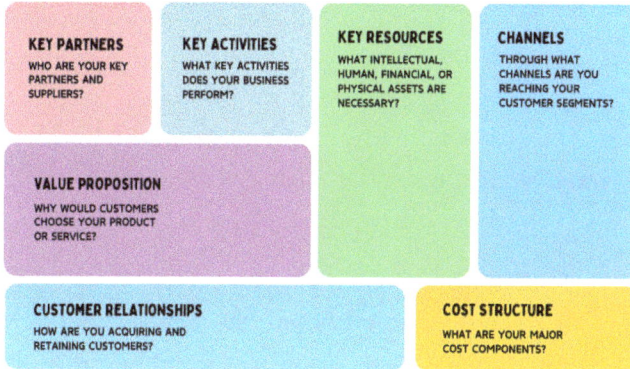

KEY PARTNERS
WHO ARE YOUR KEY PARTNERS AND SUPPLIERS?

KEY ACTIVITIES
WHAT KEY ACTIVITIES DOES YOUR BUSINESS PERFORM?

KEY RESOURCES
WHAT INTELLECTUAL, HUMAN, FINANCIAL, OR PHYSICAL ASSETS ARE NECESSARY?

CHANNELS
THROUGH WHAT CHANNELS ARE YOU REACHING YOUR CUSTOMER SEGMENTS?

VALUE PROPOSITION
WHY WOULD CUSTOMERS CHOOSE YOUR PRODUCT OR SERVICE?

CUSTOMER RELATIONSHIPS
HOW ARE YOU ACQUIRING AND RETAINING CUSTOMERS?

COST STRUCTURE
WHAT ARE YOUR MAJOR COST COMPONENTS?

You can fill it out and stick it on the wall as a general reminder of what the business represents, what you need, how you get there, what the cost structure looks like, and who will help you in this journey. Similarly to the other corresponding resources, the canvas print will be included in the book website, mbadisrupted.com.

As a digital CEO, choosing the right business model will shape your operations, your go-to-market strategy, your financial projections, and ultimately, your overall chances of success. GTM strategies will be reviewed in a separate chapter in this book.

You may be launching a new e-commerce platform. Your business model could be based on a commission-driven approach, where you take a percentage of each sale made through your platform. Or you could opt for a subscription-based model where customers pay a recurring fee to access your services. Or use the commerce platform as a forefront of a data consultancy firm behind the scenes charging enterprise retainers.

Each of these models has its unique pros and cons, and the one you choose will determine your operational processes, hiring strategy, revenue streams, customer acquisition, and ongoing execution strategy.

Types of Business Models

There is a broad list of business models across the complete business landscape, but we're focusing on digital businesses here. And while mixed in models exist (a business can provide more than one segment), I've outlined the core ones reviewed in this book:

DIGITAL BUSINESS TYPES

1 SERVICE-BASED

2 ECOMMERCE

3 SAAS

4 MARKETPLACE

5 AFFILIATE MARKETING

6 ADVERTISING

7 PUBLISHING

8 INFO PRODUCTS

9 DROPSHIPPING

10 MEMBERSHIPS

11 COMMUNITIES

12 LEAD GENERATION

For simplicity, some categories are merged into higher level tiers, but let's go through each of them separately.

Service-Based Business Model

The service-based business model is all about offering your expertise, skills, and knowledge to clients in exchange for payment. This could include consulting, agency work, freelancing, or any other professional service. The key is that you're not selling a physical product, but rather your time, ideas, and problem-solving abilities.

For example, a digital marketing consultant might offer services like social media strategy, SEO optimization, and content creation to help businesses improve their online presence. A web design agency could provide end-to-end website development, UI/UX design, and ongoing maintenance for their clients. A freelance writer could write blog posts, ebooks, and marketing/sales copy for a variety of customers.

The service-based model is often attractive because it allows for more flexibility, personalization, and control over the work you do. However, it also requires continuously generating new business, managing your time effectively, and delivering exceptional results to keep clients satisfied and coming back.

E-commerce Business Model

The e-commerce business model is all about selling physical or digital products online. This could include anything from physical goods like clothing, electronics, or home goods, to digital products like ebooks, online courses, or software. The key is that the entire sales process happens through an online platform, typically a brand's website or a third-party marketplace.

A great example of an e-commerce platform is Shopify. They provide an easy-to-use platform that allows entrepreneurs and small businesses to quickly set up and manage their online stores. Another example is WooCommerce, which is a popular e-commerce plugin for the WordPress content management system. WooCommerce allows users to easily turn their WordPress website into a fully-featured online store. Buth platforms can provide the underlying foundation for starting an online store yourself.

E-commerce businesses can leverage growth mechanisms around SEO, social media marketing, email campaigns, and automated outreach within your data analytics to drive traffic and sales, regardless of which platform they choose.

The main benefits of the e-commerce model are the ability to reach a wider customer base, reduced overhead costs compared to a physical retail location, and the opportunity to scale more easily. However, it also requires careful inventory management, logistics, and competition with other online sellers.

SaaS Business Model

The SaaS business model is all about providing access to a digital platform or software application through a subscription-based model. Instead of purchasing and installing software on their own devices, SaaS customers pay a recurring fee to access the software through the cloud, usually via a web browser or mobile app.

A prime example of a SaaS company is Salesforce, which offers a suite of customer relationship management (CRM) tools and applications that businesses can access and use online. Another example is Zoom, the popular video conferencing platform that has become ubiquitous during the pandemic. SaaS companies often focus on providing a seamless user experience, regular software updates, and scalable solutions to meet the needs of their customers.

The key benefits of the SaaS model are:

- the recurring revenue stream
- the ability to quickly add new features and functionality
- the elimination of hardware and software maintenance costs for the customer.

However, SaaS businesses also need to continually innovate, ensure high uptime and reliability, and provide excellent customer support to retain their subscriber base. Also, launch costs require initial funding. Even with the evolution of site builders or app building apps like Bubble, engineering costs are high, data retention policies are complex, scaling leads to recurring fees – and the early months require a significant investment compared to other business models.

Marketplace Business Model

The marketplace business model is all about creating a platform that connects buyers and sellers, allowing transactions and exchanges to take place. Prominent examples include Amazon, Airbnb, Upwork, and eBay. These platforms provide the infrastructure, tools, and user experience that enable efficient, secure, and scalable transactions between multiple parties.

Marketplaces can generate revenue through commission fees on sales, subscription fees for sellers, advertising, or a combination of these monetization strategies. The value proposition for both buyers and sellers is the ability to access a large, diverse pool of products, services, or talent all in one centralized location.

The main benefits of the marketplace model are the network effects that can be created, the ability to scale rapidly by leveraging the existing user base, and the potential for high-profit margins. However, marketplace businesses also need to invest heavily in trust and safety measures, customer support, and continuous platform improvements to maintain a positive user experience.

Affiliate Marketing Business Model

Affiliate marketing is a performance-based business model where individuals or websites (known as "affiliates") earn a commission by promoting and referring customers to other businesses' products or services. The affiliate doesn't own the product or provide the service. They simply drive traffic and generate sales in exchange for a percentage of the revenue.

A classic example is a blogger who includes links to related products in their content. When a reader clicks on one of those links and makes a purchase, the blogger earns a commission. Other real-world stories include social media influencers promoting products, email newsletters featuring sponsored offers, and niche websites that review and recommend relevant products to their audience.

The appeal of affiliate marketing is the ability to earn passive income by leveraging someone else's products or services. Affiliates can earn commissions without having to manage inventory, handle fulfillment, or provide customer support. However, it also requires building a trustworthy audience, selecting the right affiliate partners, and creating compelling content that drives meaningful conversions.

Advertising-Based Business Model

The advertising-based business model is all about generating revenue by displaying ads or sponsored content on your digital platforms, such as websites, mobile apps, newsletters, or social media channels. The core premise is that you're able to attract a sizable and engaged audience that advertisers are willing to pay to reach.

Examples of advertising-based models include news and media sites that feature display ads, YouTube channels that monetize their videos with ads, and influencers who post sponsored content on their social media pages. The revenue comes from the advertisers paying for impressions, clicks, or conversions generated through these ad placements.

The main benefits of the advertising model are the potential for passive income, the ability to leverage your existing audience, and the opportunity to diversify revenue streams. However, it also requires building a strong traffic base, maintaining high engagement, and carefully managing the user experience to avoid ad fatigue or annoyance.

Content/Publishing Business Model

The content/publishing business model is all about creating and distributing valuable, engaging, and informative content to attract and retain an audience. This could include media sites, blogs, digital magazines, newsletters, podcasts, and other forms of digital content. As Neil Patel said, "Create content that teaches. You can't give up. You need to be consistently awesome."

The key to success in this model is to produce content that educates, informs, and entertains your target audience. You must be committed to consistently creating high-quality, valuable content that provides genuine utility to your readers or listeners. As Patel emphasizes, you cannot simply give up – it takes persistence and a dedication to being "consistently awesome" to build a successful content-driven business.

Whether you are running a media site, blog, digital magazine, or any other form of content-focused operation (including a social media thought leadership account or newsletter), the principles remain the same. Focus on creating content that teaches, informs, and engages your audience, and does so with unwavering commitment and excellence. This is the path to attracting and retaining a loyal following that will sustain your content/publishing business model.

Successful content platforms and notable digital magazines produce a wide range of content, from news and analysis to opinion pieces and lifestyle content. They generate revenue through a combination of advertising, subscriptions, and sometimes e-commerce, data reports, consultancy, or other ancillary offerings.

Pierre Herubel is a rising B2B creator in the space who amassed over 100,000 LinkedIn followers in the B2B space in two years through engaging infographics, business charts, and bite-sized pieces uncovering the marketing funnel and buyer journeys. He crossed the 7-figure mark in 18 months through targeted and engaging content, further expanding into a paid course and a Slack community.

The key benefits of the content/publishing model are the ability to build a loyal audience, the potential for passive income through advertising and sponsorships, and the opportunity to diversify revenue streams. However, it also requires a consistent investment in high-quality content creation, effective audience targeting and engagement, and a strong understanding of SEO and distribution strategies.

Informational Products Business Model

The informational products business model is all about creating and selling digital assets that educate, inform, or provide valuable insights to your target audience. This can include online courses, webinars, ebooks, reports, masterclasses, and more.

Successful examples of this model include platforms like Udemy, Skillshare, and Teachable, which allow experts and educators to create and sell their online courses. Another example is independent authors who self-publish and sell ebooks and digital guides directly to their readers.

The key benefits of the informational products model are the ability to scale your business by creating content once and selling it repeatedly, the potential for high-profit margins, and the opportunity to position yourself as a thought leader or subject matter expert. However, it also requires significant upfront investment in content creation, effective marketing and promotion, and ongoing customer support and updates.

Dropshipping Business Model

The dropshipping business model is a type of eCommerce setup where the merchant doesn't keep the products they sell in stock. Instead, when a customer places an order, the merchant purchases the item from a third-party supplier, who then ships the product directly to the customer.

Prominent examples of dropshipping platforms include AliExpress, Oberlo, and Temu, which connect merchants with suppliers around the world. Successful dropshipping businesses often focus on niche product categories, leveraging targeted marketing and social media to drive sales.

The main advantages of the dropshipping model are the low startup costs, the ability to offer a wide range of products without holding inventory, and the potential for scalability. However, it also comes with challenges like longer shipping times, less control over the customer experience, and heightened competition in popular product categories.

Membership Site Business Model

The membership site business model is all about providing exclusive, gated access to content, community, and other valuable resources in exchange for a recurring subscription fee. This could include access to premium content, live events, private online communities, one-on-one coaching, and more.

Successful examples of membership sites include websites like MasterClass, which offers online classes taught by renowned experts, and fitness platforms like Peloton, which provide on-demand workout content and a community of fellow members. Other examples include professional associations, software user groups, and private investment research communities.

One powerful marketing community worth checking is Stacked Marketer Pro. The Stacked Marketer media network led by Emanuel Cinca and Thomas Tiroch started as a small pilot group of 15 people receiving daily emails, then growing to 2,000 subscribers, and now representing over 100,000 active readers across 3 newsletters (and counting). While the initial business models deployed were around sponsorships (advertising) and affiliate links, a growing number of subscribers now sign up for the Pro membership plan, unlocking deep dives, data stories, group forums, and detailed whitepapers for premium users.

I have been reading Stacked Marketer for nearly three years now and have invested in their 2023 seed round as I firmly believe in the growth potential of the media network.

The key benefits of this membership model are the recurring revenue stream, the opportunity to build a loyal and engaged audience, and the ability to leverage economies of scale as the membership base grows. However, it also requires consistently delivering high-value content and experiences, effectively onboarding and retaining members, and continuously improving the membership offering.

Community-Based Business Model

The community-based business model is all about building and nurturing an exclusive, engaged community of like-minded individuals who are willing to pay for access to special deals, discounts, networking opportunities, and collaboration.

Examples of successful community-based businesses include private online forums, industry-specific Slack groups, invite-only Clubhouse rooms, and exclusive Facebook groups. These communities often provide members with access to exclusive content, events, job opportunities, and the ability to connect with peers and experts in their field.

A Media Operator is a great example of such a community. I was invited to uncover deep dives in the media market, from the largest publishing companies in the world to the leading business and marketing newsletters out there. Its founder, Jacob Donnelly, spent several years in CoinDesk, following three years in Morning Brew before launching the media, and turned it into a freemium community with a Slack group for premium members, gathering the leading names in the space.

The main advantages of the community model are the potential for recurring revenue, the ability to foster deep relationships and loyalty, and the opportunity to leverage the collective knowledge and expertise of the community. However, it also requires significant time and effort to build and maintain an engaged, valuable community, as well as careful curation and moderation to ensure a positive member experience.

Lead Generation Business Model

The lead generation business model is all about collecting valuable contact information and sales leads, which can then be sold or leveraged to drive revenue for your business. This could include gathering email addresses, phone numbers, or other data from potential customers who express interest in your products or services.

Examples of lead generation businesses include outreach specialists who find and qualify potential clients for agencies, social media influencers who connect brands with their audience, and B2B companies that compile and sell sales leads to other vendors. The revenue comes from either directly selling the leads or using the data to fuel your own sales and marketing efforts.

Business directories like Clutch fall in the same bracket - providing opportunities for vendors to close new business. Max Bidna, known as "@MarketingMax" online, launched a similar niche listing service called AgencyReviews listing over 50,000 agencies with a paid listing upsell option connecting brands to verified vendors. His former background as a paid media expert and a founder of a 7-figure ad agency sold in 2021, gathering over 200,000 social followers and having been featured in Forbes, Business Insider, and a number of popular outlets, provide holistic opportunities to pipe all channels into this agency listing business as an additional source of revenue as a trusted lead generation broker.

The key benefits of the lead generation model are the potential for recurring revenue, the ability to leverage your audience or expertise, and the opportunity to monetize your data and connections. However, it also requires careful data management, compliance with privacy regulations, and a deep understanding of your target market and their pain points.

Essential Factors For Selecting Your Business Model

7 STEPS TO SUSTAINABLE BUSINESS GROWTH

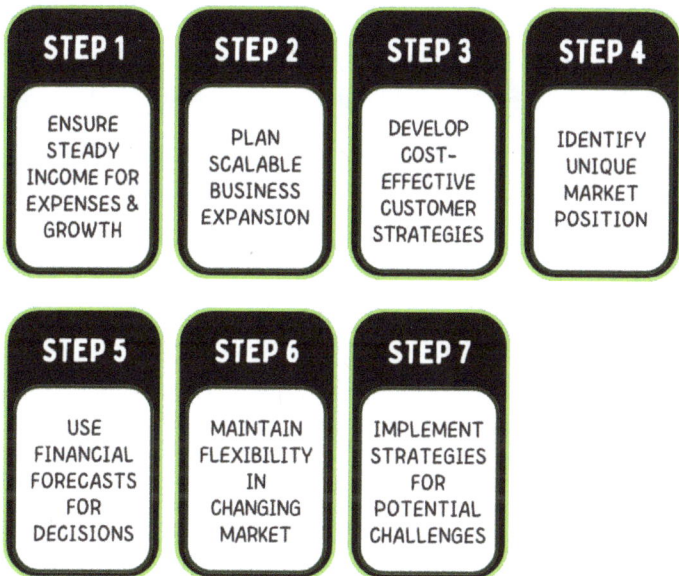

STEP 1 — ENSURE STEADY INCOME FOR EXPENSES & GROWTH

STEP 2 — PLAN SCALABLE BUSINESS EXPANSION

STEP 3 — DEVELOP COST-EFFECTIVE CUSTOMER STRATEGIES

STEP 4 — IDENTIFY UNIQUE MARKET POSITION

STEP 5 — USE FINANCIAL FORECASTS FOR DECISIONS

STEP 6 — MAINTAIN FLEXIBILITY IN CHANGING MARKET

STEP 7 — IMPLEMENT STRATEGIES FOR POTENTIAL CHALLENGES

MARIO

When starting a new business, choosing the right business model is crucial for long-term success. As you evaluate different approaches, it's important to consider several key factors that can make or break your venture. These include:

1. Revenue Streams

When selecting a business model, it's crucial to carefully consider your primary revenue sources. Will your company primarily generate revenue through one-time sales of products or services? Or will you opt for a recurring revenue model, such as subscription-based services or memberships? Understanding the pros and cons of different revenue streams is essential. For example, one-time sales may provide immediate cash flow, but recurring revenue can offer more predictability and stability. Evaluating which revenue model best aligns with your target market and long-term goals will be a key factor in your decision.

2. Scalability

Another important consideration is the scalability of your chosen business model. Can your company grow and serve more customers without proportional increases in overhead and operational costs? Highly scalable models, like SaaS or e-commerce, allow you to expand your reach and customer base more efficiently than models that require significant manual effort or physical infrastructure for each additional customer. Assessing the scalability of your business model is crucial for sustainable long-term growth.

3. Customer Acquisition

How will you attract and retain customers? The cost and effectiveness of your customer acquisition strategy will play a crucial role in the viability of your business model. Some models, like affiliate marketing or referral programs, may have lower customer acquisition costs, while others, like traditional advertising or sales teams, may require a more upfront investment. Understanding the most efficient and cost-effective ways to reach and convert your target audience is essential for ensuring your business model can generate sufficient revenue to sustain and grow your operations.

4. Competitive Advantages

What sets your business apart from the competition? Your chosen business model should leverage your unique strengths and help you stand out in the market. Perhaps your model allows for more personalized customer experiences, faster delivery, or better pricing than your competitors. Identifying and highlighting your competitive advantages will be crucial for attracting and retaining customers in a crowded marketplace.

5. Financial Projections

How will your selected business model impact your profitability, cash flow, and overall financial performance? Careful financial modeling and projections are essential to ensure the long-term sustainability of your venture. Consider factors like startup costs, operational expenses, pricing strategies, and potential revenue streams. Some models, like SaaS, require a heavy frontloaded investment in engineering. E-commerce may need a strong initial investment in product manufacturing or maintaining inventory. This financial analysis will help you determine whether your business model can generate the necessary revenue and profits to support your growth plans and operational needs.

6. Adaptability

In today's rapidly changing business landscape, it's essential to choose a model that is adaptable and flexible. Your business model should be able to evolve and adjust as market conditions, customer preferences, and technological advancements shift. The most successful companies are often those that can quickly pivot and adapt their business models to stay ahead of the curve and capitalize on new opportunities.

7. Risk Management

Every business model carries inherent risks, and it's crucial to carefully evaluate and mitigate these risks. Consider factors like supply chain disruptions, regulatory changes, or market volatility that could impact your revenue streams or operational efficiency. Developing contingency plans and risk management strategies will help ensure the long-term viability of your chosen business model.

Choosing your business model will shape the future of your company in the next few years. Whether you opt for a service-based approach, a SaaS model, a product-focused strategy, or any of the alternative models, switching pricing plans on the fly is not trivial.

Look into competitors in the space and find out what works. Review two parallel options to move forward: one that's aligned with the market expectations (stick to what works) and one disruptive option that provides a competitive edge compared to the market. You can test both out by following the market research principles in the second chapter of this book.

CHAPTER FIVE

BASICS OF INCORPORATION AND COMPLIANCE

As a new business owner or someone who's been running a company for a while, the legal and regulatory requirements can feel overwhelming and confusing. It's easy to get bogged down in all the details and paperwork. However, taking the time to understand the fundamentals of incorporation and compliance is crucial for the long-term success and stability of your business.

What is Incorporation?

When you start a new business, one of the most important steps is officially turning it into a legal entity, separate from you as the owner or founder. This process is known as incorporation, and it's a crucial step for several key reasons.

First, incorporation gives your business a formal brand separate from you as an individual. This is important because it provides legal protection. Your assets are kept distinct from the business, so you're not as personally liable for any issues or business debts that the company might face. It also allows the business to enter into contracts, open separate business bank accounts, and take other actions in its name rather than having to go through you as the owner.

Another major benefit of incorporation is the tax advantages it provides. Depending on the business structure you choose, like a corporation or limited liability company (LLC), you may be able to take advantage of certain tax deductions and structures that can save you money compared to operating as a sole proprietorship. This can make a big difference, especially as your company grows and becomes more profitable.

Now, a common question from future entrepreneurs is whether creating a company is a necessity.

I am not a lawyer or a certified accountant so you may need to explore that with the local authorities and revenue agency. There are certain jurisdictions, deal sizes, and services that may not require incorporation. You may be able to conduct business as a "sole trader" or a "self-employed individual" and report taxes under different codes in your country. Your mileage may vary, but no matter the circumstances, as your deal size goes up, founding a company is inevitable, and provides additional tax benefits or safety measures for founders that we'll review here.

What is Compliance?

While incorporation is all about establishing your business as a legal entity, compliance is about continuously adhering to all the various laws, regulations, and industry-specific rules that apply to your operations. This is an ongoing process that requires diligent attention and a thorough understanding of the requirements in your particular field and location.

For example, let's say you start an online e-commerce store selling products. You'd need to make sure you have the proper business licenses and sales tax permits required in the states or countries where you'll be selling. Properly setting up your payment processing and accounting systems would be crucial to stay on top of sales, taxes, and expenses. Neglecting areas like website accessibility guidelines or shipping hazardous materials could also lead to fines or disruptions to your business operations.

Another common compliance area is data privacy. If you collect and store any personal information from customers, clients, or employees, you'll need to ensure you're following all the relevant data protection laws, like the General Data Protection Regulation (GDPR) in Europe or the California Consumer Privacy Act (CCPA) in parts of the U.S. Getting this wrong can lead to massive penalties.

The key to compliance is to always be proactive and diligent. It's not enough to just check the boxes when you're first starting. You have to continuously monitor for changes in the law and adjust your practices accordingly. Staying on top of compliance is essential for the long-term health and stability of your business.

Establishing the Right Legal Foundation for Your Business

When you're starting a new business, one of the most important early decisions you'll need to make is choosing the right legal structure because it's crucial for ensuring the long-term success and stability of your company.

The legal structure you choose will have significant implications for things like how your business is taxed, how much personal liability you face as the owner, who has decision-making authority, and even your ability to raise capital down the line. So it's essential to carefully evaluate the pros and cons of the different options before making your choice.

The main business structures to consider are sole proprietorships, partnerships, limited liability companies (LLCs), and corporations. These may vary across countries, but we'll look into the globally recognized framework **when incorporating into the US or most of Europe**. Let's take a closer look at each one:

1. **Sole Proprietorship:** As a sole proprietor, you can directly start doing business, and there is no legal entity that is to be incorporated, which is why the owner and company are the same, that is you. You have complete control over all decision-making, and your business income is reported on your tax return. However, this also means you're personally liable for any debts or lawsuits against the business - your assets, like your home or savings, could be at risk.

2. **Partnership:** A partnership is similar to a sole proprietorship but involves two or more owners. Partners share in the profits and losses, as well as the decision-making authority. Like a sole proprietorship, a partnership doesn't have a legal separation between the business and the owners, so there's unlimited personal liability.

3. **Limited Liability Company (LLC):** An LLC offers a middle ground between a sole proprietorship/partnership and a full corporation. It provides liability protection so your assets are shielded, but you still have a great deal of flexibility in how the business is managed and taxed. LLCs are a popular choice for many small businesses and startups.

4. **Corporation:** A corporation is its distinct legal entity, separate from its owners (called shareholders). This offers the strongest

liability protection, as well as more opportunities for raising capital, going public, and expanding. Corporations also have a more complex management structure, with a board of directors and various officer roles. They're subject to stricter regulations and tax requirements compared to other structures.

As you can see, each business structure has its unique pros and cons to consider. The "best" choice for your company will depend on factors like the size of your business, your growth plans, how you want to be taxed, and how much personal liability you're comfortable with.

Setting Up Your Legal Structure

Once you've decided on the right business structure, the next step is to set it up. This typically involves registering your company with your state or local government, obtaining the necessary licenses and permits, and fulfilling various tax and administrative requirements.

The specific steps can vary quite a bit depending on your chosen structure and location. For example, forming an LLC in the US generally requires filing articles of organization, appointing a registered agent, and securing an Employer Identification Number (EIN) from the Internal Revenue Service (IRS). This process may vary across different countries, although a unique identifier (Tax ID or VAT ID) is usually required everywhere. Incorporating as a full-fledged corporation involves an even more complex process, with things like, approving the corporate bylaws, establishing a board of directors, approving important decisions through a board resolution, recording minutes of the meeting and more.

This process is cumbersome and outright stressful for every single entrepreneur trying to focus on launching a business and generating sales (instead of dealing with paperwork and legal regulations).

Some of my companies are registered in Europe due to on-site teams, payroll, expense management, office costs, team benefits and other recognizable tax regulations locally. And when it comes to incorporating in the US, my go-to choice is doola.

I discovered doola after several years of seeking a US-based solution for simplified expense management, lightweight invoice and payment processing, and additional access to payment gateways or loan providers not available in Europe. Founded by Arjun Mahadevan in 2020, the "Business-in-a-Box" provides remote incorporation services, virtual bank account setup, and tax management all year long. It takes care of any doubts and fears with the IRS and compliance troubles that both local and foreign founders can face in the process.

Regardless of the structure you choose, it's highly recommended to work closely with an experienced business attorney or accountant. They can guide you through all the necessary filings, ensure you're in full compliance with the law, and help you make the best strategic decisions for your company's unique needs and goals. If you go through doola, their CPAs will take care of the process and consult you on the go.

Essential Paperwork and Regulations for Your New Business

No matter what type of business you're starting - whether it's a sole proprietorship, partnership, LLC, or corporation - there are some very important paperwork and regulatory requirements you'll need to take care of. Skipping or mishandling these essential steps can lead to major problems down the road, including hefty fines, legal complications, and even the potential shutting down of your company.

Let's break down the key paperwork and regulations you'll need to address once you've decided on the right legal structure for your business.

Paperwork Essentials

The first critical piece of paperwork is officially registering your business with the relevant state and local authorities. This usually involves filing articles of incorporation, organization, or a "doing business as" (DBA) certificate, depending on your specific business structure. This formally establishes your company as a recognized legal entity.

In addition to the registration paperwork, you'll also need to obtain any necessary licenses and permits to operate legally in your area. These can vary widely based on your industry, location, and the specific activities of your business. Some common examples include sales tax permits, professional or occupational licenses, health department permits for food service operations, and many others. Making sure you have all the right licenses in place is essential.

Another important set of paperwork involves securing the proper tax identification numbers for your business. This starts with getting the Employer Identification Number from the Internal Revenue Service (IRS). You may also need to register for additional state and local tax IDs, depending on the requirements in your area.

Ongoing Regulatory Compliance

In addition to the initial paperwork, there are also numerous ongoing regulatory requirements you'll need to stay on top of. This includes properly collecting and remitting sales tax, filing business income tax returns, and meeting all payroll tax obligations if you have employees.

For businesses with workers, there are even more compliance areas to manage. This can involve setting up proper payroll systems, obtaining workers' compensation insurance, and adhering to all applicable labor laws around minimum wage, overtime, employee rights, and more.

The key thing to remember is that meeting these paperwork and regulatory requirements isn't a one-time exercise. It's an ongoing process, such as filing monthly or quarterly filings, that requires you to stay vigilant and adaptable as the rules and laws governing your business evolve.

New permits may be required, tax policies can change, and labor regulations are frequently updated. Falling behind on any of these compliance areas can quickly snowball into major problems. That's why it's so important to have a solid system in place for tracking deadlines, staying informed on regulatory changes, and making sure your business is always operating within the bounds of the law.

Taking the time to get all of this essential paperwork and compliance in order upfront will pay dividends in the long run. It provides the proper legal foundation for your business to grow and thrive without the constant fear of penalties or other legal issues lurking in the background.

Starting a Business in the U.S. as a Non-Resident

Are you a non-U.S. citizen considering starting a business in the United States? If so, you're in the right place. The United States offers an incredible wealth of opportunities for entrepreneurs, and the good news is that you don't need to be a U.S. citizen or permanent resident to take advantage of them.

One of the best business structures for non-U.S. residents is the Limited Liability Company, or LLC. An LLC is a versatile business entity that combines the benefits of a corporation with the simplicity of a partnership or sole proprietorship. By establishing an LLC in the U.S., you can gain access to the world's largest economy, tap into a vast customer base, and position your company for long-term growth and success.

The Advantages of a Non-U.S. Resident LLC

As a non-U.S. citizen, setting up an LLC in the United States can provide you with several key advantages:

1. **Access to the U.S. Market:** With over 330 million potential customers, the U.S. market is a vast and lucrative opportunity for businesses of all sizes. By establishing a U.S. LLC, you can position your company to tap into this thriving consumer base.

2. **Credibility and Reputation:** Operating a U.S. LLC can enhance your company's credibility and reputation, both domestically and globally. It demonstrates your business's commitment to the international marketplace and can help you forge valuable partnerships and attract investment.

3. **Limited Liability Protection:** One of the primary benefits of an LLC is the limited liability protection it offers. Your assets, such as your home, savings, and other possessions, are generally shielded from the debts and liabilities of your business, providing you with crucial financial safeguard.

4. **Tax Advantages:** Depending on your specific situation, an LLC can offer favorable tax treatment. LLCs are typically taxed as "pass-through" entities, meaning the business's profits and losses are reported on the owner's tax return, potentially leading to significant tax savings. This helps you move your basis of taxation from a high tax jurisdiction to a low tax jurisdiction and save significant taxes.

5. **Flexibility in Management:** LLCs grant you a high degree of flexibility in how you structure and manage your business. You can choose to run the company yourself or appoint managers to handle the day-to-day operations, and you have the freedom to customize the ownership and decision-making processes to suit your needs.

Preparing the Essential Documents for Starting Your LLC

When you're in the process of launching your new business as a Limited Liability Company (LLC) in the United States, there are several important documents you'll need to gather and maintain. These records will not only be crucial for getting your LLC off the ground, but they'll also be vital for your ongoing tax preparation and compliance.

6 ESSENTIALS FOR STARTING YOUR LLC

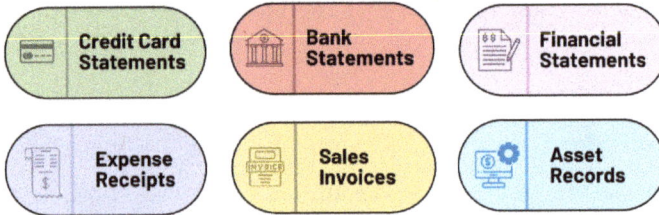

So, let's take a closer look at some of the key documents you'll need to collect as you embark on your entrepreneurial journey:

1. **Bank Statements:** Maintain detailed records of all your business banking activity, including checking, savings, and any other accounts.
2. **Credit Card Statements:** Track expenses made on business credit cards, whether a dedicated company card or your one used for business.
3. **Financial Statements:** Work with your bookkeeper or accountant to prepare balance sheets, income statements, and cash flow reports to monitor your company's finances.

4. **Expense Receipts:** Save any receipts for any business-related expenses over $75 to maximize tax deductions.

5. **Asset Records:** Document the purchase, value, and status of any physical assets owned by your LLC, like equipment or real estate.

6. **Sales Invoices:** Carefully record all invoices for products or services sold to accurately report revenue and cost of goods.

Proper documentation is essential for tax compliance and addressing any questions from authorities. Retain these records for at least three years after filing your original tax return or two years from the tax payment date. For employment taxes, the period is four years.

Staying organized with these key documents from the start will make tax season smoother and protect your assets as an LLC owner.

Setting Up a Non-U.S. Resident LLC in the United States

1. Determine Your Non-Resident Alien Status

The first step is to understand your tax status as a non-resident alien. This will have important implications for how your LLC is taxed. To qualify as a non-resident alien, you must not be a U.S. citizen, a permanent U.S. resident (green card holder), or subject to the "substantial presence test" for U.S. tax purposes.

2. Choose the Right State for Your LLC

Each U.S. state has its laws and regulations governing LLCs, so it's essential to select the state that best suits your business needs. Factors to consider include the state's LLC maintenance fees, privacy provisions, and overall business-friendly climate. Some popular and tax friendly choices for non-U.S. resident LLCs include Wyoming, Nevada, and Delaware.

3. Select a Unique LLC Name

Your LLC will need a distinct and memorable name that complies with your chosen state's naming requirements. This usually involves including the words "limited liability company" or the abbreviation "LLC" in the name. You'll also need to research and ensure the name is not already in use by another business.

4. Appoint a Registered Agent

Most states require you to designate a registered agent for your LLC, who will be responsible for receiving official documents and legal notifications on behalf of your business. As a non-U.S. resident, you'll likely want to use a professional registered agent service to handle this important task.

5. Obtain an Employer Identification Number (EIN)

An Employer Identification Number (EIN) is a unique tax ID number issued by the Internal Revenue Service (IRS). This number is essential for opening a U.S. business bank account, filing taxes, and conducting other business activities. As a non-U.S. citizen, you'll need to apply for an EIN, as you won't have a U.S. Social Security Number (SSN).

6. Prepare and File the Articles of Organization

The next step is to prepare and file the Articles of Organization, which are the foundational documents that officially establish your LLC. These forms typically require information about the company's name, registered agent, and members or managers. There's usually a filing fee associated with this process.

7. Create an Operating Agreement

While not always required by law, it's highly recommended to create a comprehensive Operating Agreement for your LLC. This document outlines the company's management structure, decision-making processes, ownership distribution, and other essential operational details. Having a well-crafted Operating Agreement is especially important for multi-member LLCs.

8. Open a U.S. Business Bank Account

Establishing a dedicated U.S. business bank account is a crucial step in managing your LLC's finances. This will allow you to keep your personal and business finances separate, simplify accounting and tax preparation, and facilitate transactions such as accepting payments and paying expenses.

9. Maintain Ongoing Compliance

Starting an LLC is just the beginning – you'll also need to stay on top of ongoing bookkeeping and compliance requirements. This may include filing annual reports, paying any required state and federal taxes, obtaining necessary licenses and permits, and ensuring you're following all applicable laws and regulations.

This chapter may be heavier with all the regulatory requirements in place, but you can't operate a successful business outside of the legal frameworks and tax requirements. Understanding the pros and cons of each option will determine the right legal setup for your venture.

I use doola for my US LLCs to ensure complete compliance, working with a capable team spending 100% of their time staying on top of recent changes and administrative requirements for managing and growing LLCs. And if you want to study the LLC process even further, I can personally recommend *"LLC Made Easy"*, Parshwa Mehta's free book including 72 pages devoted to non-US residents launching a business in the States. Both will be linked in mbadisrupted.com.

PART TWO

CHOOSING YOUR MODEL AND BUILDING THE FOUNDATION

CHAPTER SIX

SERVICE-BASED BUSINESSES

Starting a service-based business is the fastest and the easiest way to start your entrepreneurial journey as a digital CEO.

There are clear benefits of taking this path as a starting point:

- Minimal or practically zero starting costs
- Complete flexibility in working hours, weekly allotment, location
- Fully compatible with full-time jobs, parenting, stay-at-home assignments
- Fast revenue turnaround - payments within days or weeks and no ramp-up time.

This versatile business model covers a broad spectrum of solutions and service providers, including freelancers, consultants, and agencies, delivering everything from marketing and web development through creative, branding, advertising, PR solutions to accounting, legal and management consulting, M&A advisory.

According to the last Freelance Forward report conducted by the Upwork Research Institute in 2023, $1.27 trillion in annual earnings were generated by freelancers alone in the United States. 38% of the workforce was involved in freelancing - a total of 64 million Americans, compared to 60 million from 2022.

The core value proposition of service-based businesses is simple: you provide paid services for a skill in demand that you're uniquely qualified to fulfill. This could be paid marketing, development, consulting, design, ad management, SEO, or any other flavor in demand that you have an audience to serve.

This chapter will go over the best practices, pricing strategies, and client acquisition techniques that can help your service-based business thrive and flourish. We will explore the nuances of crafting a compelling service value proposition, the importance of doubling down on your core skills, and the advantages of stepping on the expertise and success stories of established service-based businesses. I will reveal specific techniques deployed successfully in DevriX as we ranked as one of the top 20 WordPress agencies worldwide back in 2016 (and still show up in the top 10 charts even if you search for the best WordPress vendors in ChatGPT or Gemini!)

As the prevailing business model covering the largest percentage of digital business providers online, let's dive into the best practices for running a service-based business, effective pricing strategies used in the market, what client acquisition looks like, and specific tactics to win proposals and close deals with a strong value proposition.

Let's start with the first one.

Best Practices for Service-Based Businesses

One of the key drawbacks of starting with a business model that's easy to penetrate is, well, everyone can do it, too.

I'm authoring an alternative MBA book because of the flaws in the current layer of education in business management when it comes to entrepreneurship, startups, or digital ventures. But the reason this problem exists in the first place is the dire need of validation - degrees, certificates, diplomas, any other way to build credibility and prove expertise in realms where everyone is free to sell anything.

You may have 30 years of IT or marketing expertise and work with an enterprise that gets pitched by 16-year-old teenagers taking a shot after passing a Udemy course online. While case studies or industry experience can be faked, formal degrees are theoretically harder to misrepresent. Certain industries - the legal and medical fields for example - cannot operate before practitioners have taken the corresponding degrees.

In service-based businesses, this is rarely the case. It's an open realm.

When you start out, this is a competitive advantage for you: low requirements to launch and easier to land the first contracts. But in order to keep scaling, close great contracts, and keep the competition behind later on, here is what you need to take care of in the coming months and, sometimes, weeks.

BEST PRACTICES FOR SERVICE-BASED BUSINESSES

1. NICHE SPECIALIZATION

2. EXCEPTIONAL SERVICE DELIVERY

3. EFFICIENT OPERATIONS

4. CONTINUOUS IMPROVEMENT

5. LEVERAGING PARTNERSHIPS

1. Niche Specialization

I have devoted the entire second chapter on defining your market, niche, and persona for a reason: differentiation matters. Service-businesses are often commoditized, with thousands of national competitors and millions of businesses offering the same service worldwide. Without niche specialization, you are as vulnerable as it gets.

Competing on price is never a winning strategy, and niching further down will help. Here are several areas to consider and narrow down even further:

- **Service Mix**: Instead of a broad "marketing" offer, think about Instagram Reels marketing or highly converting email newsletters. Refining your core service into a clear and understandable offer will deliver stronger results.

- **Target Market**: Try to isolate your market to a specific industry, segment, business size, type of persona. Marketing services for real estate agents or legal professionals is less densely populated than generic marketing, and you can supplement with success stories or unique skills to that key market.

- **Business Size**: Serving SMBs and large enterprises together is hardly possible for starting entrepreneurs. Position yourself for a specific business size. This will help you understand their core problems. Small businesses don't have talent available to deliver professional services even though their budgets are smaller. Large enterprises may be able to pay, but employing 3,000 people will likely include some marketing experts in-house who can deliver most of the work. Unless you niche down and specialize in an area they can outsource as well.

- **Location**: You can be the leading expert in your city or state. Being the go-to person in your local community is easier than competing globally. Bonus points if you niche down in a market that speaks a different language from English because this automatically filters out all US/UK/Australia-based top vendors that would normally be in the pool.

Profiling in a niche segment, market, region, language, and location will limit the competition and carve a niche you can dominate yourself. In this case, being a big fish in a small pond is the winning preservation strategy. As your business grows, you can take on other markets and expand accordingly.

2. Exceptional Service Delivery

There are two critical lessons you need to keep in mind in a service-based business:

- Retaining a client is five times cheaper than finding a new one. Providing quality service can turn your one-off clients into recurring ones by developing the right mix of pricing models.
- Word of mouth is one of the strongest lead-generation mediums for service professionals. Happy customers will refer more business to you - and that's contingent on high quality work.

Investing in excellent processes and implementation, responsive communication, and a genuine customer-centric mindset can set your business apart from the competition and foster long-term, loyal client relationships. Think about a poor telecom or a bank you've had terrible customer experience with - would you blink twice if a better vendor was available locally at the same price?

When clients engage in your service-based business, they are not just seeking a transactional exchange; they are looking for a trusted partner who will understand their unique needs, deliver exceptional results, and go the extra mile to exceed their expectations.

Customers are NOT always right, but you need to educate and lead them to the right results. Be a consultant, an educator, a professional authority guiding them based on their actual needs and the actual market opportunities.

Satisfied clients generate a steady flow of referrals and new business opportunities. This is one of the 4 core lead sources for DevriX: existing clients referring us to their partners or account managers we've worked with directly who switch jobs and invite us for another contract at their new workplace.

3. Efficient Operations

Streamlining your internal processes, automating repetitive tasks, and optimizing resource allocation can significantly enhance the scalability and profitability of your service-based business. You can deliver consistent, high-quality service while maintaining a lean and agile operation.

We will cover the principles of effective business processes in Chapter 18 and where to implement additional automation and technical solutions in Chapter 19. By the end of the book, you will have a better command of running efficient ops in your service-based business.

It may sound as a tedious future problem to have, but it's one of the key reasons enterprises are slow and get disrupted by smaller startups. Overhiring, complex workflows, slow communication, painful decision-making protocols, legal red tape take forever to solve simple problems while going through multiple stakeholders and decision makers in each division.

When discussing bloated software solutions during sales calls, I often compare them with a house of cards: you can't keep building on top of a foundation forever; it will fall apart eventually. Get this straight as early as possible.

4. Continuous Improvement

Staying ahead of the competition requires continued commitment to learning, innovation, and adaptation. Review your processes every three to six months, incorporate feedback from within and your customers, and adopt new technologies or industry trends.

One of the easiest ways to get replaced by a new market player is providing outdated services. Web technologies evolve and new frameworks pop up. SEO core algorithm changes are announced every three to six months. Email marketing regulations and tools provide new opportunities.

In the era of AI, dozens of new AI tools are released on Product Hunt every single week.

Get your operational frameworks in place and focus on the core of your business. Always strive for higher quality of service - it pays off as higher profit margins, better customer satisfaction, easier hiring and onboarding, and additional opportunities to compete in the field.

5. Leveraging Partnerships

Collaborating with complementary service providers or industry experts helps you tap into a broader pool of resources, knowledge, and client networks, ultimately strengthening your overall value proposition.

This too is one of the four key lead generation pillars my agencies utilize heavily. We have generated seven figures in revenue through collaborations and intros from our hosting agency partner Pagely. At DevriX, another $1.5M+ is attributed to introductions and mutual contracts with an ad management partner at our publishing part of the business.

We have also closed enterprise clients in automotive manufacturing, telecoms, and banks through branding agencies or security compliance providers cross-selling engineering or marketing strategy work. The opportunities are endless, and we consistently look for and carefully vet new partners, brand ambassadors, and advisors to expand into new niche markets.

Mastering Pricing Strategies for Service-Based Businesses

Mastering sales is a transferable skill that is the driving force of every single business enterprise. Once you get comfortable to attend sales meetings, run webinars, conduct discovery sessions, pitch solutions at events and plug them at speaking events, your business will pick up traction and start to accelerate.

But this process is highly related to the viability of your offer - namely, the fees involved with the transaction. How you price your services may differ, so pick the right pricing mechanism as you shape up your offers.

MASTERING PRICING STRATEGIES FOR SERVICE-BASED BUSINESSES

- VALUE-BASED PRICING
- HOURLY RATES
- PROJECT-BASED PRICING
- RETAINER-BASED PRICING
- TIERED PRICING

1. Value-Based Pricing

One of the most powerful pricing strategies for service-based businesses is value-based pricing. This approach focuses on aligning your fees with the perceived value your services deliver to the client. Once you understand your client's pain points, desired outcomes, and the transformative impact your solutions can have on their business or personal life, you can justify a premium price that reflects the true worth of your expertise.

Imagine you start a management consulting firm that specializes in helping small and medium-sized businesses streamline their operations and increase profitability. Through your in-depth analysis and tailored recommendations, you're able to help your clients achieve a 20% increase in revenue and a 15% reduction in operating costs. As long as you can communicate the tangible, measurable benefits of your services and how they directly address your client's most pressing needs, you have multiple ways to structure your offer with a clear expectation of the forecasted return on investment.

This value-based pricing model allows you to move beyond the constraints of hourly rates or fixed project fees and instead focus entirely on the output you can create for your clients. Adapting this framework, you can look for specific niches and ways to deliver $100K in extra revenue or savings and charge $10K to $20K for this service line, even if it takes you 10 or 15 hours to deploy an established framework.

This model is also known as "performance-based pricing" and often used for paid ads, lead generation, conversion rate optimization solutions. While some industry lines have carved a way into pricing this way, you may have to start with a simplified pricing that's easier to sell on.

2. Hourly Rates

The traditional hourly billing model remains a popular choice for many service-based businesses, particularly for freelancers and consultants. Hourly pricing directly correlates your time and effort with the client's investment, providing a clear and transparent pricing structure.

Hourly pricing requires careful tracking and reporting as every hour matters. You need to run a time tracking software like RescueTime, Toggl Track, or Time Doctor, or report hours manually in a spreadsheet used for invoicing afterward.

Hourly pricing is very contradictory. For some, it's the only viable way to run a business, although some clients are reluctant to pay on time. Rates aren't a great indicator of how long it takes to get a job done. Poor estimates and scoping make this hard to gauge at first, and contractors may also end up spending more time in estimates and ballparks than actually working.

That said, with specific consultations, it's easy to forecast expenses - think of legal consultations, marketing strategy, technical training, or other hourly appointments that set a clear contract for both parties and required costs.

3. Project-Based Pricing

For service-based businesses that work on fixed-scope, well-defined projects, a project-based pricing model can be an attractive option. Compared to the hourly model discussed above, this one provides clients with greater predictability and budget control, with a transparent, fixed-fee cost breakdown that clearly outlines the deliverables, timeline, and milestones of the engagement.

Project-based fees are possible only when you have a comprehensive understanding of the client's requirements and the resources needed to deliver the desired outcomes. For instance, producing 15 articles or writing a book with a pre-filled form compiling all assets by the client can be priced at a fixed rate. However, assessing a set of technical fixes for an existing platform in production, with all underlying risks of a custom code base, several years of patches by other people, and business-specific implementational details, are almost certain to exceed the scope by dozens or even hundreds of hours thanks to unexpected requirements popping in.

It's more common than not - most IT projects go out of budget and past the original deadline. The CHAOS report (an independent research group) found out that 31% of projects get canceled even before they get completed. This frightening realization justifies the move to other pricing models, agile-based solutions, retainer pricing, and alternative ways to avoid this outcome.

Moreover, with the realities of unexpected surprises, last-minute additions, delays, sick leaves, and everything in-between, even professional managers add a safety net multiplier to their initial estimates - which may be anywhere from 1.5X to 3X of the initial project scope.

Project-based pricing can be particularly beneficial for service-based businesses that offer standardized or repeatable solutions, especially ones delivered from scratch. The consultative, hourly pricing approach, is a better fit when debugging and analysis work is required before one even gets to scoping the work.

4. Retainer-Based Pricing

I've been a proponent of retainers for 15 years and this billing model was almost non-existent when we launched our business into the WordPress territory. After two years of continuous efforts, providing educational resources, comparison reports, and analyses through other business verticals (such as legal) relying on retainers, we successfully pioneered and coined "WordPress retainers" back in 2015 and helped coach over 300 agencies adopting this model after. It's still our best sold solution internally (supplemented with value-based deals and some fixed packages).

Retainer-based pricing can be especially advantageous for service-based businesses that provide ongoing support, and consultative services or maintain long-term relationships with their clients. Securing a consistent revenue source is a predictable path to planning and allocating your resources, investing in the growth of your business, and mitigating the volatility of project-based or hourly-rate engagements.

When structuring a retainer-based agreement, make sure you clearly define the scope of services, the expected level of support, and any additional fees or variable costs that may arise. This provides peace of mind for your clients and allows you to cross-sell or include additional resources internally to expand the scope of solutions and services over time.

For instance, we offer different levels of SLA for smaller retainer plans compared to large ones. Our larger contracts are eligible for a shared Slack channel with most of our leadership team in for anything that may come up in the process. Response and reaction times also depend on the arrangement. The same goes for the number of meetings or scheduled calls, strategy calls included, and any support with roadmap planning.

5. Tiered Pricing

The tiered pricing structure presents a series of options depending on different variables or accommodation to available budgets. This is particularly beneficial for service-based businesses that offer a range of services or deliverables.

For example, a digital marketing agency may offer a basic package focused on search engine optimization, a mid-tier package that includes social media management and content creation, and a premium package that provides a comprehensive suite of digital marketing solutions. Smaller packages may exclude technical SEO or strategic content guidance while larger ones can involve more strategic and due diligence work pulling in senior consultants internally or leveraging expensive data sources your team has access to.

Presenting clients with a clear menu of options, each with its own set of features and pricing, makes it easier for clients to identify the service level that best fits their needs and budget. This can help you attract a wider range of clients, from small businesses to enterprise-level organizations, as long as you can afford to maintain both audiences in terms of communication or management overhead or compliance for the enterprise segment.

Tiered pricing may be structured around other variables as well:

- **SLA:** Service-level agreements on response hours or support availability

- **Depth of Changes:** Lower plans can cover the basics while top plans involve your most experienced staff members for consulting and strategy
- **Volume-Based Pricing:** Structuring your pricing based on a number of campaigns or website pages, web traffic, number of transactions, or other resource metrics that scale with the business.

Regardless of the pricing strategy you ultimately choose to implement, make sure you thoroughly research your market, study your competitors, and establish a clear value proposition that justifies your pricing. You may pivot into new pricing models occasionally or structure an ad-hoc deal with specific clients, so keep an eye open on new opportunities during pre-sales calls.

Client Acquisition for Service-Based Businesses

One of the most common questions I receive from young agency owners, freelancers, and consultants is: "How to find more clients?"

Lead generation is top of mind for most businesses out there, but service-based ones lack the added overhead or competitive advantage of building a unique product or leveraging a magical source of data that's compelling and invites people in. Being easy to start and entirely related to time spent on serving customers, sales is naturally top of mind until a certain level of recurring revenue and ongoing profitability is secured.

And here's the thing: using densely populated channels with tons of other vendors is unlikely to work well. Whichever medium you use, try to position yourself as an authority and stay away from markets if possible. I have mentioned marketplaces as one of the possible channels since diversification is always needed, but focus on being a scarce resource when you can.

CLIENT ACQUISITION FOR SERVICE-BASED BUSINESSES

1 Leveraging Referrals and Networking

2 Targeted Outreach and Lead Generation

3 Showcasing Expertise through Inbound Marketing

4 Leveraging Digital Platforms and Marketplaces

5 Attending Industry Events and Conferences

I have provided different examples from my own agency DevriX throughout the book - cherry-pick the ones that make sense and try them out if you're starting an agency or running a freelance business.

Let's dive into several channels to start with.

1. Leveraging Referrals and Networking

One of the core methods to find new clients continuously is by building and nurturing a strong network of industry connections, past clients, and professional groups where your target audience gathers.

This may sound like a generic piece of advice, but it's a lot more tactical and methodical than you may think. Here's how to structure a flywheel process to keep your partners warm and engage new partnership opportunities:

- Make it a habit to regularly check in with your past clients, ask for feedback, and ask for referrals.
- Keep in touch with account managers or directors who switch jobs. They may be looking for a reliable vendor in their new role.
- Sign up for professional Slack communities, masterminds, local startup groups, and industry associations. Keep track of online discussions and panels and on-site meetups.
- Create a list of industry events in your area that your ideal customers attend. For example, if you provide marketing services to lawyers, consider legal conferences. Don't stick to your own bubble and professional organization.

Being methodical and reviewing these opportunities on a regular basis will present opportunities that won't require a brute force approach doing constant cold outreach.

2. Targeted Outreach and Lead Generation

Cold outreach has been around for as long as telephones and email networks have been around. They are both integral components of outbound-led go-to-market motions reviewed in chapter 14.

Aside from cold calling or sending email blasts pitching your services, this covers all available channels your prospects hang out at: LinkedIn, X or Instagram DMs, Messenger or WhatsApp texts and ads, and any other intrusive ways to get in their way and capture their attention.

Certain businesses find success in traditional brute force cold-calling, especially when campaigns are executed with some best practices in place: captivating subject lines, clear value proposition with a compelling promise in the copy, featuring a relevant case study, mentioning a competitor, or any other principles that a modern playbook includes. But pitching right away - on the very first contact - fails over 99% of the time and led to severe consequences for executives and business owners, including not picking up to private numbers once you get 10 spam calls every single day for years.

The more crowded the space is, the harder to find a prospective client that would be interested. Keep in mind that executives get blasted about development, SEO, marketing, creative, lead generation services all the time - email, social, texts, and calls. However, crafting a creative and unique offer or finding relevant contacts for introduction (or common interests/alumni groups/events you both attended) may unlock doors that cold outreach won't bypass. The better researched a prospect is - especially following specific signals they are in shopping mode - the higher the close rates are from outreach initiatives.

If you take the path of outreach, do your best to avoid spam at scale. This may get your phone numbers and email accounts blacklisted fast. Additionally, giving your brand a bad name in the long term is not what you want to be known for. Most executives look into their CRMs or email inboxes for relevant connections or brand mentions when reviewing an opportunity or a company. Your spammy blast from a decade ago may still be recorded somewhere.

Targeted outreach performs well when mixed in with personalization, longer journeys, email sequences, gradual warm up over several weeks before the initial contact, thorough research to offer a highly relevant solution in need. Any shortcuts will jeopardize the efficiency of the campaign.

3. Showcasing Expertise through Inbound Marketing

Your freelance, agency or consultancy business can grow as an authority through continuous education - both on corporate level and with a founder-led thought leadership journey.

Establishing yourself as a recognized thought leader and industry expert can be a tremendously valuable asset when it comes to attracting new clients. Allocate regular time to create and distribute high-quality content - business guides, industry research, customer interviews, whitepapers, case studies, or educational webinars. You can demonstrate your deep knowledge and expertise, build trust with your target audience, and position your service-based business as a go-to resource in your industry.

Thought leadership and executive branding have been a personal passion of mine after years of training in professional organizations like SAP, VMware, Software AG, CERN, Saudi Aramco. Having led hundreds of courses and talks, I've been repurposing existing resources into bite-sized pieces on social media and my blog. Over time, this knowledge base expands, ranks on Google, attracts more social followers, and this reaches a broader audience.

I also use these resources during sales pitches and conversations with prospects. Some of my work is published on Entrepreneur and Forbes, Inc. Authority sources featuring my content have a higher chance to seal a deal than a random opinion posted in an email thread.

4. Leveraging Digital Platforms and Marketplaces

Platforms like LinkedIn, Upwork, or Fiverr can provide service-based businesses, especially freelancers and consultants, with a much broader reach and access to a diverse pool of potential clients.

While you may end up competing with everyone in your field across the world, it's still a targeted market with job postings and freelance opportunities you can bid on directly. It's a spectacular way to polish your sales pitches, test different offers, validate pitch frameworks, test out research initiatives, see what common problems exist in your industry, and keep refining forward.

After all, other approaches listed here are either passive (you wait for clients to come and hope that an opportunity presents itself) or aggressive (cold calling and emails). In marketplaces, every client is actively looking to solve a specific problem.

Competitive marketplaces are densely populated and shining out is only getting harder, even though not impossible. Bidding on jobs will get some contract opportunities even though starter jobs may be more modest. In my early days, I took on several Upwork contracts generating tens of thousands of dollars each. One small job in 2012 started as a $1K one-off debugging contract that turned into a $6,000/mo retainer deal - and this was instrumental to slowly growing my team and diversifying my offerings down the road.

5. Attending Industry Events and Conferences

Industry-relevant events, conferences, meetups and trade shows are a great excuse to connect with and network with potential clients face-to-face.

These in-person interactions can help you build genuine rapport, demonstrate your capabilities and potentially convert some attendees into paying customers. People do business with people, and facetime can create stronger bonds compared to impersonal email or online direct messages in a cluttered inbox.

Moreover, on-site events limit the pool of competitive vendors on the ground. You always need to strive for a "blue ocean" market as discussed in W. Chan Kim and Renée Mauborgne's book, *Blue Ocean Strategy*. A blue ocean, compared to a red ocean, isn't crowded with competitors thanks to defining a unique niche, a specialized target market, and attending events with limited competition.

Regardless of which client acquisition strategies you choose to implement, you must maintain a relentlessly customer-centric approach, consistently improve, and stress on the unique value that you offer, all while delivering exceptional service to every single client. Most deals take months to close. Don't miss on opportunities and get the right relationships in place to nurture over time. As you keep scaling, your success record and growing brand will make sales easier and contract sizes will expand.

Unique Value Proposition

Providing a unique service proposition (USP) is critical for every business type, but no segment is as densely populated as service-based companies. This is why we went on a long journey on niche exploration and problem-solution definition in chapter 2, together with validating ideas and a thorough market research later in chapter 3.

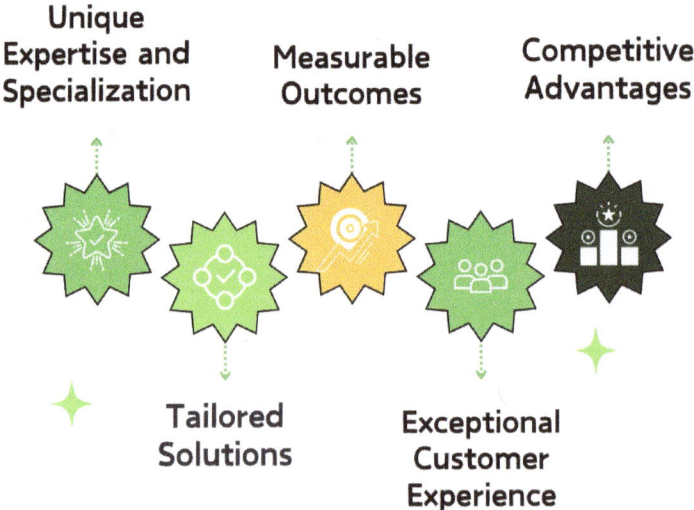

SERVICE VALUE PROPOSITION

Unique Expertise and Specialization

Measurable Outcomes

Competitive Advantages

Tailored Solutions

Exceptional Customer Experience

Crafting an effective unique value proposition (UVP) requires deep insights into your target market, a clear understanding of your client's specific pain points and challenges, and a thorough assessment of your own unique capabilities and competitive advantages. A UVP explicitly articulates why your solution is preferable over competitors' offerings and how it uniquely addresses the needs of your customers. It is critical that your offer considers all these elements to stand out in the marketplace.

In contrast, a general value proposition broadly defines the inherent value that a company promises to deliver to customers. It focuses on the benefits and outcomes that customers can expect from the entire brand or service, without necessarily highlighting what makes these benefits unique or superior to what is available from other vendors. While a value proposition is essential for communicating the core reasons a customer should choose your services, a UVP goes a step further by pinpointing and promoting unique differentiators that make your offering special.

In the early days, service-based businesses may be pressed to take on every job that comes in for revenue reasons. This isn't a great approach in the long term, but early revenue, portfolio, reviews, and referrals are everything, and closing deals is more important than ever. So being versatile and open to any job is no dirty work - don't pass on jobs if you have the time and skills to deliver.

And if it comes to a marketplace pitch or bidding against multiple other vendors, try the following ideas to differentiate yourself in the crowd.

1. **Unique Expertise and Specialization:** One of the most important things to highlight in your USP is your niche expertise, your specialized skills, and your proven track record of delivering exceptional results for your clients. What makes you the go-to expert in your field? Can you outline specific success stories in this field? Point to any examples in that niche, service segment, niche clients, former work experience.

2. **Tailored Solutions:** Your value proposition should also emphasize your ability to provide customized, client-centric solutions designed to solve real problems in the wild. How do your services accommodate custom requirements? What are your recommendations to deliver solutions that generate notable results? Can you forecast specific obstacles on the way - related to budgets, spend, design constraints, web traffic? Be a strategic partner and not an outsourced vendor following a checklist.

3. **Measurable Outcomes:** Whenever possible, rely on hard data and success stories. Whether it's increased revenue, improved efficiency, enhanced brand visibility, or something else, be sure to showcase the real-world results that your clients can expect. Clear expectations and visualizing the end results make a true difference.

4. **Exceptional Customer Experience:** Especially valid in marketplaces, make sure you go above and beyond and overdeliver as needed. This is one of the few instances where the client is always right - because you want to avoid that 1-star or even three-star review that ruins your general rating in the future. Over Communicate, help out, don't rush it - good reviews add up and help after.

5. **Competitive Advantages:** Are there other insights beyond work expertise or case studies that can be helpful? If you speak a foreign language that is used in the project, this is a specialized skill. If you have interned in hospitals before or have done door-to-door sales for medical brochures, tie this expertise into any healthcare projects for relevance. Use every bit that makes sense.

Service-based businesses are extremely easy to start and incredibly hard to grow and scale. They may present a perfect opportunity for a freelancer or a side business, but if you try to move past the seven-figures and don't account ad spend in the equation, you need to stand out from the competition and employ professional business practices here.

I have built two seven-figure service businesses from the ground up and consulted dozens of others in Growth Shuttle, my advisory firm. While moving up is not easy, it's also particularly straightforward when you keep closing deals with a great track record, grow your expertise in certain verticals, and use that momentum to keep going.

CHAPTER SEVEN

SAAS FOUNDATIONS

One of the most lucrative business models in the software industry is the concept of subscription-based solutions. Most consumers are intimately familiar (and likely customers) of subscription businesses such as Netflix, Amazon Prime, Disney+, Comcast, Spotify, DoorDash - and thousands of popular brands making a living through predictable MRR (monthly recurring revenue).

This is applicable outside of the digital realm (your cable subscription or your phone bill) and for web-based solutions - particularly rented software applications known as SaaS (Software as a Service).

Back in the late 1990s and early 2000s, we had to purchase software, install it on our local machines, and then maintain and update it over time. This is still the case for certain software applications - accounting solutions, healthcare applications, ERPs (while many are moving to cloud-based solutions as well).

SaaS has pioneered a new medium of cloud-based software delivery, where applications are hosted on remote servers and accessed by you over the internet, often through a simple web browser or a mobile app.

The SaaS model has changed the game in remarkable ways. Rather than making a one-time purchase, you can now subscribe to SaaS applications, paying a recurring fee to access the software and its features. This shift has made software much more accessible and affordable, especially for smaller businesses and individual users who may not have the resources or IT expertise to manage traditional software installations.

I vividly remember the time back when we were playing MP3 audio files in Winamp (audio player in the 90s) or BSPlayer (a multimedia player for video files). While browser-based applications started to pop up, I found it impossible to steam video or audio online, especially when WAP and GPRS connections were barely available (far before 3G, 4G, let alone 5G existed) and mobile devices were primitive at best.

Nevertheless, Shopify and Netflix changed the games, and it's been a decade since I last used my audio player with wired headphones instead of streaming YouTube on my bluetooth buds.

The benefits of SaaS go far beyond just cost savings. The cloud-based nature of these applications also makes them highly scalable, as you can easily add or remove licenses as your needs change. SaaS providers can also ensure that their software is always up-to-date, with the latest features and security patches automatically rolled out to all users.

Complex and heavy SaaS applications can run calculations and do processing on expensive cloud servers that exceed the capabilities of an average laptop, and present the output in a web interface straight in the browser. This resembles a Remote Desktop session to a powerful machine that does the heavy lifting for you.

By eliminating the need for costly infrastructure and maintenance, SaaS companies can focus their resources on continuously improving their products and delivering exceptional user experiences. This has led to a surge of new and innovative SaaS solutions, catering to a wide range of industries and use cases.

As the adoption of SaaS continues to grow, it's clear that this cloud-based software delivery model is here to stay. You, as a business owner or individual user, are embracing the convenience, scalability, and cost-effectiveness that SaaS offers, transforming the way you access and utilize software tools and applications. Moving on, we will explore the core foundations that underpin a successful SaaS business:

Lean Product Development

Developing a successful SaaS product requires a smart and flexible approach. This is called lean product development, and it focuses on quickly creating a basic version of your product, getting feedback from your early customers, and then improving the product based on what you learn.

The key idea behind lean product development is the Minimum Viable Product (MVP). This means you create a very simple version of your product that has only the most essential features. You then launch this MVP and see how your early customers react to it. What do they like? What do they not like? What other features do they want?

By getting this feedback from your customers, you can then make changes and improvements to your product. You don't have to spend a lot of time and money building out a ton of features upfront. Instead, you can test your product with real customers, learn what's working and what's not, and then keep refining and adding to your product over time.

This is a much more effective approach than trying to build out a huge, complex product all at once. SaaS companies need to be nimble and adaptable. The market is constantly changing, and customer needs can shift quickly. By using a lean, iterative approach, you can stay ahead of those changes and make sure your product is always meeting the needs of your customers.

For example, let's say you're building a new project management SaaS tool. Instead of trying to build every single feature you can imagine, you might start with just the most basic functionality - the ability to create tasks, assign them to team members, and track progress. You launch this simple MVP, get feedback from your early users, and then start adding more advanced features like reporting, calendar views, and integrations based on what your customers say they want.

This allows you to get your product out there quickly, start generating revenue, and get valuable insights from real users. It's a much more efficient way to develop a successful SaaS product than trying to build everything upfront. Stay lean, stay flexible, and always keep your customers at the center of what you're doing.

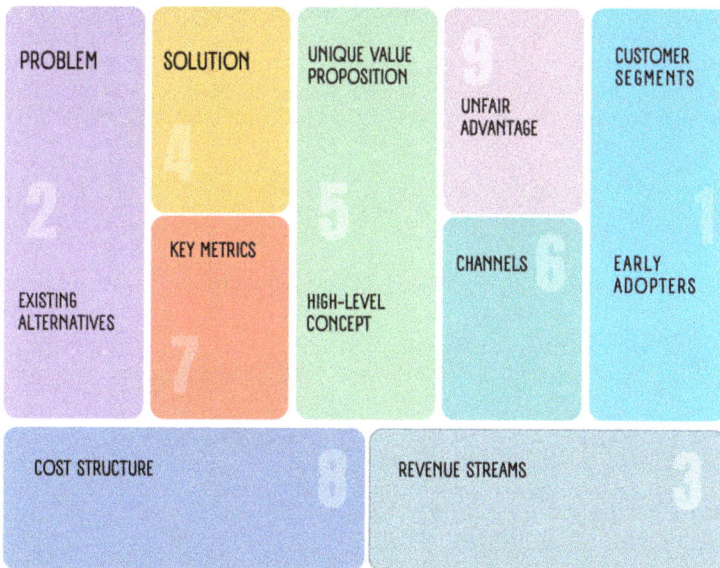

I have authored several guides on product development and building MVPs that will provide you with a more comprehensive process on structuring your engineering process and resources - for planning the technical stack (programming languages or frameworks) to necessary starter components (login forms, user management, data safety), to the ability to scale and launch an MVP forward. Having published thousands of pages of content across blogs and Q&A sites like Quora over the past decade. I will link the additional guides on the book's website, mbadisrupted.com.

Pricing Models

Pricing is a crucial part of running a successful SaaS business. As a SaaS company, you need to carefully consider your pricing strategy to make sure your business is profitable and can keep growing over the long term.

I've compiled several strategic pricing buckets in the following concept map:

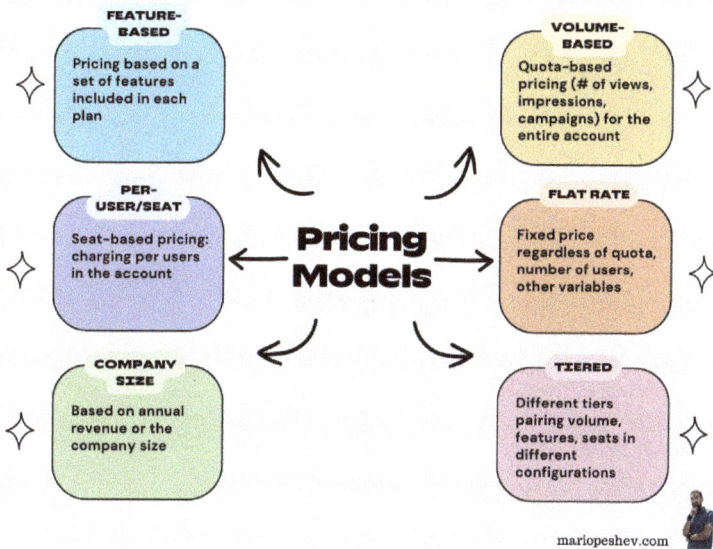

FEATURE-BASED	VOLUME-BASED
Pricing based on a set of features included in each plan	Quota-based pricing (# of views, impressions, campaigns) for the entire account

PER-USER/SEAT	FLAT RATE
Seat-based pricing: charging per users in the account	Fixed price regardless of quota, number of users, other variables

Pricing Models

COMPANY SIZE	TIERED
Based on annual revenue or the company size	Different tiers pairing volume, features, seats in different configurations

mariopeshev.com

We can simplify and group them into 4 core categories analyzed below.

1. Subscription-Based Pricing

With this model, your customers pay a recurring fee, usually monthly or annually, to access your SaaS platform. This gives you a steady, predictable stream of revenue. It also allows your customers to easily scale up or down their usage as their needs change. For example, a project management SaaS tool might offer a basic subscription plan for $9 per user per month, and then higher-tier plans with more features for $19 or $29 per user per month. Customers can choose the plan that fits their team size and requirements.

2. Usage-Based Pricing

Here, customers pay based on how much they use your SaaS platform. This could be things like the number of users, the amount of data storage used, or the number of transactions processed. The key is that the pricing is directly tied to the value the customer is getting from your product. A good example is a cloud storage SaaS - customers might pay \$5 per month for up to 1TB of storage, and then an additional \$2 for every extra 500GB they need. This keeps the pricing fair and aligned with how much the customer is using.

3. Tiered Pricing

With this model, you offer different pricing tiers, each with its own set of features and capabilities. This allows customers to choose the plan that best fits their needs and budget. It can also encourage customers to upgrade to higher tiers as their requirements grow. Tiered plans can provide access to premium features at the higher plans that aren't available in the starter ones, so your customers may opt in for the more expensive option even if they don't max out the quota limits for the starter plans.

4. Freemium Model

In this model, you offer a basic version of your SaaS product for free, and then charge for a premium version with additional features. The free version helps you attract new users and build your customer base, while the paid version generates revenue. A note-taking app is a common example. The free version might have limited storage and features, while the paid version unlocks unlimited storage, advanced formatting tools, and team collaboration.

As a digital CEO building a SaaS company, you'll need to carefully evaluate factors like your target customers, the perceived value of your product, your competition, and your costs to determine the right pricing strategy. The goal is to find a model that is both attractive to your customers and profitable for your business.

Initial Traction

Initial traction is super important for SaaS companies, especially when you're just starting. It shows that your product is viable and that people are interested in using it.

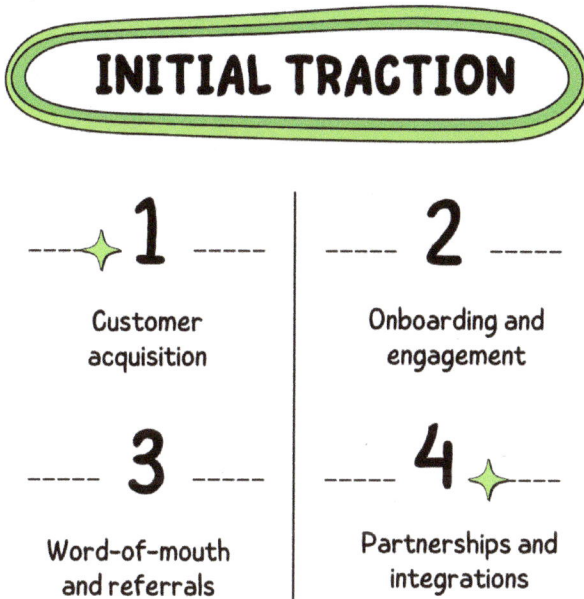

INITIAL TRACTION

1 Customer acquisition

2 Onboarding and engagement

3 Word-of-mouth and referrals

4 Partnerships and integrations

Initial traction refers to the early signs that your SaaS product is starting to gain some real interest and momentum from customers. It's that crucial first step in proving that your product is viable and people are willing to use it. Getting that initial traction lays the groundwork for your business to grow and succeed in the long run. So, how do you go about getting that initial traction? Well, it usually involves a few different strategies:

1. **Customer acquisition:** The first step is identifying your target audience - the people who are most likely to be interested in and benefit from your SaaS product. Then you need to figure out the best ways to reach them, whether that's through content marketing, search engine optimization, social media, or partnering with other businesses.

2. **Onboarding and engagement:** Once you get those initial customers signed up, you must provide them with a smooth and helpful onboarding experience. Walk them through the key features of your product, make sure they understand how to use it, and provide ongoing support. This will help keep them engaged and make them more likely to stick around.

3. **Word-of-mouth and referrals:** Happy customers are your secret weapon when it comes to building that initial traction. Encourage them to spread the word about your SaaS product to their networks. Offer incentives like discounts or credits for referrals, and make it easy for them to share your product with others.

4. **Partnerships and integrations:** Teaming up with other businesses, apps, or industry influencers can be a great way to expand your reach and tap into new audiences. Integrating your SaaS product with other popular tools your customers already use can make your solution even more valuable to them.

Building that initial traction is an ongoing process. You'll need to constantly experiment, analyze your results, and tweak your strategies to find what works best for your unique SaaS business and your target customers. If you stay focused, get creative, and put the customer experience first, you'll be well on your way to achieving that crucial early momentum.

SaaS businesses are very effective as a progression to a different business model or when diversifying solutions.

- You can productize a solution into a report generator, a calculator, form builder, a premade website, a marketing report generator or an email funnel designer. This cuts down on service time and delivery every time in exchange for a monthly fee.
- SaaS provides scalability opportunities that service-based businesses cannot afford an offer. You can service hundreds or even thousands of clients with a team of 5-10 people managing product operations, stability, and marketing. Compared with hourly pricing or project-based fees, this model scales fast.
- Turning an educational or onboarding experience into a self-guided one. This cuts down onboarding and training time and enables customers to self-train themselves.

Instead of creating visuals from scratch, our micro SaaS YVisuals.app provides a collection of minimalist visuals we can quickly update in the browser and share on social media. The AI-generated experience can pick the right chart from the database depending on different criteria and populate this for you. It's a great primer on how SaaS saves time and delivers.

One of my successful exits was an order tracking Shopify app in early 2024 serving nearly 3,000 stores with a small team of a dozen people. The scaling potential is endless even with a nimble team. This model works well within evolved marketplaces, site builders, or hosted ecommerce platforms in a similar fashion if you're servicing this market.

Just like other models, SaaS has pros and cons. We'll review several other business models that may be more aligned with your vision and strong suit.

CHAPTER EIGHT

BUILDING COMMUNITY

I am a very strong proponent of branding: personal and professional, executive branding, and thought leadership.

Strong brands build loyal communities and grow valuations. This proposition alone leads to opportunities to close strategic partnerships, amplify campaigns, organize impressive launches, and maintain profitability while onboarding some of the best people on the planet.

As a digital CEO or a serial entrepreneur, building a strong, engaged community around your product or business is one of the most crucial elements in growing the business. This is not just about acquiring customers. It's about nurturing a loyal following of passionate advocates who truly believe in your mission and are invested in your success. This involves staff members, partners, customers, journalists, influencers, and other community supporters.

When you build a strong community, you unlock a wealth of invaluable benefits. Your community members can provide you with crucial feedback, generate word-of-mouth promotion that amplifies your reach, and even contribute to the ongoing development and improvement of your offerings.

I'm in over a dozen Slack communities, several Skool groups, two Circle groups for investors - all serving different purposes for different cohorts of people. These have been instrumental to solving specific problems, hiring staff, shortlisting tools and vendors, uncovering partnership opportunities, and building close relationships with other players in the space.

There are two forms of communities we're reviewing in this chapter:

- **A product/brand-based community:** Building a cohort of loyal users, partners, and ambassadors for a brand, a SaaS product, or a marketplace.
- **Community as a business model:** Launching a niche community with people with shared interests or professional inspirations and monetizing this through paid subscriptions, courses, webinars, mastermind groups, consulting services, on-site events, affiliates, and promotions.

In both cases, if community building is top of mind, there are certain considerations you need to go through to make it possible.

Choosing the Right Community-Building Platform

As a digital CEO or entrepreneur, the platform you choose can have a profound impact on the success and growth of your community, so it's essential to carefully consider your options.

CHOOSING THE RIGHT COMMUNITY-BUILDING PLATFORM

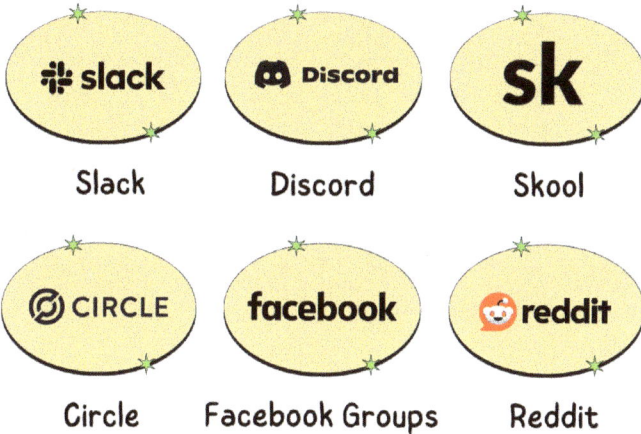

Slack   Discord   Skool

Circle   Facebook Groups   Reddit

Let's explore some top platform choices for building a community:

1. **Slack:** Slack is a popular messaging and collaboration platform that allows you to create private and public channels for your community. It enables real-time communication, file sharing, and integration with various other tools, making it an efficient way to keep your community connected and organized. Slack has a long history, launching in 2013 and later being acquired by Salesforce, and has since become a widely used tool for teams and communities of all sizes. It's powerful and popular in business, though its free plan does not retain history forever and paid plans start at $8.75/user/month.

2. **Discord:** Discord is a versatile communication platform that is particularly popular among online communities and gaming enthusiasts. It offers features such as text, voice, and video chat, as well as the ability to create custom roles and permissions for community members. Discord has been around since 2015 and has become a go-to platform for building and maintaining engaged online communities. Recently, AI communities, NFT/metaverse groups, and even investor groups have been signing up for Discord as their platform of choice. One of my accounting firms maintains a startup community for its own clients in Discord as well.

3. **Skool:** Skool is a community-driven platform that focuses on collaborative learning and knowledge sharing. It allows you to create private or public groups, host live sessions, and engage in discussions around specific topics or interests. Skool has a strong emphasis on fostering a sense of community and facilitating knowledge exchange among its users. I participate in an agency accelerator Skool community hosted by Eric Siu, the founder of Single Grain and the co-host of the Marketing School podcast.

4. **Circle:** Circle is a community platform that enables you to create private or public spaces for your community members to connect, share content, and engage in discussions. It offers features such as forums, events, membership management, and integrations with other tools like Slack and Zapier. Circle has been in the market since 2019 and has gained popularity among community-driven organizations and businesses. Our SeedBlink investment community is hosted on Circle.

5. **Facebook Groups:** Facebook Groups provide a familiar and widely used platform for building and managing online communities. They allow you to create private or public groups,

share content, and engage with your community members through various features such as discussions, events, and polls. Facebook Groups have been around for years and continue to be a popular option for community building. Find out if your audience is using Facebook actively and decide accordingly.

6. **Reddit:** Reddit is a social news aggregation and discussion platform that offers the ability to create and manage subreddits (community-based forums). It allows you to engage with your community through discussions, content sharing, and the upvoting/downvoting system. Reddit has a long history, dating back to 2005 before the IPO in early 2024, and has become a hub for online communities and discussions on a wide range of topics.

When choosing the right platform, consider factors such as the feature set, user experience, integration capabilities, and the overall fit with your community's needs and goals.

Some communities host successfully on Telegram or even WhatsApp. Find out what mediums look more native and familiar to your existing audience. Experiment with different platforms, gather feedback from your community, and continuously optimize your approach to ensure the success of your community-building efforts.

Developing Effective Growth Strategies for Your Community

Building a thriving, engaged community around your business doesn't happen overnight. It requires a well-crafted and consistently executed growth strategy. When you approach that with a business mentality, hiring a community manager may be the first logical role to bootstrap this venture. Look for someone devoted to connecting with industry peers, compiling insights, keeping the community alive, cross-posting stories, and creating conversations.

Even if you take on this personally in the early days, it necessitates a tactical results-based approach, not chaotic ad-hoc actions.

DEVELOPING EFFECTIVE GROWTH STRATEGIES FOR YOUR COMMUNITY

LEVERAGE EXISTING NETWORKS

Involve friends, colleagues, and industry peers.

1

2

DEVELOP TARGETED CONTENT

Create blogs, videos, and discussions.

INCENTIVIZE PARTICIPATION

Provide exclusive content, discounts, or merchandise.

3

4

FOSTER INFLUENCER RELATIONSHIPS

Partner with influencers for enhanced credibility.

EXPLORE CROSS-PROMOTIONS

Co-host events and webinars.

5

6

MAINTAIN ENGAGEMENT

Keep up regular interactions and feedback loops.

STRATEGIC OUTREACH

Employ direct messaging, emails, and press releases.

7

8

REGULAR UPDATES

Offer continuous updates and exclusive deals.

MARIO PESHEV

mariopeshev.com

Let's explore some proven growth strategies that you can leverage to steadily build momentum, attract new members, and turn your community into a vibrant, self-sustaining ecosystem.

1. Leveraging Existing Networks

Start with your personal network, including friends, former colleagues, partners, vendors, and social media followers. Make a connection and invite them to join your community. This personal touch can go a long way in kickstarting your community's growth, as people are often more inclined to engage with something that's been recommended by someone they know and trust.

Imagine you've just launched an online community for aspiring entrepreneurs in the tech industry. Start by reaching out to your personal network, reconnecting with former colleagues, classmates, and even friends who might be interested in your community. Encourage them to join and participate, and ask them to share the community with their networks as well. This ripple effect can help you quickly build a solid foundation of engaged members who can then become advocates for your community, further expanding its reach.

I launched my Slack community for Daily Creators through my personal network on LinkedIn and Twitter and expanded from there. While there are a handful of groups for industry experts, our niche circle revolves around content amplification strategies, hooks, algorithm changes, content frameworks, engagement mechanisms, impression rates, and very specific topics that other groups simply don't discuss.

2. Targeted Content and Outreach

Identify the pain points, interests, and aspirations of your ideal community members, and develop content that addresses these needs. This could include informative blog posts, educational videos, or controversial discussions on industry-relevant topics.

Once you've created your content, actively promote it through various channels, such as social media, guest blogging on industry-leading platforms, and participation in relevant online forums. Press releases can be an amplification mechanism to spark some interest. Supplement that with targeted outreach through direct messages or emails to your ideal customers that may be a good fit.

3. Incentivizing Participation

Engaging your community members and encouraging their active participation is crucial for the long-term success of your community. One effective way to do this is by offering incentives that motivate them to contribute, share, and collaborate.

These incentives can take various forms, such as exclusive content, discounts on products or services, recognition for their contributions, or even rewards like merchandise or experiences. Gamifying that community experience will contribute to a sense of ownership and investment, which can lead to increased engagement, loyalty, and word-of-mouth promotion.

4. Fostering Influencer Relationships

Partnering with industry influencers, thought leaders and subject matter experts can be a powerful way to amplify your community's reach and credibility. Influencer impact cannot be understated, and we can gauge that via celebrities like The Rock (running a $3.5B tequila brand), the Kardashians (several billion-dollar stories behind different family members), or Ryan Reynolds (Mint sold for $1.35B and he is actively involved with multiple businesses outside of his acting career).

You probably don't have close relationships with ultra-high-net-worth influencers, but there are niche experts and respected figures in each network. Identify some subject-matter experts who are respected and influential within your target market and explore opportunities to collaborate with them. Bringing several of them on board will amplify the exposure and solidify the trust factor.

Once in, invite them to host live Q&A sessions, contribute guest articles, or even lead specialized workshops or masterclasses for your community members. Tapping into the authority (and networks) of key opinion leaders helps to attract new members, increase engagement, and position your community as a go-to resource within your industry. This could be an extra growth and revenue channel for them if they launch new courses or SaaS, need early feedback on a product or recently wrote a book.

I participate in more networking and collaborative activities over the past few months to raise additional awareness for the book and build more personalized connections rather than spending $10K/mo on Facebook ads to reach random users online.

5. Leveraging Cross-Promotional Opportunities

Exploring partnerships and cross-promotional opportunities with complementary businesses or communities can be a highly effective way to tap into new audiences and drive mutual growth.

This includes joint webinars, content collaborations, or even co-hosted events that outline unique perspectives and trigger interest in both networks. Through these cross-promotional efforts, you can introduce your community to new potential members and foster mutually beneficial relationships that contribute to the overall success of your business.

This is specifically common in newsletter groups, podcasts, and even video channels - not to mention social media and creating circles of trust and engagement with like-minded individuals. But we have seen similar results in the events space, too: a WordPress meetup we host locally sees shared exposure or co-hosted meetups with PHP framework communities; we invite other platform guests to our conferences and get invited as keynote guests for other site builders and frameworks to increase awareness or adoption of a broader suite of solutions.

Even if there is some overlap, there is usually enough room for collaboration and members joining multiple communities at the same time.

6. Continuous Engagement and Feedback

Maintaining consistent engagement with your community members and actively soliciting their feedback is crucial for the long-term growth and relevance of your community. Regularly engage with your members, respond to their questions, and encourage them to share their ideas and suggestions. Nobody wants to be a member of a virtual ghost town - you have to proactively engage and interact internally (along with the rest of your team).

Keep a close pulse on your active community members. Listen to their feedback, ideas, suggestions, and critiques. This will shape your network going forward.

Consider implementing regular community surveys, hosting live Q&A sessions, or creating dedicated feedback channels where your members can share their thoughts and ideas. This ongoing dialogue will not only strengthen your relationships with your community but also provide invaluable insights to help you drive the growth and development of your business.

You can incentivize moderators with a monthly or quarterly stipend for engagement or offer some rewards to the most active community members. It is a valid approach in some communities. For instance, in my early days in the 2000s, I was promoted to a moderator or even administrator of national subject matter forums, participating in meetup organizations and landing freelance or writing opportunities thanks to this visibility.

Remember, building a thriving community is a continuous process that requires a well-rounded, multi-faceted growth strategy. Keep your active users close, attract new members, build deeper engagement, and transform your community into a self-sustaining ecosystem that drives the long-term success of your business.

Monetization Options for Community-Driven Businesses

As a community-driven business, you have a unique opportunity to leverage the power of your engaged audience and turn it into a sustainable revenue stream. Here are several common monetization options that communities rely on.

MONETIZATION OPTIONS FOR COMMUNITY-DRIVEN BUSINESSES

- Membership Subscriptions
- Sponsorships and Partnerships
- Virtual Events and Workshops
- Premium Content and Services
- Community-Driven Products or Merchandise
- Community-Driven Crowdfunding

1. Membership Subscriptions

Allow your most dedicated community members to access exclusive content, features, or benefits by offering tiered membership plans. Popular platforms like Skool, Discord, and Circle offer built-in membership and subscription management tools to facilitate this. For example, you could offer a basic free membership, a pro membership with additional features at $9 per month, and a premium membership with VIP access and personalized support at $19 per month. You further expand your tiered offerings by introducing private channels to premium individuals for weekly check-ins, monthly webinars, or 1:1 sessions. Providing incremental value at each tier, you can cater to different levels of engagement and willingness to pay within your community.

2. Sponsorships and Partnerships

Reach out to businesses, influencers, or brands that align with your community's interests and offer them sponsorship opportunities. This could include banner ads for the site, sponsored content or "ask me anything" (AmA) sessions, or integrations within your community platform. You could partner with a leading industry publication to have them sponsor a monthly Q&A session with your community members or work with a relevant software provider to offer discounted access to your community.

3. Virtual Events and Workshops

Organize engaging virtual events, webinars, or workshops that provide value to your community members. You can charge attendance fees or offer premium access to these events.

Platforms like Skool and Circle make it easy to host and monetize virtual events. Consider hosting a monthly webinar on a trending topic in your industry or offering a quarterly workshop series on a specific skill or area of interest for your community.

4. Premium Content and Services

Create and sell exclusive, high-value content, such as e-books, courses, or specialized guides. Offer premium services, like one-on-one coaching, consulting, or community-based support. You could develop an in-depth course on building a successful online community or provide personalized consulting services to help other businesses navigate the challenges of community management.

5. Community-Driven Products or Merchandise

Develop and sell branded merchandise, such as t-shirts, mugs, or accessories that resonate with your community. Some communities take swag seriously and love to support a brand and associate with it publicly. Consider designing merchandise that reflects your community's values, interests, or inside jokes, and offer it exclusively to your members.

This could increase brand awareness with printed merchandise that goes viral on social media, too.

6. Community-Driven Crowdfunding

Engage your community to crowdfund new projects, initiatives, or product developments. This not only generates funding but also strengthens the community's investment and ownership in your endeavors. You could crowdfund the development of a new feature or tool that your community has been asking for, or raise funds to expand your community's reach and resources.

A strong community is not just about getting customers. It's about having loyal supporters who believe in your mission and are invested in your success. Explore the right monetization models and test them with your loyal customers. Find a scalable approach that keeps you invested or makes it possible to hire community managers to maintain the community in the future.

CHAPTER NINE

CONTENT PUBLISHING SUCCESS

Some of the most successful businesses you can think of are media companies. Digital magazines, newsletters, blogs, TV networks and YouTube channels, radio shows, podcasts, social accounts with vast following offer the ability to reach and connect with a large audience.

Successful media companies can control the narrative. They set trends, influence decisions, and set precedents. Large media networks have always been a key target for important events like elections, enforcing trust and uniting people around contradictory topics and raising awareness around socioeconomic challenges.

A 2024 Super Bowl ad was priced at roughly $7 million for 30 seconds of TV time. President election propaganda hits hard for months from political opponents and their parties, including international governments or cyberterrorists impacting voters.

The bottom line: media is power, and content publishing can build a significant audience that listens to editorial teams on top.

As a digital CEO, you could:

- Focus entirely on a media-based business and form your company around publishing
- Supplement a different business model with content channels like YouTube, a podcast, or a newsletter
- Work with other content publishing networks via partnerships, owning a small stake and offering strategic cross-promotion

- Launch an executive brand offering thought leadership to supplement the efforts on the core business model

Business entrepreneurs like Gary Vaynerchuk or Alex Hormozi employ entire teams around their own personal presence online: videographers, content creators, researchers, data analysts, and algorithm experts across different channels. This has proven to be extremely effective to fuel their businesses. YouTubers like Mr. Beast have used the social algorithm trends to amplify their reach, monetize through ads, hire teams, diversify into other channels, and then invest in or build other parallel businesses. The opportunities are endless.

Content-Driven Models

When it comes to building a successful online publication or a media network, your content is the most important part. Instead of just randomly writing articles or recording videos, a content-driven model focuses on creating valuable, engaging content that connects with your audience. This is what will make your content stand out and keep readers coming back.

The core of a content-driven model is deeply understanding your audience, what information they need, what challenges they're facing, and what type of topics will educate, entertain, or inspire them. By focusing on these key things, you can create content that provides real value and makes your publication a trusted, respected resource in your industry.

Whether you're writing informative articles, conducting interviews with industry leaders, or sharing thought-provoking opinions, your content should always be centered around giving your subscribers or first-time readers an exceptional experience. Don't just create content for the sake of it. Take the time to truly understand your audience and give them what they want.

I've been managing some satellite media sites or networks on autopilot for years. It's only after investing focused effort, defining a specific set of topics, crafting unique, powerful, highly valuable content for months that channels start to slowly pick up thanks to a gradual interest of followers consistently seeing high value content or algorithms starting to recognize the premise of the network.

THREE EFFECTIVE WAYS TO GATHER READER FEEDBACK

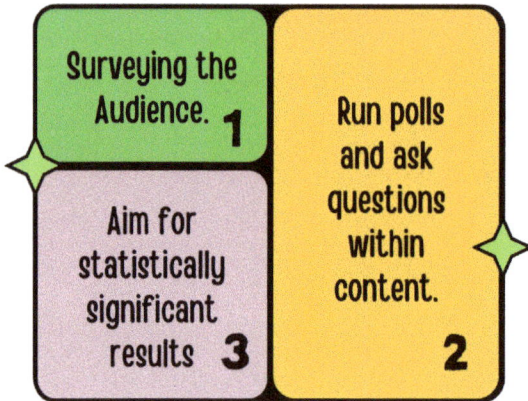

Surveying the Audience. **1**

Run polls and ask questions within content. **2**

Aim for statistically significant results **3**

One great way to do this is by regularly getting feedback from your readers. This can be achieved in three different ways:

- **Surveying the audience**: Run polls, ask questions in your content, seek feedback directly and continuously to find out what resonates and what doesn't. You need statistically significant results that align with your vision; ad-hoc, individual opinions may be biased and unrelated to the bigger picture here.

- **Sourcing 1:1**: Direct messaging or emailing people who engaged with your content. Instead of the "feedback blast," touch base with readers or listeners directly. Ask them what they think of your content and what topics work best for them. If and when possible, try to meet for 15 minutes to get to know them better. It's a similar premise to interviewing ICPs for other business models we covered in previous chapters.
- **Analytics**: Every media network relies heavily on data to make strategic decisions. For websites, it's Google Analytics traffic, bounce rates, number of pageviews per session. On YouTube, creators look into watch times, subscribers, engagement rates, and unique viewers. Social media networks track down engagements per view, comments, number of followers, or saves.

The more feedback loop mechanisms you can employ, the better. Remember - we have an entire chapter on market research in this book. Use it wisely and refer to it whenever you need to undertake this process.

A content-driven model doesn't have a one-size-fits-all approach. The type of content that works best will depend on your niche, your brand's unique voice, and the preferences of your specific readers. Some publications might thrive on long, in-depth articles, while others do better with concise, actionable tips in a newsletter. Experiment, look at the data, and adapt your content strategy as you learn what resonates most.

How Creators Leverage the Content Model

A prime example of an individual thriving in the content-driven business model is Sahil Bloom. As the writer and creator behind the popular bi-weekly newsletter The Curiosity Chronicle, Sahil has built a massive following of millions who eagerly consume his insightful and engaging content.

Sahil's success stems from his ability to leverage his extensive expertise as an investor and entrepreneur to produce strong and engaging narratives on a wide range of business, finance, and personal development topics. His content resonates deeply with his audience due to its mix of intellectual substance and authentic, relatable delivery.

There are millions of successful individuals who never crack the social game. Sahil grew successfully on Twitter (now X), expanded his email list as a first-party data source, and launched LinkedIn and Instagram a year later to cover multiple channels simultaneously. He reached 400K subscribers in 36 months and now has over 1 million X followers alone.

His tactical methods have been covered by other shrewd creators like Chenell Basilio, the author of Growth in Reverse. Chenell studies creators and reverse-engineers their successful strategies in deep dives in her weekly newsletter - a great collection of case studies by top creators and one of the best sources of intelligence in the social and newsletter growth space. She launched her own newsletter in December of 2022 and grew past 30,000 subscribers and 18,000 followers in a little over a year, with compounding returns and a snowball effect following after.

As you work on creating your thriving online publication, keep your content at the forefront. Treat it as the lifeblood of your operation and use it to propel your publication to new heights of success. With a commitment to creating content that truly resonates, you'll be able to build a loyal following and scale that as a full-time revenue stream or the fuel you need to grow a different venture of yours.

I will link to the established creators and newsletter authors in the resources section of the book's website, mbadisrupted.com.

Building Authority

Building authority refers to the process of establishing yourself as a trusted, reliable, and respected expert within a specific niche or industry. It involves developing a deep, comprehensive understanding of your subject matter through continuous learning and experimentation and then consistently sharing your expertise through the creation and distribution of high-quality, valuable content.

There's an alternative path to growth called "build in public" or learning on the go. Documenting your journey is the entrepreneurial version of a reality TV show with business outcomes and lessons on the go. This path does not require you to start as an authority leader. Instead, you can learn alongside your followers, taking one step at a time, and growing an audience of other people in the same path (just a few months behind). While this route is less authoritative and takes longer to achieve results and reach profitability, the lessons learned from sharing personal stories, trials, and tribulations can be utilized in your journey of expertise and education.

You can look up some examples on Twitter. Just search for the #buildinpublic hashtag and browse around.

Another example of a notable creator who elevated his brand through niche positioning and authority is Justin Welsh. Justin Welsh is a former sales executive turned CRO who has now become an entrepreneur, teaching solopreneurs how to bootstrap and balance their high-margin businesses with quality life.

Justin Welsh takes an operational approach to accelerating revenue and propelling businesses forward through professionally crafted content frameworks, massive loads of content, and affordable courses that generate close to $5M in annual revenue (for a solopreneur with no employees). He has a big-picture understanding of how every department within a company supports revenue generation, and he teaches his clients to build cross-functional plans that can generate tens of millions in revenue each year.

Replicating The Model to Establish Authority

The first step is to develop an in-depth, comprehensive understanding of your niche. Let's say you're an expert in digital marketing. You'll need to have a deep knowledge of the latest trends, strategies, and best practices across areas like search engine optimization, social media marketing, content creation, and more. Without this solid foundation of expertise, it will be challenging to establish yourself as a credible authority.

Once you've built up that critical knowledge base, the next phase is to proactively and consistently share your insights with your audience. This could involve creating informative how-to videos, writing detailed blog posts that tackle common digital marketing challenges, or even hosting webinars that dive into cutting-edge industry developments. Consistently providing valuable, actionable content is key to positioning yourself as a go-to expert.

But simply publishing content isn't enough. You also need to build and maintain a genuine connection with your audience. When someone reaches out with a question or leaves a comment on your posts, make sure to respond thoughtfully and engage with them. Show that you're not just broadcasting information but that you truly care about helping people and addressing their specific needs. This personal touch will go a long way in building trust and loyalty.

Finally, immerse yourself in the broader digital marketing community. Join social communities, participate in industry events and conferences, connect with other leaders in your space, follow their content and engage with their stories, even start your own community. The more visible you are and the more you interact with your peers, the more people will start to recognize you as a leading voice in your field. This level of involvement and recognition is what solidifies your status as a respected authority.

You need consistency, grit, determination, focus, proactive networking to make it work. Moreover, you have to study algorithms and network trends on a regular basis - regardless of whether you publish on LinkedIn/X, run a newsletter, or grow a media site with SEO. Algorithms change every few months, introducing new best practices or featured content formats, discarding certain content types and giving additional reach to others. You can't stay on top of your game without a strong network of other active creators, a consistent content calendar, and zealous data tracking to capture shifts in behavior or engagement rates.

For context, I have five full-time people on my Growth Shuttle team experimenting full-time across all media channels for multiple profiles to validate against bias, monitor trends, and experiment based on news and algorithm change reports. This includes content marketing, SEO, newsletter development, multiple social networks (LinkedIn, X, Instagram, TikTok, YouTube), and even Quora and Reddit. As a business advisor, it's my professional duty to keep my clients informed and up to speed with the latest developments online, especially as it relates to the channels they use for generating pipelines, forming partnerships, recruiting team members, announcing product launches, or diversifying with new service and product lines.

Building a Successful Digital Publication as a Revenue Stream

Starting your own digital magazine, newsletter, a podcast or a video channel can be an exciting and rewarding venture. However, what differentiates a real business from a hobby is the ability to continuously generate revenue through a certain channel.

Similar to other types of businesses, we're bound to have overlap between business models, and that's fine. Here are the key revenue generation mechanisms for content business types.

KEY REVENUE GENERATION MECHANISMS FOR DIGITAL PUBLISHERS

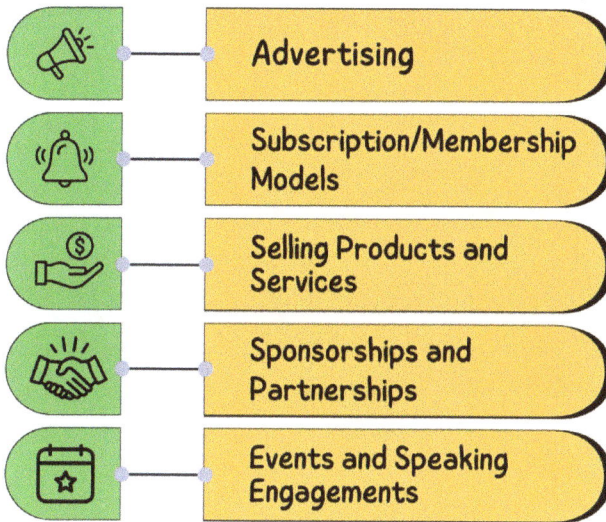

- Advertising
- Subscription/Membership Models
- Selling Products and Services
- Sponsorships and Partnerships
- Events and Speaking Engagements

1. Advertising

One of the most common and effective ways to earn money from a digital publication is through advertising. This can include different types of ads:

- Banner ads on your website (in-post, on top of the site, in the sidebar, wallpaper ads)
- Sponsored content with specific brands on custom articles or other promotional materials (including podcast shoutouts)
- Self-hosted content ads or featured blocks for affiliate marketing programs (earning a commission for purchases)

- Automated ad inventory networks like Google AdSense, Ezoic, and Playwire place relevant ads on your web pages or within your newsletters
- YouTube ads if you host video content.

2. Subscription/Membership Models

Another effective revenue stream is offering subscription or membership plans for your digital publication. You can move some of your premium or exclusive content behind a paywall so that readers have to pay a monthly or annual fee to access it. You can also create different tiers of subscription plans with varying levels of access and additional benefits for your most loyal and engaged readers. This allows you to generate recurring revenue from your audience rather than relying solely on one-time payments or advertising.

For instance, if you have a digital newsletter about personal finance, you could offer a basic free version that includes general tips and articles. But then you could also have a premium subscription that gives readers access to in-depth guides, personalized advice from financial experts, and exclusive Q&A sessions. Subscribers to the premium plan would pay a monthly or yearly fee to get this enhanced content and services.

3. Selling Products and Services

In addition to monetizing your content, you can also generate revenue by selling your products and services. This could include digital downloads, like e-books, guides, templates, or online courses that you've created based on your expertise and the needs of your audience. You could also sell consulting services, webinars, or other offerings that align with your brand and the interests of your readers.

For example, if you run a digital magazine about home design, you could create and sell an e-book with 10 easy DIY home projects or offer an online course on interior decorating. Or if you have a newsletter about productivity, you could sell a template library with customizable schedules, checklists, and workflows.

4. Sponsorships and Partnerships

Collaborating with other businesses or brands can be another lucrative revenue stream for your digital publication. This could involve creating sponsored content, where a brand pays you to produce an article or other promotional material that features their products or services. You can also explore affiliate marketing partnerships, where you earn a commission on any sales or leads that you generate through your platform. Brand ambassador deals can pay you a flat monthly retainer plus commission fees to represent the brand on social and within your content.

5. Events and Speaking Engagements

Finally, you can monetize your digital publication by hosting your events, such as in-person or virtual conferences, workshops, or webinars. This allows you to engage your audience in a more interactive and immersive way while also generating revenue through ticket sales, sponsorships, and other event-related offerings. Additionally, you can explore opportunities for your team members to speak at industry events or be featured on podcasts, which can help raise your profile and open up additional revenue streams.

Building a successful and sustainable digital publication, podcast, or video channel requires consistency, regularity, building an audience, making friends in the space, and introducing different monetization strategies until you find the right mix for the audience. Just like most other business verticals, practice makes perfect, and results take time to achieve. Content and publishing businesses are about resilience. In a competitive space, the strongest players survive. The good news is, that most give up or go out of business within the first few months or a year, and the odds of making this work increase with every new article or episode you publish.

There are over two million podcasts out there. However, nearly 90% of them have only produced about three episodes. And 99% of all podcasts have fewer than 21 published episodes. As long as you stay consistent and keep going with a weekly podcast, you'll reach the top 1% after month 5.

Other networks and channels may take longer to elevate. Plus, not all of the top 1% of media sites or channels are highly profitable. But this aims to showcase the compounding results of staying consistent. Similarly to seniority at work, the longer it works, the better you become, the larger your audience and the more opportunities pop up with time.

CHAPTER TEN

AFFILIATE MARKETING

Affiliate marketing is a fantastic business opportunity for digital CEOs who don't consider themselves inventors or product creators. It allows you to earn commissions by promoting and selling other companies' products or services. This is a win-win situation. You get to earn a percentage of the sales you generate, while the product or service owner expands their customer base.

HOW AFFILIATE MARKETING WORKS

1 Person visits your website

2 Person clicks your link and buys

3 You get credited for the sale

4 You get paid your affiliate commission

Imagine this scenario: you've found a powerful new software that helps small businesses streamline their operations. Once you become an affiliate for this software, you can start promoting it to your audience and earn a commission every time someone clicks on your unique affiliate link and makes a purchase. This is a simple yet effective way for you to generate passive income and diversify your revenue streams.

Popular businesses who follow a similar shared paradigm:

- Uber doesn't own automobiles
- Amazon doesn't own most of the inventory sold on their website (besides a few of their own products like Kindle or Alexa)
- Facebook monetizes thanks to your content
- Airbnb doesn't own homes
- Google Search indexes global content.

Just like real estate agents broker deals between buyers and sellers, affiliate marketers connect product or service businesses with their prospective buyers.

The beauty of affiliate marketing is that it's scalable. As you build your audience and promote more products, your earning potential can grow exponentially. You can promote as many or as few products as you like, and you can work at your own pace. Whether you have a few hours a week or a few hours a day to dedicate to your affiliate marketing efforts, you can still see significant results.

One traditional path to starting an affiliate business is on top of an existing community or a publishing business. Media sites, social media accounts, and newsletters often include affiliate links in the mix.

However, agencies and other service-based providers also include affiliate or referral deals in their contracts. For example, web development and design agencies tend to recommend hosting companies they work with and take a commission. Some build one-off projects and then outsource maintenance for a 10% cut to a corresponding vendor.

Being a brand ambassador for Flippa, the largest marketplace for buying and selling businesses, I've brokered deals over $50K and made $3K - $5K in commissions for connecting a buyer to the right listing. This aims to illustrate that while most affiliate transactions generate a few dozen dollars per sale, high ticket deals also exist.

Another creative affiliate model I found through Flippa is an upsell through a series of affiliate and referral relationships. While Flippa sells everything from cheap domains to eight-figure digital businesses, one category for aspiring entrepreneurs is "startup websites." You can purchase a starting site for a social media agency or a web development firm for under $1,000 and offload operations completely. The sellers close the deal and then provide a playbook on how to run the operations: where to host the site, vendors to work with and outsource (referral fees), paid media freelancers for paid ads (affiliate), tools to use for traffic monitoring or AI content creation (affiliate), and so on. This is the purpose of this book: keep your mind open to alternative forms of deals you won't find in online tutorials and traditional courses.

Starting with traditional affiliate marketing, you'll need to find products or services that align with your audience's interests and needs. This could be anything from software and online courses to physical products and services. Once you've identified the right products, you'll need to sign up as an affiliate and get your unique tracking link. Then, you can start promoting the products to your audience through your website, social media, email marketing, and other channels.

Individual providers to products, SaaS solutions, or courses often list down affiliate campaign sign up forms on their websites. Additionally, you can look up PartnerStack, Impact, Amazon, or other networks with tens of thousands of deals or products you can list down directly.

As you build your affiliate marketing business, it's important to focus on providing value to your audience. Don't just promote products for the sake of earning commissions. Instead, focus on recommending products that you genuinely believe will be helpful to your audience. This will not only increase your chances of making sales but it also builds trust and loyalty with your audience.

Niche Selection

To find your profitable niche, start by thinking about your passions and hobbies. What are you knowledgeable about? What kinds of problems do you enjoy helping others solve? These are great starting points for identifying a niche that you'll be genuinely excited about promoting.

Next, do some research on the market to see what the competition looks like and how much demand there is for products or services in your potential niche. Look for niches with a good balance of high demand and relatively low competition. This sweet spot will give you the best chance of standing out and earning commissions.

SELECTING YOUR NICHE: A Checklist for Affiliate Marketers

1. TARGET MARKET SIZE	✓ Estimate the number of potential customers ✓ Evaluate market saturation
2. COMPETITION LEVEL	✓ Assess the number of competitors ✓ Analyze market share distribution
3. PRODUCT TYPES	✓ Identify available product categories ✓ Consider product diversity
4. PRICE & COMMISSIONS	✓ Review product pricing range ✓ Compare commission structures
5. GROWTH TRENDS	✓ Look at historical market growth ✓ Predict future market trends

Remember, we have devoted the entire chapter 2 on defining your niche and target audience. These core principles and skills are applicable for every business type. Use them wisely and make the most out of extracting the right value proposition.

For example, let's say you're interested in health and fitness. You could look into the weight loss niche, which has a lot of demand but also a lot of competition. Or you could focus on a more specific area like keto diet products, which have been growing in popularity but may have less competition. This could be a great niche for you if you have expertise and passion for the keto lifestyle.

Another example could be in the personal finance niche. This is a broad category, but you could find a more specific angle, such as helping young adults manage their money or providing tips for small business owners on saving and investing. The key is to find a niche that you're excited about, and that has enough potential customers without being overly saturated.

Once you've identified a few potential niches, do some deeper research to evaluate things like:

- The size of the target market
- The level of competition
- The types of products or services being sold
- The average sale prices and commission rates
- The potential for growth and trends in the industry.

This will help you narrow down your options and choose the niche that has the best opportunity for you to succeed as an affiliate marketer.

In some cases, you may explore opportunities outside of your area of interests. If you have access to thousands of prospective buyers in a specific industry, you can still compile strategic guides or connect a few services together that solve their problem. This could be packaged as an infomercial product (an ebook or a course) bundled with affiliate products and referral agreements to reliable vendors and partners.

And don't forget, it's critical to run affiliate campaigns that deliver value. It's easy to find high commission deals selling placebo or even illegal products. You don't want to end up in a legal battle or jeopardizing someone's health for a few extra dollars. Stay in the clear at all times and only focus on value added deals.

Partner Strategy

Picking individual services or products is a great way to start. But elevating to the higher ticket deal size requires a more comprehensive strategy - often aligned with signing strategic partners on board.

When selecting affiliate partners, look for companies that offer non-competitive products or services that align with your niche and your audience's needs. You'll also want to focus on partners that have a generous commission structure and a solid reputation in the industry. This will ensure that you're promoting offerings that your audience will truly value and that you'll be able to earn a fair commission for your efforts.

For example, let's say you're in the health and fitness niche, and you've identified a company that sells top-notch workout equipment and supplements. This could be an excellent affiliate partner for you, as their products would likely appeal to your audience, and they may offer a lucrative commission rate to incentivize you to promote their offerings.

On the other hand, you'll want to steer clear of partners that have a history of poor customer service, shady business practices, or low-quality products. These kinds of partnerships can harm your reputation and rank your business. The reviews and feedback carry over to any other ventures or business opportunities you want to explore. Approach this with a long-term mindset. You're not just looking for a quick transaction; you need a scalable business model with compounding returns. This means taking the time to get to know your partners, understanding their goals and values, and finding ways to collaborate that create value for both of your businesses.

For example, you might offer to promote your partner's products to your email list in exchange for exclusive discounts or early access to new releases, or you could work with them to create co-branded content that educates and engages your audience. The key is to find creative ways to leverage your partnership to drive results for both of your businesses.

As you build out your affiliate partner network, keep an eye on performance and be willing to make adjustments as needed. Monitor your sales, track your conversion rates, and stay in close communication with your partners. If a particular partnership isn't producing the results you had hoped for, don't be afraid to move on and explore new opportunities. This is a common problem with partnership marketing. Some deals don't pan out or partners aren't equally invested in the relationship. Aligned incentives are what make this possible, and you can supplement this by running webinars or cross-promoting content on social media, sponsoring campaigns together, launching industry reports, or joining podcasts as a group.

Back in the day, my agency DevriX worked in a power trio with a hosting company and a reputable ad management vendor. We worked on over a dozen deals together with publishers who needed professional engineering services and ad implementation, scaling hundreds of millions of monthly views (which requires a stellar hosting provider). Since we worked together and exchanged leads, we all marketed our services as a group, had internal communication protocols (VIP Slack channels for escalations or fixes), and managed a bulletproof value proposition for publishers in need. Our ad partner made a successful exit and no longer provides the same services, but we still manage a number of massive accounts together with our hosting provider.

Maximizing Your Affiliate Income

To maximize your earnings from affiliate marketing, you'll need to use a mix of different strategies and approaches. Here are the key tactics you want to explore in the process:

- **Find the most effective partners**: While testing out hundreds of products or services, vet down your top 5-10 affiliate solutions or partners that resonate with your audience.
- **Iterate on high-quality content**: Figure out what content works best with your audience. Adapt your other offers accordingly. Play with openers, call to action, deal definition length, listing down prices or percentages or dropping them to measure performance.
- **Analyze**: Speaking of measurement, continuous analysis and keeping a close eye on affiliate performance is critical. Avoid seasonal deals that work for a month or two and dry out after. Keep your offers fresh and timely.
- **Diversify channels**: If you find a successful channel for your deals, try to diversify and develop other channels as well. If your website performs well, try X. Or start a newsletter. Think about starting other affiliate sites to cross-promote or niche down into other territories.
- **Capture your top buyers**: Following Paretto's 80-20 principle, 80% of the results often come from 20% of your

audience. Try to incentivize your top buyers to sign up for your email list or join your webinars. Compiling a list of active buyers is easier to upsell and cross-sell to with a higher success rate.

- **Work on deals and offers**: Deals are evergreen. Coupons, offers, discounts are always in fashion. This is why Black Friday works so well. If you can compile affiliate deals that provide discounts for bundles, seasonal offers, or anything else that invokes scarcity and FOMO (fear of missing out), this will generate better results.

It's not going to be a quick or easy journey, but if you focus on delivering value, building trust, and exploring new opportunities, you'll be well on your way to achieving your goals and unlocking your earning potential through affiliate marketing.

CHAPTER ELEVEN

MASTERING E-COMMERCE

E-commerce is one of the most important business models in the world today. It has completely transformed the way we think about commerce and how businesses operate. As an entrepreneur and an upcoming digital CEO, you simply cannot afford to ignore the power of e-commerce.

E-commerce originally started in 1979 with a sale of a Sting album from NetMarket. Considering the almost non-existent Internet access (or computer availability) for years to come, it took 15 years for Netscape Navigator to arrive as the first web browser, Amazon in 1995 and PayPal in 1998 as the first mass adopted payment system.

Even though the space has been moderately new (compared to traditional businesses like breweries or restaurants available for virtually thousands of years), retail e-commerce generated over a trillion dollars in sales in 2013 and 5.78 trillion in 2023, projected to surpass 8 trillion USD by 2027.

Think about it, with a basic website and an online store, you can offer your products to people in other countries, even on the other side of the planet. This opens up unparalleled opportunities to manufacture locally and sell globally, arbitrage products from one country to another, run package deals with box products combining multiple solutions - all online, with supported payment gateways and logistics providers in each country.

E-commerce also allows you to streamline your sales and distribution processes. Instead of having to physically store and ship products from a brick-and-mortar store, you can simply process orders online and have them delivered directly to your customers. This can save you a lot of time and money and make your business much more efficient.

So if you're a business owner or aspiring digital entrepreneur, e-commerce can be the right business model for you.

10 ESSENTIAL STEPS FOR LAUNCHING YOUR E-COMMERCE BUSINESS

Platform Selection (1)

Choose a suitable e-commerce platform (e.g., Shopify, WooCommerce, Magento).

Understand Your Market (2)

Identify customer demographics, preferences, and needs.

Market Research (3)

Analyze industry trends and competitor strategies.

Supplier Relationships (5)

Cultivate partnerships for better pricing and supply terms.

Pricing Strategy (4)

Set product prices, accounting for costs and expenses.

Use Marketplaces (6)

Utilize Amazon, Etsy, etc., to boost visibility and sales.

Optimize for Mobile (7)

Ensure a mobile-friendly shopping experience.

Plan for Scalability (8)

Choose a platform that supports business growth.

Customer Support (9)

Ensure access to reliable and responsive support.

Marketing and SEO (10)

Implement strategies to improve visibility and engagement.

Platform Selection

When it comes to selling your products or services online, you've got a wide variety of e-commerce platforms to choose from. Some of the most popular options include Shopify, WooCommerce (on top of WordPress), Wix, Squarespace, BigCommerce, Magento. Each one has its own unique set of features and capabilities.

For instance, Wix and Squarespace are incredibly user-friendly website builders that make it super easy to create a professional-looking online store, even if you don't have any technical skills. They have hundreds of pre-designed templates and drag-and-drop tools that allow you to customize your site without any coding knowledge. These platforms are great for small businesses or individual entrepreneurs who want to get an online shop up and running quickly.

On the other hand, platforms like BigCommerce and Magento are a little more robust and complex. They're better suited for larger, enterprise-level businesses that need advanced features like multi-channel selling, complex inventory management, and sophisticated analytics. These platforms give you more flexibility to customize every aspect of your e-commerce experience, but they also tend to have a steeper learning curve.

Then you've got two of the leading e-commerce platforms which are WooCommerce and Shopify. WooCommerce is a plugin that integrates with the popular WordPress content management system. This gives you the ability to build a highly personalized online store that seamlessly fits with the rest of your website. It's great for businesses that want a lot of control and customization options.

Shopify, on the other hand, is a complete, cloud-based e-commerce solution. It's incredibly easy to set up and use, with tons of built-in features like secure payment processing, inventory tracking, abandoned cart recovery, and more. Shopify is an excellent choice for entrepreneurs and small business owners who want a simple, turnkey e-commerce platform that just works. A great example is Peg and Awl, a small home goods company that was able to build a thriving online store using Shopify.

So when you're trying to decide which e-commerce platform is right for your business, there are a few key factors you'll want to consider:

1. **Your technical skills**: If you're not very tech-savvy, you may want to go with an easier, more user-friendly platform like Wix, Squarespace, or Shopify.

2. **The level of customization you need:** If you want to be able to customize every aspect of your online store, WooCommerce or Magento might be better options.

3. **Your budget**: Some platforms are more affordable than others, especially when it comes to things like transaction fees and monthly subscription costs.

4. **The features and functionalities you require**: Make a list of all the must-have capabilities you need, like inventory management, shipping tools, marketing integrations, etc.

5. **Scalability:** Think about how much your business might grow in the future, and choose a platform that can easily handle increased sales and traffic.

6. **Customer support:** When issues come up, you'll want to make sure the platform provider offers reliable, responsive support

7. **Mobile optimization:** In today's world, your online store has to look great and function seamlessly on mobile devices.

Evaluating all of these factors will help you determine the best e-commerce platform to build your online business.

My digital agency DevriX has built a number of WooCommerce stores and currently manages several brands selling eight figures of inventory annually through their WordPress-based shops. Some of the enterprise brands we manage run their B2B solutions on WordPress while separately running their e-commerce on BigCommerce or Magento. And Rush, the order tracking SaaS, powered thousands of Shopify stores before we sold the business in early 2024.

Both platforms are proven to work and scale significantly. And everything you read in this book is a combination of best practices and principles studied by industry experts combined with my personal know-how and experience of running companies and managing teams specializing in these corresponding business models.

1. Understand Your Target Market

Your first step is to deeply understand your target customers. Who are they? What are their needs, preferences, and pain points? This knowledge will help you identify products that align with your interests. For example, if you're selling health and fitness products, you'll want to focus on items that cater to people passionate about living a healthy lifestyle.

2. Conduct Market Research

Thorough market research is crucial. Analyze industry trends, study your competitors' offerings, and read customer reviews. This will give you insights into the types of products that are in high demand and have the potential to be profitable.

When in doubt, head back to chapters 2 and 3 where we dive deep into niche definition, ideal customer profiles, and extensive principles of running market research studies of all types.

For instance, if you're selling home decor, you might discover that minimalist, Scandinavian-inspired furniture is a popular trend right now. Make sure your production facilities and manufacturing take that into account.

And studying the reviews can spark ideas for problems that other competitors don't solve (but you do) or narrative you need to include in your product description copy.

3. Establish a Pricing Strategy

Evaluate the wholesale price, shipping costs, and other expenses to determine the potential profit you can make on each product. This will help you identify the items that offer the best return on your investment.

E-commerce pricing isn't easy and you'll need to assess that over time. Consider other areas such as packaging and labeling, warehouse storage costs, what volume of inventory you need to keep in stock, degradation or malfunction or materials or devices, chargebacks and return rates. Include additional expenses for licenses, platform fees, paid ads, vendors, contractors. Make sure your business model is sustainable first and foremost.

4. Build Supplier Relationships

Spend the time to develop and nurture strong relationships with reliable manufacturers, logistics companies, carriers, payment gateway providers. This can lead to better pricing, priority access for new products, and improved delivery times. Some of your products may ship with complimentary candy, handcrafted jewelry, books, or other products you need sourced through partners.

5. Leverage Online Marketplaces

Aside from self-hosted experience on your own store, don't neglect e-commerce marketplaces like Amazon, Etsy, and eBay. Most marketplaces allow you to run your own store and still list with them. While they take steep commission fees for the opportunity to list, this is a separate channel for generating traffic and sales and potentially developing a funnel of returning customers for your products.

The key component of e-commerce we go over in this chapter is shipping your own goods and physical products. Another popular segment of e-commerce is dropshipping: sourcing products from third-parties and reselling through your own store. We will review this separately in the next chapter, but the principles of traffic generation, brand building, and digital campaigns are similar.

Driving Traffic to Your E-Commerce Store

Just as pipeline generation is imperative to running a successful service business and community building is how communities and membership sites grow, e-commerce stores require digital foot traffic, potential buyers, and an optimized the journey as traffic grows.

THE SALES FUNNEL

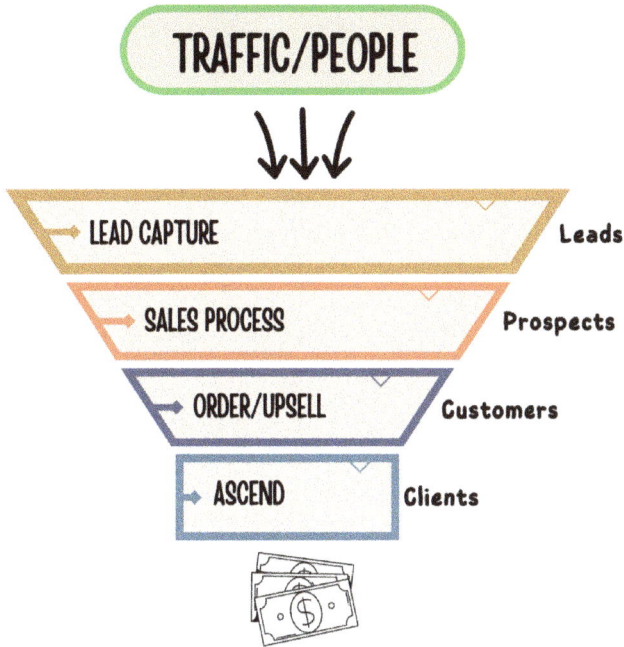

TRAFFIC/PEOPLE

↓↓↓

LEAD CAPTURE	Leads
SALES PROCESS	Prospects
ORDER/UPSELL	Customers
ASCEND	Clients

Here are the most common traffic acquisition channels for e-commerce businesses.

1. Search Engine Optimization (SEO)

Before we head into SEO, I'll preface it with the following:

Search Engine Optimization requires proactive content development efforts, persistence, and patience to slowly get organic visitors to your site. It's no immediate way to grow, but every successful business aims to develop a strong brand and generate traffic on autopilot. And SEO enables that (and makes it easier for larger stores with enough products to rank for transactional keywords).

Detailed product descriptions, FAQ and educational articles, and other industry-wide resources online help your store and products show up higher in search results, making it easier for people to find you. The key SEO tactics include using relevant keywords, creating high-quality content, and making sure your site is fast and mobile-friendly. For example, if you sell handmade jewelry, you'll want to optimize your product pages around keywords like "custom earrings" or "unique necklaces."

Once you have successfully driven traffic to your site, it's crucial to focus on conversion rate optimization (CRO) to convert visitors into customers. This includes strategies like visual merchandising and pricing automation.

Visual Merchandising: This involves strategically arranging products and optimizing the layout of your online store to enhance the visual appeal and improve the customer experience. Effective visual merchandising can guide visitors through your site, highlight key products, and encourage purchases by creating attractive product displays and promotional graphics. For example, showcasing best-selling items on the homepage or using high-quality images for feature products can significantly impact buyer decisions.

Pricing Automation: Leveraging analytics-driven tools for pricing automation allows you to dynamically adjust prices based on market conditions, competitor pricing, and demand. This strategy ensures that your pricing is always competitive and maximizes profit margins without constant manual intervention. Automated systems can also help you implement promotional pricing strategies at optimal times to boost sales conversions.

2. Social Media Marketing

Promoting your e-commerce store on social media platforms like Instagram, Facebook, and TikTok is a great way to reach a wider audience and build brand awareness. Successful stores post great looking product photos, engaging videos, user guides and relevant information tailored to your target customers. Interacting with your followers, running contests, and collaborating with influential users in your industry can also help drive traffic back to your online store. Just think about your ideal customer - what kind of content would they enjoy and find valuable?

Social media is not limited to traditional company account posting. Don't forget Facebook groups or communities like Reddit or Quora. Many online stores engage proactively and build an audience in similar groups by providing value and dropping a guide or a product link every now and then. Maintaining a quality level of enough value between product drops is important. Otherwise, you'll be flagged for spam, and access will likely be rejected.

3. Paid Advertising

Running targeted ads on search engines, social media, or other relevant websites can be an effective way to drive more qualified traffic to your e-commerce store. Platforms like Google Ads, Facebook Ads, and Instagram Ads allow you to laser-focus your messaging and targeting to reach the exact people you want to sell to. Ads require an upfront investment, but with the right strategy, paid ads can deliver a great return on your money. For example, you could run a Facebook ad campaign showcasing your newest product line and offering a special discount to first-time buyers.

Most e-commerce stores start with paid ads and diversify from there. This is the fastest channel to validate the need, get feedback fast, generate some sales and optimize the value proposition sooner. If you end up keeping stock for a year until SEO picks up or you get enough prospects to your email list, it may be too late at this point.

4. Email Marketing

Building an email list is the best investment in the long term (right next to phone numbers). Emails and texts tap into first-party data: having direct contact to your customers at all times.

As algorithms evolve and shift over time, you can't rely solely on the mercy of SEO or how Facebook ads will perform. Keeping emails and phone numbers handy - and growing that list - bypasses the middleman and provides unique opportunities to connect directly with your clients, offer personalized discounts, and keep cross-selling later.

Email is also beneficial for product launches, special offers, educational content, and any valuable tips that keep your customers engaged. Emails can be used to retarget former customers or prospects who typed in their email but never completed a purchase. Think of related product emails that Amazon or Etsy send a few times a week to their audience.

5. Influencer Marketing

Partnering with relevant influencers in your industry can be a powerful way to expand through their existing followers and supplement the credibility of your brand. Whether it's a popular lifestyle blogger, a social media celebrity, or a YouTube creator, collaborating with the right influencers can introduce your products to a whole new set of potential customers. Just make sure the influencers you work with truly align with your brand and have an engaged, loyal following

Starting businesses is all about trust. Successful e-commerce stores are featured across the web, gather thousands of reviews, list down media exposure or strategic partnerships. New store owners have to fast-track this entire journey through guest blogging for logos, media contacts for features, and working with influencers to form the trust factor until real users get to buying and reviewing products later.

There are other growth channels available, including affiliate marketing, seasonal sales, promo deals with partners, product bundles with other brands (to name a few). But starting with the core mix is a good starting point until you get some traction.

Explore the Different E-Commerce Models and Selling Digitally

E-COMMERCE MODELS:
PROS AND CONS COMPARISON

MANUFACTURING

PRO: Complete control over product design and supply chain.

CON: Requires significant upfront investment in production and distribution.

PRINT-ON-DEMAND

PRO: Low inventory risk and highly scalable.

CON: Limited control over product quality and fulfillment speed

DIGITAL PRODUCTS

PRO: Minimal overhead with global reach, 24/7.

CON: Highly competitive market requiring unique content.

PHYSICAL PRODUCTS

PRO: Wide product range and tangible customer value.

CON: Complex logistics and significant inventory management.

As a business owner, you have a variety of e-commerce models to choose from, and each one comes with its unique advantages. Let's explore some of the different options you can consider:

1. **Manufacturing:** If you can produce your products, this model makes all the sense for e-commerce digital founders. It gives you complete control over the entire supply chain, from designing the

products to distributing them to your customers. This can be a very rewarding and fulfilling path, especially valid for inventors, creative designers running their own product lines, or technical professionals launching innovative physical solutions. For example, if you're a skilled woodworker, you could create and sell your line of handcrafted furniture through your online store. The same goes for bakeries for birthday or wedding cakes, crafted jewelry, greeting cards, and 3D printed models.

2. **Print-on-Demand:** This model is perfect if you want to sell customized products without the hassle of maintaining a large inventory. With print-on-demand, you can offer a wide variety of items, like t-shirts, mugs, or phone cases, and have them printed and shipped directly to your customers as orders come in. This is a low-risk and highly scalable option, as you don't have to worry about storing and managing a ton of inventory. If you're an artist, you could create designs and sell them on a variety of print-on-demand products without the stress of keeping hundreds of items in stock.

3. **Digital Products:** Selling digital products, such as e-books, online courses, or software, can be an incredibly profitable and scalable e-commerce strategy. These types of products have minimal overhead, as you don't have to worry about manufacturing, warehousing, or shipping physical goods. Plus, you can sell your digital products around the clock, reaching customers all over the world. If you're an expert in a particular field, you could create an online course and share your knowledge with students globally.

4. **Physical Products:** Selling physical products, whether you source them from wholesalers, manufacturers, or distributors, can also be a successful e-commerce model. This option allows

you to offer a wide range of tangible goods to your customers. However, it does require more inventory management and logistics considerations. For instance, if you want to sell home decor items, you'll need to find reliable suppliers, manage your stock levels, and ensure your products are shipped safely to your customers.

Regardless of the product type you choose, one of the great benefits of e-commerce is that it allows you to sell both locally and internationally. This means you can expand your reach and tap into new markets, potentially growing your customer base and your business. When selling internationally, it's important to consider factors like currency conversion, shipping logistics, customs regulations, and cultural differences, to ensure a seamless and positive experience for your customers.

E-commerce is one of the fastest growing ecosystems on the market. At the moment of writing, **Shopify hosts over 4.4 million stores and WooCommerce reports another 4.7 million.** Amazon has 9.7 million sellers worldwide too, some cross-selling on Amazon and their own website.

Similarly to other business models reviewed earlier, e-commerce can be supplemented and run in parallel with other venture lines. At DevriX, we manage publishing websites with e-commerce stores for partner products, creator blogs and video channels shipping merchandise, and affiliate websites, including dropshipping in the mix.

Speaking of dropshipping, let's dive into the next chapter exploring the reseller model.

CHAPTER TWELVE

DROPSHIPPING DYNAMICS

When we reviewed affiliate marketing in chapter nine, one of the key benefits of this model revolved around selling other products and taking a commission without caring about manufacturing, logistics, or operations. Just like Uber and Airbnb don't own cars or real estate, affiliate marketers can nurture their audience and plug different products and services in exchange for commission.

Dropshipping follows a similar model and allows you to sell products without the hassle of managing inventory or shipping. Instead, you work with suppliers who handle the entire fulfillment process for you.

Before we dive into the key principles of this business model, don't forget that outsourcing fulfillment requires the same level (if not higher) of investment and proficiency in driving demand and generating leads. The lack of differentiation means that your customer acquisition skills should always be top of mind. Fulfillment partners are less efficient with low volume compared to high transaction volumes. And more competitors can launch quickly and target the same audience.

Nevertheless, dropshipping remains a viable model and the preferred entry to digital businesses for millions of entrepreneurs every year.

Let's start with the basics. Dropshipping is a way of selling products where you, the retailer, don't keep the products you sell in stock. Instead, when a customer places an order with you, you pass that order along to your supplier, and they ship the product directly to the customer. This means that you never have to handle the physical product yourself or worry about storing inventory.

THE DROPSHIP MODEL

Customer places order pays you retail price ($200)

YOUR STORE

Forward order to your supplier and pay wholesale ($150)

Keeps $50 Profit

CUSTOMER

SUPPLIER

Supplier ships the product directly to your customer

Imagine you want to start an online store selling electronics. In a manufacturing world, you need to be an inventor and creator of electrical equipment, building your own devices with IP and trademarks, working with factories abroad, and ensuring high product quality. With a traditional retail model, you would have to buy a large number of products, rent a warehouse, and manage the entire process of shipping and fulfillment.

Now, with dropshipping, you can simply partner with a supplier who specializes in electronics. When a customer orders a product from your store, you forward that order to your supplier, and they take care of the shipping and fulfillment. The only thing you need to focus on is marketing, customer service, and growing your business.

The Benefits of Dropshipping

Dropshipping offers several benefits that make it an attractive business model for entrepreneurs:

1. **Low Startup Costs:** With dropshipping, you don't need to invest in a large inventory or warehouse space. This means you can start your business with relatively low upfront costs.

2. **Flexibility:** Since you don't have to worry about managing inventory, you can easily expand your product offerings or pivot your business strategy as needed.

3. **Scalability:** As your business grows, you can easily add more suppliers and products to your offerings without the hassle of managing a complex logistics operation.

4. **Reduced Risk:** With dropshipping, you don't have to worry about unsold inventory or products that become obsolete. Your suppliers handle all of that, which reduces your financial risk.

5. **Possible Expansion:** Dropshipping does not limit you from running a traditional e-commerce model. You can sell two of your own products and 50 other supplied ones, and expand your own selection over time.

Finding the Right Suppliers

One of the most important parts of running a successful dropshipping business is finding reliable and trustworthy suppliers. You want to work with suppliers who offer high-quality products, fast shipping times, and great customer service. Here are some tips to help you find the right suppliers for your business:

FINDING RELIABLE DROPSHIPPING SUPPLIERS

RESEARCH ONLINE MARKETPLACES
- AliExpress
- Oberlo
- Spocket
- Temu

ATTEND TRADE SHOWS AND NETWORKING EVENTS

REACH OUT TO MANUFACTURERS DIRECTLY

1. Research Online Marketplaces

Websites like AliExpress, Oberlo, Spocket and Temu are great places to start your search for dropshipping suppliers. These platforms connect you with a wide range of suppliers, making it easier to compare products, pricing, and shipping times. You can browse through different product categories, read supplier reviews, and even reach out to potential partners directly through these marketplaces.

2. Attend Trade Shows and Networking Events

Getting involved in the dropshipping community, both online and in-person, can help you discover new suppliers and build valuable relationships. Attend industry events, conferences, and local meetups to connect with other entrepreneurs and suppliers. This can give you insider knowledge and access to suppliers you might not find through online searches alone. Luckily, a lot of online communities are also available - from Facebook groups through online courses, Discord communities, and Telegram channels for products suitable for sourcing.

3. Reach Out to Manufacturers Directly

Sometimes, the best deals and most reliable suppliers can be found by reaching out to the manufacturers themselves. This allows you to negotiate better terms and establish a direct relationship with the source of the products. You can often get better prices and more control over the fulfillment process by cutting out the middleman.

4. Vet Your Suppliers Thoroughly

Before you commit to working with a supplier, you must take the time to thoroughly vet them. Check their product quality, shipping times, customer reviews, and overall reliability. This will help you avoid any potential issues down the line, such as delays, poor product quality, or unhappy customers.

VETTING DROPSHIPPING SUPPLIERS THOROUGHLY

- ✓ High-quality products
- ✓ Fast shipping times (ideally 7-14 days or less)
- ✓ Positive customer reviews
- ✓ Responsive customer service
- ✓ Transparent communication about policies and processes

When vetting suppliers, look for things like:

- High-quality, durable products
- Fast shipping times (ideally 7-14 days or less)
- Positive customer reviews
- Responsive customer service
- Transparent communication about their policies and processes.

Taking the time to find the right suppliers is one of the most important steps in building a successful dropshipping business. By partnering with reliable, high-quality suppliers, you'll be able to provide your customers with a great experience and set your business up for long-term success.

Don't skip this part of the process. The suppliers you choose will have a big impact on the success of your dropshipping venture, so don't be afraid to be picky and do your due diligence. With the right suppliers in place, you'll be well on your way to building a thriving online business.

Fulfillment Challenges and Solutions

Once you've found reliable suppliers, the next hurdle you'll face is managing the fulfillment process. Dropshipping may seem like a hands-off approach, but there are still some challenges you'll need to navigate. Let's take a closer look at some common fulfillment challenges and how you can address them.

1. Shipping Times

One of the biggest pain points for dropshipping customers is long shipping times. Customers today expect fast delivery, and if your products take too long to arrive, it can lead to unhappy customers and hurt your business. To address this, work closely with your suppliers to find ways to optimize the shipping process. This could involve using faster shipping methods, such as expedited or express delivery, or exploring local fulfillment options that can get products to customers more quickly.

2. Product Quality Control

Since you're not physically handling the products, it's important to establish a clear quality control process with your suppliers. You want to make sure that the items your customers receive are of high quality and meet your standards. Set clear quality standards with your suppliers and regularly check sample products to ensure consistency. This will help you avoid issues like damaged, defective, or low-quality items reaching your customers.

3. Inventory Management

Even though you don't hold physical inventory, you still need to have a system in place to track product availability and avoid overselling. Integrate your online store with your suppliers' systems so you can maintain real-time visibility into inventory levels. This will allow you to promptly update your product listings and prevent frustrated customers from placing orders for items that are out of stock.

4. Customer Communication

Transparent communication with your customers is crucial in a dropshipping business. Keep them informed about order status, shipping times, and any potential delays. Use automated email workflows and chatbots to streamline the process and ensure your customers always feel informed and supported. This will go a long way in building trust and loyalty with your customers.

5. Technical Support and Integrations

I exited a Shopify app called Rush that managed thousands of Shopify stores, many of them being traditional dropshippers. Rush is still actively growing under its new ownership and provides automated order tracking and notifications to customers, sending intermediate updates as remote packages fly around the world, supports over 1,300 different carriers for global shipments, provides estimated delivery times based on historical sales with a vendor, and so much more.

This is possible for Shopify merchants, and WooCommerce or BigCommerce solutions exist for similar reasons (with varying success connecting to carriers or dropshipping partners). The largest commerce platforms support direct integrations with marketplaces such as AliExpress via apps like DSers or a myriad of other vendors through Sell The Trend (including US and European suppliers with shorter delivery times).

Building the right stack, including commerce platform, delivery integration, suppliers, requires some initial legwork. But once the process is in motion, scaling it is faster than other business models.

Scaling Your Dropshipping Business

As your dropshipping business starts to gain traction and grow, you'll need to think about scaling your operations. This can present its own set of challenges, but with the right strategies and mindset, you can successfully grow your business to new heights. Here are some tips to help you scale your dropshipping venture:

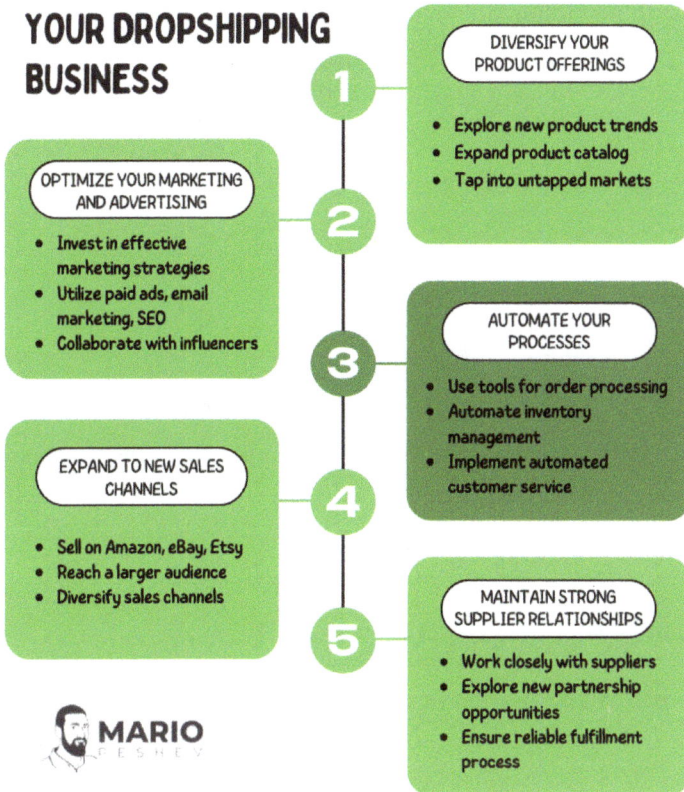

ROADMAP TO SCALING YOUR DROPSHIPPING BUSINESS

1. DIVERSIFY YOUR PRODUCT OFFERINGS
- Explore new product trends
- Expand product catalog
- Tap into untapped markets

2. OPTIMIZE YOUR MARKETING AND ADVERTISING
- Invest in effective marketing strategies
- Utilize paid ads, email marketing, SEO
- Collaborate with influencers

3. AUTOMATE YOUR PROCESSES
- Use tools for order processing
- Automate inventory management
- Implement automated customer service

4. EXPAND TO NEW SALES CHANNELS
- Sell on Amazon, eBay, Etsy
- Reach a larger audience
- Diversify sales channels

5. MAINTAIN STRONG SUPPLIER RELATIONSHIPS
- Work closely with suppliers
- Explore new partnership opportunities
- Ensure reliable fulfillment process

MARIO PESHEV

1. Diversify Your Product Offerings

Don't rely on a single product or niche. Keep browsing for new product trends and expand your product catalog to appeal to a broader customer base. Look for untapped markets. Watch TikTok videos about products that are rising in popularity in China but aren't yet available in the US or Europe. Follow trendsetter influencers in categories like consumer electronics, beauty, luxury and pull comparable products at a low price for larger audiences.

211

2. Optimize Your Marketing and Advertising

Investing in effective marketing strategies is crucial to driving more traffic and sales to your business. Follow the key models recommended in the previous chapter: paid ads, email marketing, SEO, working with influencers. Produce educational content. Leverage the assets from suppliers for video and image campaigns on social media.

3. Automate Your Processes

As your business scales, manual tasks can quickly become a bottleneck. Explore tools and software to automate various aspects of your operations, such as order processing, inventory management, and customer service. Automating these repetitive tasks will free up your time and resources so you can focus on the higher-level strategy and growth of your business. We will dive deeper into processes and automation later in the book in chapters 18 and 19.

4. Expand to New Sales Channels

Don't limit yourself to just your online store. Explore selling your products on marketplaces like Amazon, eBay, or Etsy to reach a larger audience and diversify your sales channels. This can help you tap into new customer bases and increase your overall sales potential.

5. Maintain Strong Supplier Relationships

As your business grows, your need for reliable and responsive suppliers will only increase. Work closely with existing suppliers and continuously explore new partnership opportunities. Maintaining a strong network of high-quality suppliers will ensure you can meet the demands of your expanding customer base without any serious disruptions in the fulfillment process.

Having been involved personally with every single business model covered in this book, I can confidently say that picking the right one is a matter of personal preferences and available opportunities. Spending over 15 years in service businesses, I've met thousands of SaaS or marketplace executives who can't fathom the idea of working with individual clients, reviewing briefs, and analyzing different business models every time. Managing a company with tons of dropshipping clients, I worked with people spending 10 hours a day watching videos looking for trends, browsing supplier catalogs, comparing products, and iterating on video creatives for TikTok ads.

The same principles are valid for content and publishing businesses, affiliates, or marketplaces. Some executives get excited about producing content and connecting with like minded individuals on social media while others avoid it like plague.

Find out what keeps you up at night and align your business to the corresponding traits. The last thing you want is ending up building a company with day-to-day operations differing too much from your personal value map.

PART III

LAUNCH AND EARLY GROWTH

CHAPTER THIRTEEN

CREATING & TESTING OFFERS FAST

As a business leader, whether you're an entrepreneur or a digital CEO, you understand the importance of being agile, responsive, and ahead of the competition. The ability to create and test offers quickly can be the driving force behind your success.

This is why we took on offer development and early tests in the second chapter of this book and uncovered the necessity of extensive market research right after, in chapter three.

Let's define what we mean by "creating and testing offers quickly." This refers to the process of **rapidly generating ideas, creating prototypes, and validating your products, services, or value propositions with your customers**. Compared to the slowly progressing enterprise workflows and tedious budget approval processes, you'll be able to gather crucial feedback, refine your offerings, and make data-driven decisions – all in a fraction of the time it would take using traditional methods.

Experimentation and agility are mandatory for every starting business. Finding your "product-market fit" takes time until you refine your product offer and establish your ideal customer profile. The faster you move, the easier it is to get this process straight. Especially for bootstrapped businesses that cannot afford to spend years making it work and don't have spare millions to run ads indefinitely until they get it right (or not).

Imagine you're a SaaS founder who wants to launch a new project management tool. Rather than spending months building the complete solution, you could start by creating a simple landing page, outlining the key features, and gauging customer interest through email signups or pre-orders. Based on the feedback you receive, you can then decide whether to proceed with a more comprehensive development process or explore a different direction altogether.

Following this "create and test offers quickly" mindset, you'll be able to respond to market shifts, test innovative ideas, and bring your most promising offerings to life with lightning speed. This approach not only gives you a competitive advantage but also helps you minimize risks and maximize your return on investment.

This method isn't limited to starting businesses, either. I work with seven and eight-figure businesses on launching new product and service lines, pivoting new pricing models, and adapting existing products to niche markets and industries. Where enterprises lack the processes for quick experimentation, we make this possible - both through Growth Shuttle with business advisory and strategy consulting and at DevriX by taking care of the entire process, including competitor and market research, designing and creating landing pages, A/B testing results, working with media buyers and paid ad vendors on iterating offers, updating CTA buttons or landing page copy weekly, measuring success through analytics and heatmaps.

In the following sections, we will explore the specific frameworks and validation methods you can use yourself to make this process as efficient and effective as possible.

Offer Frameworks

Before we discuss the different types of offer frameworks, let's first understand what exactly an offer framework is. Imagine you're running an online clothing store and want to create a new product offering. An offer framework would be the structure or template that helps you define the key elements of that offering, such as the problem it solves, the unique value it provides, and how it's packaged and presented to your customers.

With tried and tested offer frameworks, you can quickly generate, evaluate, and refine your business ideas, ensuring that your offers are laser-focused on meeting your customers' needs. Let's explore some of the most effective offer frameworks you can leverage to drive rapid growth for your digital business.

1. The Problem-Solution Offer Framework

This framework starts by clearly identifying the specific problem or pain point your customers are experiencing. For example, let's say you run an online productivity app. Using the problem-solution framework, you would first clearly articulate the problem your customers face, such as "struggling to stay organized and on top of their tasks." Then, you would position your app as the ideal solution that solves this problem by providing features like task management, to-do lists, and real-time collaboration.

2. The Value Proposition Offer Framework

The focus here is on clearly communicating the unique benefits and value your offer provides to your customers. For instance, if you're running an online fitness subscription service, your value proposition might be "Achieve your fitness goals with personalized workout plans and expert coaching, all from the comfort of your home." By highlighting the specific value you deliver, you can create offers that truly resonate with your target audience.

3. The Bundled Offer Framework

Sometimes, combining complementary products or services into a single offer can provide even more value to your customers. Imagine you're an online education platform offering various courses on digital marketing. Using the bundled offer framework, you could create a "Digital Marketing Mastery" package that includes courses on SEO, social media marketing, and email automation. This bundled approach can make your offers more appealing and valuable to your customers.

There are different offer frameworks available and product managers, marketers, founders end up piloting their own variations as well. But I want to provide some baseline principles that point your attention in the right direction: defining a clear value proposition and coming up with a compelling offer that resonates with your customers. You often end up having one shot with a visitor or a prospect over a sales call or a conference: getting this right can make or break a sale.

Rapid Validation Methods

As a digital entrepreneur or business owner, it's crucial to quickly gather customer feedback and refine your offerings to ensure they resonate with your target audience. This is where rapid validation methods come into play. These methods allow you to test your ideas, gather valuable insights, and make informed decisions to improve your products or services.

Let's say you have an idea for a new online course or a digital tool that you believe can solve a pressing problem for your customers. Before you invest a significant amount of time and resources into building the full product, you can utilize rapid validation methods to gauge interest, gather feedback, and refine your offer. Let us examine some of the most used Rapid Validation Methods:

VALIDATION TOOLBOX:
CREATING & TESTING OFFERS FAST

CUSTOMER INTERVIEWS
Understand pain points, preferences, and reactions.

MINIMUM VIABLE PRODUCTS (MVPS)
Test stripped-down versions with a small subset of the audience.

LANDING PAGE EXPERIMENTS
Gauge interest, gather data, and inform strategy.

DRIVING TRAFFIC TO YOUR LANDING PAGE
Utilize various channels for promotion.

MEASURING INTEREST AND CONVERSIONS
Monitor metrics closely for performance.

A/B TESTING
Experiment with variations to optimize conversions and engagement.

1. Customer Interviews

You may notice that this principle keeps circulating in different chapters in this book. Once again, one of the most effective validation techniques is conducting one-on-one conversations with your potential customers. Scheduling prospect interviews you can deeply understand their pain points, preferences, and reactions to your offer. For example, if you're planning to launch an online course on digital marketing, you could interview a few individuals in your target audience to understand their specific challenges, the type of content they're interested in, and their willingness to invest in such a course. These insights can be invaluable in shaping the final product.

2. Minimum Viable Products (MVPs)

Another critical goal for founders is creating a Minimum Viable Product (MVP). An MVP is a stripped-down version of your offer that you can test with a small subset of your target audience. This allows you to gather feedback and make iterative improvements without investing significant resources upfront.

For instance, if you're developing a new project management tool, you could start with a basic version that showcases the core functionality and get feedback from a group of early users. This can help you identify the features that resonate most with your customers and guide your development roadmap.

I will link additional guides I've authored on launching products and developing MVPs on the book website, mbadisrupted.com.

3. Landing Page Experiments

Veteran growth hackers end up selling products, courses, and solutions before they even come to life. You can copy this model and quickly build landing pages to gauge customer interest, gather email signups, or even collect pre-orders for your offer. The data you collect from these landing page experiments can then inform your overall go-to-market strategy.

Let's take a closer look at the three landing page platforms I can recommend for setting up a landing page or a starter site:

1. **WordPress:** WordPress is a highly versatile platform that can power almost any web project. The core WordPress platform is free to use, with the main costs coming from hosting your website and any paid add-ons or themes you choose to enhance your site. While the ongoing development costs will grow as your business scales, starting with the free WordPress platform is easy and doesn't require a rebuild or an expensive migration later on. WordPress currently powers an impressive 43% of all websites on the Internet. As a long-term investment, launching your digital project on WordPress is often worth it, as it also plays well with other recommended landing page tools.

2. **OnePage:** OnePage is a beautiful landing page builder that originated in Europe. I recently discovered this platform through a coaching group friend, and I've been impressed with its capabilities. It's powering a number of landing pages for my email lists, my advisory program, my brand ambassador services and more.

3. **Instapage:** Instapage is a powerful landing page platform that I can't omit from the list. This tool has helped me bring in nearly 2,000 students to my business accelerator course and secure 6-figure contracts for our Experimentation as a Service retainer. Instapage offers a comprehensive set of features and tools to help you create, test, and optimize your landing pages for maximum impact. While it may be overkill for some early-stage experiments, Instapage is an excellent choice for businesses that are ready to invest in a more advanced landing page solution.

Regardless of which platform you choose, the key is to leverage Landing Page Experiments as a rapid validation method to quickly gauge customer interest, gather valuable feedback, and inform your overall go-to-market strategy.

4. Driving Traffic to Your Landing Page

Once you have your landing page set up, the next crucial step is to drive relevant traffic to it.

Industry data shows that the average conversion rate for landing pages is around 2-3%. This means that for every 100 people who visit your page, 2 to 3 of them will typically take the desired action, such as signing up for your email list or booking a consultation call.

It's important to keep in mind that **conversion rates can vary significantly** depending on the industry, your target audience, and the type of offer you're presenting. For example, a free lead magnet or consultation offer will generally have a higher conversion rate than an offer for an expensive service.

Since you're in the testing phase of your idea, it's best to start with a lower-commitment offer that provides value to your potential customers without requiring an upfront payment. This could be something like a free resource, a questionnaire, or a short preview of your course or service. These types of offers tend to have higher conversion rates, as they make it easier for people to engage with your business. To gather traffic to your landing page, you can utilize a variety of channels, including:

- Reaching out to your network (friends, former colleagues, LinkedIn and Twitter connections) and asking for introductions or shares
- Leveraging social media, both through organic posts and paid advertising on platforms like Twitter, Facebook, Instagram, and TikTok
- Utilizing SEO if you have an existing blog or website that can drive relevant traffic
- Participating in online communities, such as Reddit, Quora, Facebook groups, Slack communities, and Discord channels (but be mindful not to come across as spammy)
- Asking friends or colleagues to share your offer in their email newsletters

Promotion is often the most challenging and expensive part of the validation process. If you've already established a digital presence and built a community around your idea, you may have an easier time driving organic traffic. If not, starting your journey and building your online presence earlier can pay dividends when it's time to promote your idea.

I'm also tempted to dive deeper into running paid ads at scale, but their success is highly dependent on the business type, the audience, and the unique traits of the founder. Some businesses sell easily on Facebook while others require a sales-led motion. Founder-led businesses can be truly impactful for business leaders who enjoy this journey. Therefore, different creative strategies work for different founders, which is what we're covering broadly in this alternative MBA book listing down a large variety of options you can narrow down and refine to ensure a successful venture.

5. Measuring Interest and Conversions

Once you start getting traffic to your landing page, it's crucial to closely monitor your metrics to understand how your offer is performing. Use the various tools and analytics available to track your traffic and conversion rates (e.g., email signups, consultation bookings, or any other desired actions).

A core marketing skill in large organizations (often outsourced to individual contributors, service-based businesses, or automated subscription products) is CRO (conversion rate optimization). It's equally important for B2B and B2C businesses, delivering strong results for high ticket offers, subscriptions, courses, ecommerce products.

CRO professionals run continuous experiments by applying hypotheses and best practices designed to increase the number of conversions for the same volume of visitors. Think about a landing page selling professional services or a product page for a tech device: iterating on button sizes or colors, call to action text, incorporating additional proof (reviews/testimonials), removing distracting links or menu items, decreasing the number of fields in the contact or purchase form are just a few of the thousands experiments professionals run to maximize the effectiveness of existing traffic (free or paid).

Aim to hit that 2-3% conversion rate benchmark, as it can serve as a good starting point for your validation process. If your conversion rates are significantly lower, don't be discouraged. Instead, take the opportunity to clone your landing page and experiment with different variations, testing various pain points, promises, and messaging to see what resonates best with your target audience.

The key is to find the right balance between providing genuine value and triggering the emotional need that justifies a purchase or subscription. Just make sure that you can deliver on the promises you make, as building trust and credibility with your potential customers is crucial for the long-term success of your business.

6. A/B Testing

Finally, A/B Testing is a powerful technique that allows you to experiment with different variations of your offer, messaging, or marketing approaches. By comparing the performance of these variations, you can determine the most effective strategies for driving conversions and engagement. For instance, if you're launching a new subscription-based software service, you could test different pricing models, trial periods, or onboarding experiences to identify the most compelling approach for your target audience.

Adopting a "create and test offers fast" mindset is crucial for launching a profitable business and staying competitive. Large companies understand their flaws and the inability to move fast and make rapid changes when established processes and tens of thousands or more employees are following a specific paradigm. Sundar Pichai, Google CEO, has been open about the risks of disruption from fast-moving organizations. In a Stanford interview in early 2024, asked about startups taking on Google, his response was, "It's a question which has always kept me up at night through the years. You're always susceptible to someone in a garage with a better idea."

The key to building a powerful startup is to move quickly, learn from your experiments, and continuously refine your offers. Embrace agility, data-driven decision-making, and a customer-first approach. This will help you unlock rapid growth for your business.

CHAPTER FOURTEEN

GO-TO-MARKET STRATEGIES

As an entrepreneur, you should be aware that success isn't just about having a great product or service, it's about effectively reaching and engaging your target customers. That's where go-to-market strategies come into play. These strategies are the backbone of your business growth, and they'll determine how you'll successfully connect with, attract, and acquire the customers you need to thrive.

Go-to-market (GTM) strategies are the plans and tactics you put in place to introduce your product or service to the market and drive sales. These strategies include everything from your marketing and advertising efforts to your sales processes and customer acquisition channels. In essence, your go-to-market approach is the roadmap that guides you in getting your offering in front of the right people, at the right time, and in the right way.

Think of it this way: you've just developed the most innovative software solution for streamlining project management. It's a game-changer in your industry, but if you don't have a solid go-to-market strategy, how will your potential customers even know it exists? *"Build it and they will come"* is a wrong fallacy that's been pondered online for years - but you can't count on that.

There are different schools of thought as it comes to the available GTM strategies on the market. You can discover and explore niche propositions in each segment, but the core motions applicable to all businesses are:

MAXIMIZING YOUR
GO-TO-MARKET STRATEGY

---

1. PRODUCT-LED
- Product virality
- Word of mouth from early adopters
- Focused on customer satisfaction

---

2. SALES-LED
- Empowered sales teams
- Business developers' outreach
- Targeting corporate clients

---

3. INBOUND
- Educational content
- Guides and tutorials
- Establishing thought leadership

---

4. OUTBOUND
- Paid advertising
- Email outreach
- Scalable prospect connection

---

5. PARTNERSHIPS
- Strategic collaborations
- Brand ambassador programs
- On-site initiatives for visibility

---

6. EVENTS
- Tradeshows and exhibitions
- Industry meetups
- Webinars and virtual conferences

Sales Motions

- **Product-Led**: Product virality and word of mouth from happy early adopters
- **Sales-Led**: Empowering executive sales teams and business developers to reach out and sale to corporations

Marketing Motions

- **Inbound**: Educational content, guides, resources, tutorials, and thought leadership
- **Outbound**: Paid ads, email outreach, and other external services to connect with prospects at scale
- **Partnerships**: The power of strategic partnerships, collaborations, brand ambassador deals, and on-site initiatives
- **Events**: Heavy focus on tradeshows and industry events, meetups, webinars, and virtual conferences.

Some strategist distinguish separate motions as they make more sense in certain verticals. Community-led is often references as a unique mechanism to grow communities and use their velocity for sticky products, niche membership groups, or other models with a strong mission and high relevance to their users. Founder-led is also picking up traction, stressing on the importance of founders to lead the way not just internally, but externally; sharing trials and tribulations, teaching, building relationships separately, and providing thought leadership to prove their worth and grow transparently as fast as possible.

One incredible resource on GTM deep dives is Maja Voje's book, *Go-To-Market Strategist: Everything You Need to Reach Product-Market Fit*. Maja has been a prominent coach, trainer, and thought leader in the GTM space with a growing LinkedIn audience and dozens of applicable worksheet and checklists focused entirely on go-to-market motions. The link to the book will be available along with the other resources on mbadisrupted.com.

Bain & Company are an earlier contributor to go-to-market motions over the past 20 years, managing their own framework and a solution suite called Coro specifically designed to aligned B2B GTM teams. Michael Skok taught a class on startup go-to-market in Harvard and his strategic talk has gathered a million views since 2013 on YouTube.

Bottom line, launching and scaling businesses is common problem that's studied extensively for years. High-level strategic frameworks provide the base areas you should consider for your venture. Every business model and niche vertical uncovers specific tools, channels, or concepts unique to the space that you have to study separately as you go.

In the meantime, I will go over the core principles of these and provide some examples for each motion. In a startup's early days, starting with a single engine to gain market traction is often the right bet. Go with one that's proven to work for your audience and in your market. Established enterprises often engage in multiple motions heavily once they can afford to allot sufficient resources to each initiative.

Inbound Marketing

Inbound marketing is a smart approach to attracting potential customers to your business. Instead of interrupting people with cold calls or ads, inbound marketing focuses on creating valuable content that draws people in and builds relationships with them. So, what exactly is Inbound Marketing?

Inbound marketing is a methodology initially coined by HubSpot, one of the leaders in the CRM and marketing automation space online. It is all about creating content that your potential customers want to engage with. This could be anything from informative blog posts to helpful how-to videos, to interactive online tools. The key is to provide value upfront, without directly pitching your products or services.

For example, let's say you run an e-commerce store that sells high-quality kitchen gadgets. An inbound marketing approach might involve creating a series of blog posts with tips and recipes for home cooks. By offering genuinely useful information, you're building trust and establishing yourself as an authority in the kitchen gadget space. Over time, readers who find your content helpful are more likely to become customers when they're ready to make a purchase.

The Benefits of Inbound Marketing

Inbound marketing has a lot of advantages over traditional "outbound" marketing tactics like cold calling or TV ads. For one, it's a more cost-effective way to reach your target audience. Instead of spending money to interrupt people as they browse around or call them while in meetings, you're creating content that naturally draws people in. This helps you connect with the right customers, rather than just casting a wide (and expensive) net.

Inbound marketing also tends to be more effective at building long-term relationships with customers. By providing value upfront, you're positioning yourself as a helpful resource, not just a company trying to make a sale. This can lead to more loyal, engaged customers who are more likely to become advocates for your brand.

Content Strategies

As part of your inbound marketing approach, developing a strong content strategy is crucial. Your content is the foundation for attracting and engaging your target audience. When done well, it can position you as a trusted authority in your industry and help build lasting relationships with potential customers.

So, what goes into an effective content strategy? The key is to create content that truly resonates with your audience. This means taking the time to deeply understand their pain points, questions, and interests. What problems are they trying to solve? What information are they searching for online? By tapping into these insights, you can develop a content plan that provides genuine value.

Some common types of content that work well for inbound marketing include:

- ❖ Interesting blog posts that educate and inform
- ❖ How-to guides and tutorials
- ❖ Engaging videos that showcase your expertise
- ❖ Insightful industry reports and white papers
- ❖ Interactive tools and calculators
- ❖ Podcasts that offer thought leadership.

No matter what format you choose, the content should be high-quality, relevant, and aligned with your audience's needs. Consistency is also important. Aim to publish new content on a regular cadence to keep your audience engaged.

In the long run, the goal of your content strategy isn't just to promote your products or services. It's about establishing trust, building relationships, and positioning yourself as a valuable resource. When you prioritize your audience's interests over your own sales objectives, you'll see much better results in the long run.

Building an Audience

Once you've developed a strong content strategy, the next step is to get that content in front of the right people. This is where audience building comes into play.

The key is to meet your potential customers where they already are, whether that's on search engines, social media platforms, industry publications, or elsewhere online. This could involve tactics like:

* Search engine optimization (SEO) to improve the visibility of your content in organic search results
* Sharing your content on social media channels frequented by your target audience
* Guest posting on relevant industry blogs to reach new readers
* Collaborating with influencers or industry leaders to expand your reach
* Leveraging email marketing to nurture relationships with your existing audience.

You want to slowly but steadily build awareness and credibility with your target market. As more people discover your valuable content, you'll start to see your audience grow.

Audience building is an ongoing process. You'll need to continually experiment, analyze your results, and refine your approach to find what works best. This follows the principles uncovered for content/publishing businesses in chapter 8 and communities in chapter 7.

As a founder of a service-first business, inbound marketing has been the leading go-to-market motion for both DevriX and Growth Shuttle. Slowly but steadily, we kept producing business guides for executives and marketing leaders, bridging the gap between technology, marketing, and business execution in the digital landscape. This thought leadership model brought in tens of thousands of links from authority sources, business leaders, successful startups, and universities.

Growth Shuttle used a similar flywheel model while helping SMEs and startups unlock new revenue streams, automate internal processes, and save capital through our expertise in inbound marketing. My team of experienced professionals develops targeted content strategies, optimizes our clients' online presence, leverages search engine optimization (SEO), and implements lead-generation tactics that attract the ideal customers. Our case studies, strategic guides, tutorials, educational video content, and consistent social media publishing with frameworks and blueprints keeps generating leads and adds success stories to our portfolio of advisory clients.

Outbound Marketing

Outbound marketing refers to traditional marketing strategies where a company initiates the conversation and sends its message out to an audience. This type of marketing typically involves techniques such as paid ads, cold calling and email blasts, TV and radio commercials, podcast and newsletter sponsorships.

The key characteristic of outbound marketing is that it's a proactive approach where the company taps into existing communication channels trying to convert customers on the spot. It's often contrasted with inbound marketing, which focuses on creating valuable content and experiences tailored to draw customers in naturally.

Outbound is both lucrative and highly criticized at the same time. On the one hand, it provides better data layers to track down direct conversions, sales velocity, ad spend, or SDR payroll. On the other, there are thousands of ways you can get this right - from inefficient campaigns or inexperienced SDRs to poor benchmarking, lead attribution, and chasing the wrong signals in the process.

A key influencer in the space I can recommend is Chris Walker, the founder of Pasetto and Chairman at Refine Labs. Chris has spent the past few years analyzing sales data for enterprise companies and revealing different flaws in the data attribution process: from website prospects wrongfully attributed to marketing to absurdly expensive paid ads resulting in customer acquisition costs in the five figures, to the important of "dark social" conversations bringing enterprise-grade contracts without clear attribution. His podcasts, B2B Revenue Vitals, is one of my favorite Spotify resources I follow.

Outbound marketing can be very effective, particularly in reaching a wide audience quickly, but it's often seen as less targeted and more interruptive compared to inbound techniques. With the rise of digital marketing and the ability to personalize messages, outbound marketing has evolved to be more sophisticated, incorporating data-driven insights to improve targeting and relevance.

Outbound is often used in e-commerce due to the quick transaction cycles or self-served SaaS with free trials and innovative solutions that solve a customer's product quickly. Communities and publishing businesses may also benefit from this model, but service companies in crowded markets rarely see strong return on investment with outbound.

With outbound marketing, you take the initiative to reach out to your target customers. There are several ways you can do this:

1. **Cold Outreach:** You directly contact potential customers through phone calls, emails, or even social media messages. This allows you to introduce your products or services and start a conversation with them directly.

2. **Email Campaigns:** You create and send targeted email messages to your contact list. These emails can provide valuable information and offers to your potential customers. Email campaigns can help you build relationships and turn leads into paying customers.

3. **Direct Sales:** Your sales team actively reaches out to prospects, either in person or online, to showcase your products or services and try to close deals. For smaller startups, this initiative still falls into outbound. Enterprise teams develop enterprise-grade sales-led motions going through more complex journeys.

Using AI-powered tools can speed up the outbound marketing process. Tools like Apollo can provide detailed data analytics and personalization, allowing you to create highly targeted and effective outreach campaigns that resonate with your ideal customers.

You still need effective playbooks that work - the ability to conduct a process manually from the start, analyze what works, and then implement AI to deliver at scale. The false promise of blasting hundreds of thousands of emails and generating millions in sales is flawed and may ruin your brand, blacklist your domain, and get you flagged in various online systems and reputation tracking networks.

Event-Led Growth

Event-led growth is very efficient for executives and teams able to attend events, sponsor booths, and present with strategic talks. This motion combines both virtual and in-person events to engage with your target audience, build brand awareness, and generate valuable leads that can turn into sales. Let's take a closer look at how you can use different types of events to drive growth for your business.

ELEVATING YOUR GO-TO-MARKET STRATEGY WITH EVENT-LED GROWTH

WEBINARS

- Demonstrate expertise
- Generate leads
- Build customer relationships

VIRTUAL SUMMITS

- Collaborate with experts
- Increase reach
- Showcase industry leadership

IN-PERSON EVENTS

- Network with customers
- Raise brand awareness
- Strengthen customer connections

1. Webinars

Webinars are an excellent way for you to demonstrate your knowledge and expertise to your audience in a highly interactive format. By hosting informative, value-packed webinars, you can position yourself as an authority in your industry, generate new leads, and build stronger relationships with potential customers.

For example, let's say you own a software company that provides project management tools. You could host a webinar walking your audience through the key features of your software and sharing best practices for using it effectively. This allows you to show off your product's capabilities, answer questions in real-time, and build trust with the attendees. Over time, these webinar participants may turn into paying customers as they see your team's expertise and the value your software can provide.

2. Virtual Summits

Another powerful event-led growth strategy is to organize virtual summits. These online events allow you to collaborate with industry experts and deliver a series of informative presentations and workshops. By tapping into new audiences and showcasing your brand alongside respected thought leaders, you can significantly increase your reach and positioning as a leader in your field.

You can host a virtual summit that focuses on the latest trends and best practices in your industry. Invite other experts to share their insights and advice and create a can't-miss event for your target customers.

Capturing some hot industry topics like AI, automating B2B processes, mass-generated content, recent changes or trends on social, email marketing, data privacy - or anything that's top of mind for individuals in your audience today - can be a great reason to gather several partners and organize a full virtual conference with deep dives on each topic.

3. In-Person Events

While virtual events have their advantages, in-person events are still the preferred medium of sales for traditional organizations and enterprises. Participating in industry conferences or trade shows gives you the chance to network with potential customers, raise brand awareness, and even generate direct sales leads through on-site demonstrations and interactions.

These face-to-face experiences allow you to make lasting impressions and develop meaningful connections with the people who matter most to your company. Imagine setting up a booth at a major industry event where you can showcase your products or services and have engaging conversations with attendees. This is a fantastic way to not only attract new leads but also deepen relationships with your existing customers.

Back in the day, one of my ambassador roles for a global hosting company required several event appearances annually where I presented as a speaker and managed the booth with one or two of my colleagues. We used to hand discount fliers for free trials or discount coupon codes for our services to hundreds of attendees, meeting partners on-site, scheduling future collaborations during podcasts or co-hosted webinars. While events are time-consuming and may require international travel, facetime and limited competition during the event can nurture specific connections that last through the years. I still send occasional selfies from years ago to partners and friends as follow-up conversations every now and then.

Regardless of the event format you choose, the key is to focus on delivering an exceptional, value-driven experience that resonates with your target audience. It's easy to start regurgitating topics that are beaten to death or provide low-quality high-level tips that chatbots can answer today. Sharing the secret bits and pieces from actionable strategies that work, along with industry data and real stories, is a powerful driver for attendees.

Partner-Led Growth

Another powerful approach you can leverage is on as your Go-to-market strategy is partner-led growth. This means forming strategic partnerships with other businesses, whether they are complementary service providers or large enterprise platforms, to help you accelerate your growth and access new markets. There are several key ways you can use partner-led growth to your advantage:

LEVERAGING PARTNER-LED GROWTH IN GO-TO-MARKET STRATEGIES

CHANNEL PARTNERSHIPS

- Tap into existing customer bases
- Integrate offerings seamlessly
- Expand product offerings

STRATEGIC COLLABORATIONS

- Co-create content and host webinars
- Boost brand visibility and credibility
- Tap into new audiences

IDENTIFYING OPPORTUNITIES

- Find businesses with overlapping audiences
- Offer complementary products or services
- Unlock growth opportunities

1. Channel Partnerships

One exciting opportunity to explore is channel partnerships, where you sell your products or services through the platforms of large SaaS providers. This allows you to tap into their existing customer base and integrate your offerings seamlessly into their established ecosystem.

Imagine, for example, if your accounting software company partnered with a popular project management platform like Jira or Asana. You could offer your invoicing tools as an integrated add-on within their platform, giving you access to a whole new audience of potential customers who are already using and trusting the partner's software. This type of channel partnership is a win-win, as it allows the SaaS provider to expand their product offerings while also enabling you to reach a larger customer base through their distribution channels.

Another great example of a successful channel partnership is the integration between HubSpot, a leading CRM and marketing automation platform, and Canva, a popular design tool. HubSpot users can seamlessly access Canva's design features right within the HubSpot interface, making it easier for marketers to create visually stunning content. This integration has been hugely beneficial for both companies, as it allows HubSpot to provide more value to its customers while also exposing Canva to a vast new audience of potential users.

2. Strategic Collaborations

Another powerful approach to partner-led growth is to form strategic collaborations with industry influencers, content creators, or complementary businesses. Think of co-creating content, hosting joint webinars, or cross-promoting each other's products and services where you can significantly expand your reach and tap into new audiences.

Let's say you run a digital marketing agency specializing in social media management. You could partner with a popular social media influencer in your industry to co-host a series of educational workshops or live streams. This allows you to leverage the influencer's established following and boost your own brand visibility and credibility. The influencer, in turn, can offer valuable insights and strategies to their audience, positioning themselves as a thought leader in the space.

Strategic collaborations may go sideways, and one of my favorite examples is Shopify and its relationships in the email marketing space. Mailchimp and Shopify were partnering up for years, until some data policy regulations led to Mailchimp pulling out and refusing to abide by the new data sharing requirements at the end of 2019. Two years later, Mailchimp was acquired by Intuit for $12 billion so their journey was headed into a different path at the time.

Shopify, on the other hand, brought in Klaviyo as a recommended partner and now Klaviyo is the leading e-commerce marketing automation platform not just for Shopify, but across most commerce platforms on the market. In 2022, Shopify invested $100M in Klaviyo to further cement the relationship and profit off the referral business sent their way. A year later, Klaviyo got listed on the New York Stock Exchange and has a $5.94 billion market cap today.

Successful partner-led growth means identifying businesses or individuals whose target audiences overlap with your own, and who can offer complementary products, services, or distribution channels. Similarly to Shopify and Klaviyo's story, you can unlock tremendous opportunities for growth that would be much harder to achieve on your own.

At Rush, we invested heavily in partner-led activities with both channel partners and strategic partnerships. SaaS startups often double down on this approach, just like e-commerce vendors list on marketplaces and service-based businesses get listed on professional directories like Clutch or agency portals.

Product-Led Growth

One approach that has gained significant traction in recent years as startup growth accelerated thanks to massive funding opportunities is the concept of product-led growth (PLG). This dynamic strategy places your product at the very heart of your growth efforts, leveraging the power of the customer experience to launch and grow a self-sustaining cycle of user acquisition, retention, and expansion.

Product-led growth is a fundamental shift in how businesses approach growth and go-to-market strategies. Rather than relying solely on traditional marketing tactics or an outbound sales-driven model, PLG puts the product itself at the forefront, allowing it to become a powerful acquisition channel that can organically attract and convert new users. Here are some of the key strategies involved in this motion.

MAXIMIZING GROWTH WITH PRODUCT-LED STRATEGIES

FREE TRIALS AND FREEMIUM EXPERIENCES

- Lower barriers to entry
- Build trust and credibility
- Limited need for outbound sales staff

VIRAL GROWTH MECHANISMS

- Leverage user-generated content
- Encourage network effects
- Tap into users' natural desire to share

1. Offering Free Trials and Freemium Experiences

One of the default starting points of a successful product-led growth strategy is the use of free trials or freemium product offerings. Providing self-served demos without any initial financial commitment, you significantly lower the barriers to entry and make it easier for clients to get started without long and tedious sales qualification journeys.

Imagine you're the founder of a cloud-based project management software company. Instead of asking users to commit to a paid subscription right away, you could offer a free trial that allows them to explore the tool's features and functionalities for a limited period. This "try before you buy" approach not only builds trust and credibility but also gives users a chance to see the tangible benefits your product can provide, making them much more likely to convert to a paid plan down the line. This also limits the need for outbound sales staff as many PLG startups are almost entirely driven through marketing and customer experience teams.

Alternatively, you could opt for a freemium model, where you offer a stripped-down version of your product for free, with the option to upgrade to a premium plan that unlocks additional features and capabilities. The freemium approach is particularly effective for B2B SaaS companies, as it allows users to get acquainted with your product and gradually realize its value before deciding to invest in a paid subscription.

One popular video creation product today is OpusClip, an AI-driven tool that splits a video file into chunks for reels, stories, and shorts, incorporating visually engaging captions automatically, and turns the video production and posting experience into a semi-automated journey (including scheduled posting within their platform).

They approach that with a free self-served trial and a limited number of AI minutes for trying out several videos before switching to a paid plan or staying at a limited forever free plan with a watermark under each video.

2. Incorporating Viral Growth Mechanisms

The watermark model above completely justifies keeping the "always free" plan on for OpusClip. Providing immense value resulting in tons of videos online with the Opus logo has the viral effect the founders seek: acquiring users for free thanks to happy users gladly sharing the results of their work.

Slack, the popular team communication and collaboration platform, follows a similar model. Slack's seamless user experience, integrated workflows, and the ability to share channels and files make it incredibly easy for users to invite their teammates to join. Companies invite their vendors, freelancers, contractors, partners into a Slack workspace. As more and more people discover Slack and experience its benefits, they naturally invite their colleagues to join, further amplifying the platform's reach and user base.

Similarly, Dropbox, the cloud storage and file-sharing service, famously achieved remarkable growth in its early days by offering users additional free storage space for each friend they invited to the platform. This referral-based approach tapped into users' natural desire to share useful products with their networks, creating a viral growth loop that propelled Dropbox's expansion.

Whether you're a SaaS startup, an e-commerce business, or a company looking to expand your digital footprint, embracing a product-led growth strategy can keep your growth curve in place without investing additional funds in paid ads or spending half of your time at events. Even though PLG is not applicable to all types of businesses, when it fits, it often becomes a priority for founding teams.

Community-Led Growth

The idea behind community-led growth is quite simple. It's all about building and nurturing a thriving community around your product or brand. Creating an engaged and loyal group of users, you can gather ongoing feedback, get additional exposure and help promote product updates and announcements, and aggregate referrals on the go. This can help fuel your company's growth sustainably and organically.

One alternative segment of community-led ventures is a "founder-led" motion, the ability for prominent thought leaders and business figures to build their own community by continuously publishing online, hosting a video channel or a podcast, sharing transparent data with their audience, and shaping a successful community of supporters that translates to companies ran by the founders.

COMMUNITY-LED GROWTH STRATEGIES

ESTABLISH ONLINE ENGAGEMENT HUBS

- Dedicated online spaces (website, social media, specialized platforms)
- Foster connections and gather feedback
- Promote collaboration and partnerships

HOST COMMUNITY EVENTS

- Organize in-person and virtual meetups, workshops, conferences
- Facilitate networking and education
- Integrate GTM strategies for business growth

EMPOWER USER INVOLVEMENT

- Encourage user-generated content (blog posts, tutorials, support)
- Strengthen brand connection through user participation
- Utilize user-to-user support to ease customer service burdens

1. Creating Online Hubs for Customer Engagement

A common solution to building a thriving community is to establish a discussion group for your customers. This could be a dedicated space on your website, a social media group, or even a specialized community platform.

Within this digital hub, your customers can connect, share their experiences, ask questions, and offer support. Happy users can bond together and achieve a sense of belonging (community users churn less once they connect with others) but it also provides you with valuable insights into their needs, pain points, and ideas for product improvements.

I've been in different product groups myself and still keep an eye on some of these:

- Buffer's Slack community
- HubSpot's discussion network
- Beehiiv's Slack
- SeedBlink's Circle group
- Market Brief's Discord community.

Great products, media brands, SaaS groups can gather users and partners together in a collaborative experience that delivers extra value to everyone. Users can uncover new ways to use a product, learn about integrations, help other vendors integrate better with the product, collaborate on user guides together, get invited to relevant podcasts or video channels with partners, and join Ask Me Anything sessions with partners in these groups.

2. Organizing In-Person and Virtual Community Events

While online communities are incredibly valuable, there's also immense power in bringing your customers together in physical or virtual spaces. Most community-led groups organize in-person meetups, workshops, or user conferences where members can connect better, share specific challenges they face at the time, and use the brand as an intermediary to their roadmap for solving their problems.

Imagine you run a SaaS company that provides sales and marketing automation tools. You could host an annual user conference where customers can network, attend educational sessions, and provide direct feedback to your product team. Or, you could organize a series of virtual workshops focused on specific features or best practices, inviting your most engaged users to participate and share their insights.

You can quickly see that both GTM motions and business models can be combined and intertwined in some cases. This can lead to interesting opportunities to build a more creative business that isn't stuck back in time but progresses with the needs of its target audience. Your community-led approach can grow a SaaS business or a publishing portal, but it can also turn into a separate business venture, generating a significant amount of recurring revenue at the same time.

3. Empowering User-Generated Content and Support

Another powerful perk of community-led growth is facilitating user-generated content, such as blog posts, tutorials, or even user-to-user support, among your community members.

For example, if you run an e-commerce platform that sells handmade artisanal products, you could create a section on your website where your customers can share their DIY projects, product reviews, or even tips and tricks for using the products. This not only provides valuable content and inspiration for other users, but it also strengthens their connection to your brand, as they feel empowered to contribute and share their experiences.

Site builders can compile successful case studies and site builds from their users. Email automation platforms can gather and brag about successful newsletters run on their stack. Opportunities exist in almost every business vertical.

A bonus point when enabling user-to-user support within your community is relying on your customers to help address common questions or issues, reducing the load on your customer service team

No single GTM strategy will work indefinitely for your business during the scaling phase. The most successful companies rely on multiple growth levers, adapting the core playbooks to the unique needs and opportunities of their market. Find out what motion resonates the most with your own philosophy and what works successfully for your ideal client. Some are easier than others in different markets. Trying to force outbound for commodity services or community-led if you are deeply introverted may result in poor results compared to proven strategies that competitors in the space apply successfully.

CHAPTER FIFTEEN

REVENUE & PROFITABILITY

Starting entrepreneurs often spend the first months on the two opposing ends of the business evolution process: launching a product from zero and scraping for the first customers, then skipping through the whole operational journey of "making it work" up until the expectations of a successful exit or a profitable, self-managed, dividend-generating business.

But that intermediate process is about tactical, operational work, careful financial planning, keeping a close eye on expense reports and revenue opportunities, maintaining safety nets, analyzing late payments, supporting credit lines as buffers, and other areas where operationally strong executives, COOs, CFOs spend most of their time on.

P&L Statements

Company financials are driven by Profit & Loss (P&L) statements. That's what founders, C-level executives, and accountants follow closely to monitor company performance or build forecasts for future profits. P&L statements can be used as a baseline for forecasting and predictive analysis, annual roadmap and budget planning, and investment decks when raising money.

The earlier you start tracking your revenue channels and expense breakdowns, the better. I've spoken to hundreds of founders running companies and teams for a year or two without any visibility on incoming revenue or what expenses get incurred as a result. They understand the high-level cost items, including payroll, rent, general spend for Facebook ads, but that's about it.

Many of them failed because they spent more than they earned, not accounting for one-off costs running in the red or forecasting based on campaign sales and not true income reports. Especially in e-commerce, examples of scaling ads based on the difference between ad spend and product cost, without accounting for product manufacturing costs, taxes, refunds and chargebacks, shipping and packaging, and plenty of sunk costs in the process.

P&L statements are ideally managed monthly, which allows you to maintain a feedback loop and track down growth and decline, seasonality, remaining funds, or account for one-off expenses. Spreadsheets - Excel or Google Sheets - are the most common form for storing and managing these as accounting can run calculations and generate charts and gather insights based on them.

Tools like QuickBooks or Xero that help manage invoicing or accounting fees can generate these automatically based on data stored within. There are mobile apps or CRMs that can take care of the process, but unless your accountants recommend a specific software suite, spreadsheets are powerful and extensible as you keep adding more line items in each bucket.

Here are the high-level items you want to keep a close eye on as summarized lines on your P&L sheet:

PROFIT & LOSS STATEMENT LAYOUT

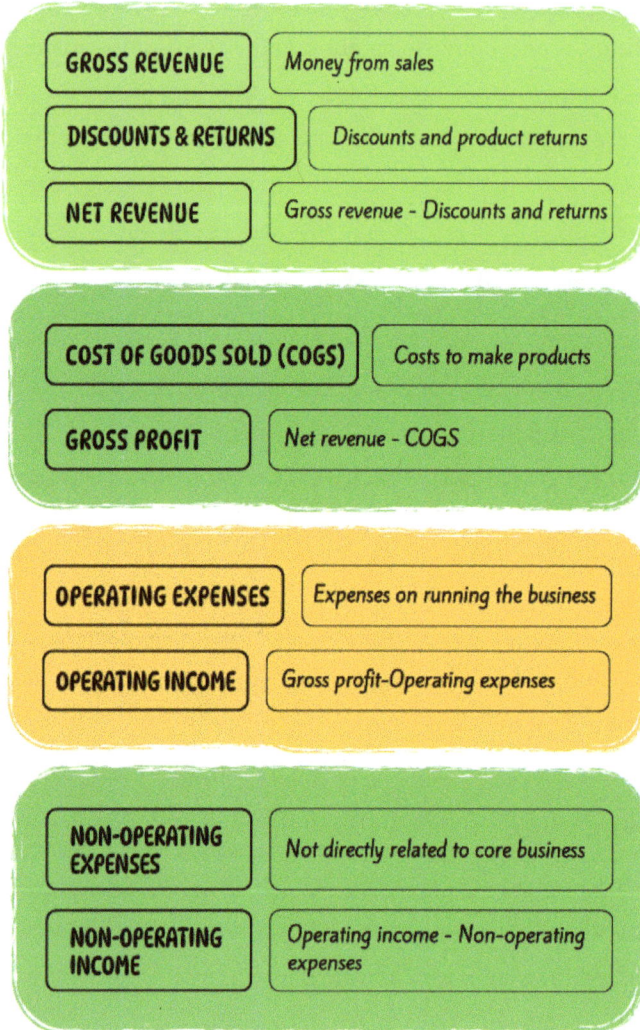

GROSS REVENUE	Money from sales
DISCOUNTS & RETURNS	Discounts and product returns
NET REVENUE	Gross revenue - Discounts and returns

COST OF GOODS SOLD (COGS)	Costs to make products
GROSS PROFIT	Net revenue - COGS

OPERATING EXPENSES	Expenses on running the business
OPERATING INCOME	Gross profit-Operating expenses

NON-OPERATING EXPENSES	Not directly related to core business
NON-OPERATING INCOME	Operating income - Non-operating expenses

On a high-level, we track down the following categories:

- **Gross Revenue:** The total revenue generated from the business.

- **Net Revenue:** Often similar to gross, but minus discounts, refunds, returns at the cost of the business.

- **Gross Profit:** The remaining amount excluding the so-called COGS, or "cost of goods sold."
  - For product businesses, that's materials, packaging, and everything directly related 100% to producing the product.
  - For service businesses, this is full-time employees entirely tied to the service execution (designers, developers, marketers with no other admin functions). Some financial experts recommend that to go into Opex below, but it's often blended with non-billable roles doing so.

- **Operating Expenses:** Any other expenses required to keep the company around. Think of rent, team perks/bonuses, admin staff that doesn't directly execute billable work but is integral (accounting, legal, cleaning), 3rd party vendors, ad budgets, events. All of your expenses not included in COGS.

- **Gross Income:** Revenue minus every other expense so far.

- **Net Income:** the gross revenue minus all other expenses ever incurred, or simplified - all of your revenue that hits the bank minus all payroll, materials, ad/vendor costs, rental, and everything you pay for. Taxes are also included as a cost cut between the gross income and the net income.

Let's take an e-commerce company as an example. You run a product manufacturing business that crafts and sells wooden toys. A toy costs $50. You sell 100 of these, which generates $5,000. That's your **gross revenue**. If you have discounts baked in, your net revenue will be $5,000 minus the discounts.

The cost of goods sold includes product materials and 100% labor to produce. If you have one part-time employee for $1,000/mo crafting and packaging, and each toy requires $10 in wood, packaging, and shipment labels, that's $1,000 in product materials and $1,000 for directly related labor to COGS, or **$2,000 in COGS**.

So, your **gross profit is $3,000** ($5,000 in revenue minus $2,000 in COGS).

You may be paying $1,000 monthly in ads, maintaining your software fees, website licenses, ad fees, credit card fees, and other tedious expenses to make this happen. **Operating profit** goes down to $2,000. Consider CPA or legal expenses, subscriptions, and others here (it may go up.)

Now, taxes are extremely complicated and vary drastically across countries, states, and types of corporations. Averages can vary drastically from 10% to 40%, including personal taxes, double charging, and lots of other hoops. You can reinvest in the business in different ways or pay taxes in different forms based on revenue or profit, depending on how you split proceeds. Let's take 25% as an average.

25% out of $2,000 is $500 for **non-operating expenses**.

You end up with a **$1,500 net income** you can cash out or reinvest in the business. Congratulations!

This is a very simplified example, but it determines how P&L sheets are structured and how expenses are managed. As soon as you start allotting ads/marketing budget or hire freelancers or staff, it gets allotted to the corresponding buckets (and additional expense items such as 401Ks or health insurance or pension funds fees get included in the mix).

There are tons of P&L templates you can start with. I will provide several examples on the book's website, mbadisrupted.com

In order to maintain profitability and keep growing, deciding on the right pricing model early on will help you establish the right go-to-market mechanisms to keep growing revenue with the best practices available for the specific pricing model.

Each business segment may provide specific considerations with regards to pricing (niche models applicable to the corresponding category).

Your product or solution can provide multiple price categories depending on your ICP. You can start simple and expand later – or introduce new pricing models to new service tiers you launch over time.

Profit Distribution

Best-case scenario, your business model is profitable: you generate more revenue than your expenses + taxes require, and profits keep piling up.

One of the key questions remains: what is the best way to distribute profits, how often, and how much?

First, if you end up taking funding in the process, you will always be under heavy scrutiny for any profit distributions and payouts outside of your agreed salary. Funding rounds share equity in exchange for capital, and your investors become shareholders in the business. They have the right to claim ownership or expect profit distribution as well in the event of an exit, annual dividend payouts, or a liquidation.

This is very, very, very important to understand. Some founders end up raising and diluting their ownership over and over, then moving to profitability, but being unable to cash out or allocate funds outside of their predefined agreement.

Your mileage may vary here. Investors and partners usually don't want to deal with media scandals or the burden of replacing CEOs or any other conflicts, but your shareholders agreement likely prevents you from paying yourself extra. Also, booted CEOs still exist. Think of the Ubers or WeWorks of the startup space and how some founders were detached from operations.

For bootstrapped businesses, you are free to distribute funds however you deem appropriate when you own 100% of your company. But even in this case, there are three possible ways to manage company profits:

- **Profit Sharing:** Taking some or all of the profit individually or distributed to other parties (leadership team, key players, bonus structures, any other ways of additional payouts)
- **Runway/Buffers:** Keeping enough funds in the bank as a safety net. It's always best to retain several months of full company expenses in the bank in the event of losing business, late payments, legal/tax fees, bonus payments, opportunities to sponsor events or invest in campaigns, and generally survive through unexpected surprises.

- **Reinvesting Capital:** Investing capital back in the business.

Especially in the first years of the business, reinvesting almost everything back in the business is the industry norm. At a later stage, dividend payouts or bonuses may be more common, especially as businesses stabilize and optimize for profitability. But in the growth stage, which can last from several years to the entire lifetime of a company, reinvesting is the best option for a business.

What are some key areas that executives should keep reinvesting in (and consider expanding)?

1. Product Development

One of the most common and impactful ways to reinvest in your business is by developing new and existing products or services. This could involve creating entirely new offerings, improving and expanding on your existing products, or adding complementary items to your lineup. Investing in product R&D shows your customers that you're committed to continuously enhancing the value you provide.

2. Technology Upgrades

Reinvesting profits into upgrading your equipment, software, and digital infrastructure can make your operations more efficient, your products or services more advanced, and your customer experience more seamless. Running better and more optimal servers, providing high availability with backup systems, and integrating better accounting or customer support software are some common examples.

3. Expanded Marketing

Another common reinvestment area is your marketing and advertising efforts. Taking some of your profits to beef up your digital presence, social media strategy, SEO, content creation, and other promotional initiatives can help you reach new customers and strengthen your brand awareness. If a channel works, just double down on it. Make sure you don't overburden your existing team with twice as much work without the ability to scale, automate, or outsource.

4. Team Development

Your employees are the heart of most small businesses, and it's only fair to share proceeds with them in different capacities. This could mean providing more robust training and professional development opportunities, offering better compensation and benefits, or adding new key roles to your team. Investing in your people helps you attract and retain top talent, which in turn drives better business outcomes.

5. Expansion into New Markets

I'm a strong proponent of diversification having spent years in the field of risk management. So moving into new markets, developing new channels, launching parallel services to upsell are all areas that resonate with me.

You can expand into new geographic regions, industries, or customer segments. Untapped opportunities are available globally if you look for them. Don't neglect the cost of market entry. You may need to set up individual LLCs locally, obey with the local tax laws, translate your site/products to a different language, or employ additional resources unique to the market. It's often worth it in the long run, but the initial investment requirements may be higher.

6. Acquisition or Partnerships

In some cases, the best reinvestment strategy is to acquire another complementary business or form a strategic partnership.

There are 3 core strategies to increase revenue:

- Find new customers
- Upsell your existing customers
- Partner or acquire a business.

Go-to-market strategists can bend the P&L additionally - through operational efficiency, automations, expanding a contract's amount or duration, landing referrals and recommendations. As for revenue growth, a common executive question is: "Should we build or buy?"

Acquiring other players in the space - smaller companies or businesses that work with the same ICP - is a tried and tested strategy and a viable exit plan for startups raising money today. Business leaders can ballparks the cost to start a relevant brand, build a competitive product, hire a team, grow to the same level and replicate the model from start to end. Oftentimes, it ends up costing more, distracting the core team with launching new companies, delaying other initiatives in the works, and risking the end outcome as similar actions may take years and go through different macroeconomic cycles.

As a digital CEO, keeping an eye on new acquisition opportunities is a great way to quickly accelerate, tap into new markets, expand your service portfolio, and tick several of the boxes here in one go.

I became a Flippa ambassador in early 2023 after completing nearly 40 acquisitions on the marketplace for my own brands and facilitating several high-scale transactions for other businesses. Flippa is the largest digital acquisition marketplace where buyers can acquire content and publishing sites, e-commerce stores, SaaS apps, newsletters, mobile apps, agencies, and everything in-between. This allows successful founders to diversify into other business models (an e-commerce buying an affiliate site), or multiply their properties (running several stores or publishing sites), grow their brand visibility (a service company acquiring a newsletter), supplement different revenue lines (community group buying an agency to upsell services).

Our partnership combines their endless pool of offers while plugging into my network of startup founders, VC funds, angel investors, and other executives I work with on a daily basis, exploring growth options and not thinking about acquisitions as a viable channel.

There are no right or wrong ways to distribute profits for a cash flow positive business. Ultimately, it's at the discretion of the founder for a bootstrapped business or the shareholders/board of directors for funded ones. You want to mitigate as many risks as possible, including churning clients or team members, negative reviews, inefficient processes, or many other areas we are about to review in the next chapter.

CHAPTER SIXTEEN

THE BIGGEST BUSINESS CHALLENGES AND HOW TO OVERCOME THEM

Businesses of all sizes are facing different obstacles in different stages of their growth curve. No matter how well you've planned things out, there will always be unexpected twists and turns that can throw you off course.

According to the SBE Council, 89% of all businesses have fewer than 20 employees. That shows just how many small and medium-sized companies are out there, all fighting to stay afloat, survive, and stabilize.

The truth is, even once you've figured out your business model and achieved a certain level of stability, you'll still face a whole bunch of recurring challenges that can keep you up at night. These challenges can pop up in different areas of your business, from your overall strategy and marketing to hiring and managing your team. But don't lose hope! With the right mindset and smart strategies, you can overcome these hurdles and take your digital business to new heights.

Strategic Challenges

As your digital business grows, you might find that the systems and processes you used to rely on are no longer working as well. You might struggle to streamline your operations, make your workflows more efficient, and ensure your team is working as productively as possible. To solve this, you'll need to invest time and resources into developing strong, scalable systems that can support your business as it grows.

STRATEGIC DEVELOPMENT

✓ Have you established a clear, long-term vision for your company?

✓ Are your competitive strategies based on thorough market analysis?

✓ Do you have mechanisms in place to quickly adapt to market changes?

✓ Is your leadership development program designed to reduce founder dependence?

✓ Do you balance quality control with growth initiatives?

✓ Are you leveraging external consultants to enhance business insights?

1. Lacking Direction or Vision

Without a clear, well-defined vision for your business, it's easy to get lost in the day-to-day grind. You might find yourself chasing after the latest trends or making decisions without a true understanding of your long-term goals. To fix this, take the time to create a compelling vision for your business and communicate it clearly to your team. This will

266

help you stay focused and make strategic choices that align with your overall objectives.

I will link to additional guides on defining mission and vision statements, along with core values for the organization, in the additional resources section of the book's website, mbadisrupted.com.

2. Competing in the Market

In the digital world, the competition can be fierce. You might find yourself going up against larger, more established players or nimble startups that are constantly innovating. To stay ahead of the curve, you'll need to closely monitor your competitors, figure out what their strengths and weaknesses are, and develop a unique value proposition that sets your business apart.

3. Keeping Up with Market Changes

The digital landscape is constantly evolving, and if you're not careful, your business could quickly become obsolete. Stay on top of industry trends, new technologies, and changing customer preferences, and be prepared to adjust your business strategy as needed to stay relevant.

4. Reducing Dependence on the Founders

As your digital business grows, you'll need to start building a strong, capable team able to take on more responsibilities. This can be a tricky transition as you might be used to being the one calling all the shots. To overcome this, focus on developing your team's skills, delegate tasks to them, and empower them to make decisions that align with your overall vision.

5. Balancing Quality and Growth

It's easy to get caught up in the pursuit of rapid growth, but if you're not careful, you might end up compromising the quality of your products or services. Find a way to strike a balance between growth and maintaining high standards. Don't be afraid to slow down or even scale back if it means preserving your reputation and delivering exceptional value to your customers.

6. Leveraging Consultants and Advisors

Running a digital business can be incredibly complex and overwhelming at times. That's why it can be really helpful to work with consultants or business advisors who can provide valuable insights, strategic guidance, and practical advice to help you navigate the challenges you're facing.

Marketing Challenges

In the crowded digital world, it can be tough to create marketing strategies that truly resonate with your target audience. You'll need to do thorough market research, understand your customers' needs and preferences, and develop a multi-channel marketing approach that consistently provides value to your audience.

We have reviewed the core principles in separate chapters of this book, but remember, continuous assessment and experimentation are integration to keeping your business afloat.

MARKETING EFFECTIVENESS

Are your marketing resources allocated based on data-driven insights?

Do you have effective metrics in place to assess marketing initiatives?

Is your brand identity strong and clear across all platforms?

Does your marketing strategy directly support your sales pipeline?

1. Properly Allocating Marketing Resources

With limited budgets and resources, you must use your marketing dollars wisely. Experiment with different marketing channels, track your results and focus your efforts on the strategies that are giving you the best returns on your investment.

2. Measuring Marketing Initiatives

Measuring the effectiveness of your marketing is integral to understanding what's working and what needs to be improved. Use analytics tools and set clear, measurable goals to help you track the performance of your marketing campaigns and make data-driven decisions.

3. Building a Strong Brand

In the digital age, your brand is one of your most valuable assets. Dale Harrison, a veteran marketing leader with diverse background in physics, finance, and engineering, authored a great piece, "Brand Marketing is SEO for Human Brains." It's an insightful read you can find in his LinkedIn articles and I'll reference it in mbadisrupted.com.

Site and app builders, along with prototyping tools and AI bots able to code in real-time, enable founders to launch competitive solutions in a matter of days. This crushes any forms of competitive advantage from a technological standpoint. Develop a strong, consistent brand identity that resonates with your target audience, and use it to stand out from the competition.

4. Relying on Marketing for Pipeline Generation

While marketing is crucial for driving awareness and engagement, you'll also need to have a solid lead generation strategy to turn those leads into paying customers. Try out different tactics, like lead magnets, webinars, and content marketing, to consistently attract high-quality leads to your business. As a digital CEO, you're equally responsible for bringing additional business and integrating all departments effectively to maximize results.

Recruitment Challenges

Human capital is one of the most volatile areas that businesses have to navigate today. While systems, processes, pricing, or funnels can be controlled and defined, building a strong team is incredibly challenging.

TALENT ACQUISITION AND RETENTION

- ☑ Is your hiring process optimized to attract top talent?

- ☑ Are your department structures planned to support growth effectively?

- ☑ Do you have retention strategies that promote career development?

- ☑ Is your workplace environment inclusive and diverse?

- ☑ Are you actively working to nurture a positive company culture?

1. Hiring New Employees

As your digital business grows, you'll need to expand your team. But finding the right talent can be a tough initiative, especially in a competitive job market. Invest time and resources into developing a robust hiring process that helps you identify candidates with the right skills, experience, and cultural fit for your organization.

2. Building New Departments

With more initiatives in the works and an increasing headcount, you may need to create new departments or functions to support your growth. This can be a complex and delicate process, as you'll need to make sure these new teams are properly integrated and aligned with the rest of your organization.

3. Retaining Top Talent

Keeping your best employees engaged and motivated can be an ongoing struggle. Offer competitive compensation, opportunities for growth and development, and a positive, supportive work environment to help you hold onto your top performers.

4. Embracing Diversity

Building a diverse and inclusive workforce can bring a wealth of perspectives, skills, and experiences to your digital business. However, it also requires a concerted effort to create a culture that values and celebrates diversity.

5. Nurturing a Thriving Company Culture

A strong, positive company culture can be a powerful differentiator for your digital business, helping you attract top talent, boost employee engagement, and develop a sense of purpose and belonging. Invest time and resources into cultivating a culture that aligns with your values and supports the growth and development of your team.

Management Challenges

As a business owner or an executive leader, your time is a precious and limited resource. Develop effective workflows for navigating standard tasks, nurture and grow your team, delegate responsibilities, and minimize distractions to stay focused and productive.

MANAGEMENT EXCELLENCE

- ✓ Are you dedicating time to work on strategic business planning?

- ✓ Is there effective communication across all levels of your organization?

- ✓ Do you regularly recognize and motivate your employees?

- ✓ Are your leaders equipped to inspire and guide with a clear vision?

- ✓ Have you established supportive policies for a hybrid work environment?

- ✓ Are you focused on maintaining core business objectives?

1. Working ON the Business

It's easy to get caught up in the day-to-day operations of your digital business, but if you want to drive long-term growth, you'll need to spend time working on the business, not just in it. Set aside dedicated time to focus on strategic planning, innovation, and high-level decision-making.

2. Effective Communication

Clear, effective communication is essential for aligning your team, addressing challenges, and driving progress. Invest in developing your communication skills, and create channels and processes that enable open, transparent dialogue throughout your organization.

274

3. Motivating Employees

Keeping your team engaged, productive, and motivated can be a major challenge, especially in a digital environment where face-to-face interactions may be limited. Develop strategies to recognize and reward your employees, fostering a positive, supportive work culture.

4. Strategic Leadership

As the key leader of your digital business, you'll need to make strategic decisions that shape the direction and success of your organization. Cultivate your strategic thinking skills, stay informed about industry trends and competitive landscapes, and make decisions that align with your long-term vision.

5. Managing Hybrid Work

The shift to hybrid and remote work models has presented new challenges for business leaders. You'll need to find ways to maintain productivity, keep collaboration going, and ensure your team feels connected and engaged, even if they're not physically in the same location.

6. Maintaining Focus

In the digital age, it can be increasingly difficult to maintain focus and avoid distractions. Develop strategies to help your team stay on track, such as implementing focused work periods, minimizing interruptions, and encouraging mindfulness practices.

Sales Challenges

Acquiring new customers is the lifeblood of any digital business, but it can also be one of the most challenging and time-consuming tasks. Develop a comprehensive sales strategy that relies on multiple channels, from marketing-led initiatives like content marketing and educational resources to networking, strategic partnerships, and outbound campaigns for new clients.

To address the evolving challenge of acquiring new customers in a digital business, it's crucial to understand that modern buyers increasingly trust recommendations from peers more than direct advertising from vendors. This shift in behavior demands a refined approach that includes creating high-quality, shareable content, building engaging online communities, encouraging customer advocacy through referral programs, strategically partnering with complementary businesses, personalizing outbound campaigns to foster relationships, and actively participating in networking to cultivate genuine connections.

SALES PERFORMANCE

- ✓ Do you have strategies in place to enhance customer lifetime value?
- ✓ Are you facilitating word-of-mouth through excellent customer experiences?
- ✓ Are you exploring and developing new sales channels?
- ✓ Have your sales teams been trained in effective pricing negotiations?
- ✓ Are you building and maintaining strategic business partnerships?

1. Retaining Customers (Lifetime Value)

Acquiring new customers is important, but keeping them engaged and coming back is just as crucial. Focus on delivering exceptional customer experiences, nurturing strong relationships, and finding ways to increase the lifetime value of your customers.

2. Maximizing Word-of-Mouth

In the digital age, word-of-mouth marketing can be a powerful driver of growth. Encourage your satisfied customers to share their experiences with their networks and find ways to incentivize and amplify their positive recommendations. Work on case studies and share PR stories together for additional reach and exposure.

3. Identifying New Sales Channels

You will need to continuously explore new sales channels and distribution models to reach your target audience. Keep a close eye on emerging trends, technologies, social networks and communities, and be willing to experiment with different approaches to find the ones that work best for your business.

4. Handling Pricing Negotiations

Striking the right balance between profitability and customer satisfaction can be a delicate dance. Develop a clear pricing strategy, be prepared to negotiate, and focus on delivering exceptional value to your customers to justify your pricing.

5. Building Strategic Partnerships & Networking

Forming strategic partnerships and building a strong professional network can be a powerful way to expand your reach, access new markets, and drive growth for your digital business. Invest time and resources into cultivating these valuable relationships.

Technology Challenges

For modern startups in the digital space, technology is both a blessing and a curse. While it can help you and your team work more efficiently, it can also be a source of distraction and frustration. Identify and address the specific productivity challenges your team is facing, and implement tools and processes to help them stay focused and on track.

TECHNOLOGY UTILIZATION

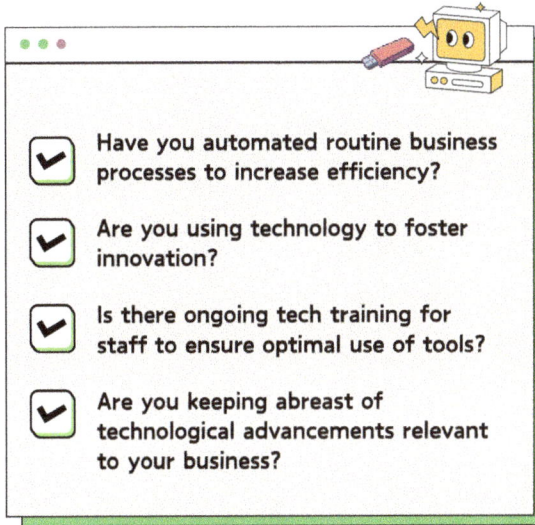

- ✔ Have you automated routine business processes to increase efficiency?
- ✔ Are you using technology to foster innovation?
- ✔ Is there ongoing tech training for staff to ensure optimal use of tools?
- ✔ Are you keeping abreast of technological advancements relevant to your business?

1. Automating Business Processes

Automating repetitive, time-consuming tasks can free up your team to focus on more strategic, high-value work. Explore the various automation tools and technologies available, and implement solutions that can streamline your operations and boost your efficiency. Don't sleep on AI innovations that your competitors now adopt.

2. Deploying Technology for Innovation

To stay competitive in the digital landscape, you'll need to continuously innovate and find new ways to deliver value to your customers. Experiment with emerging technologies, such as AI, machine learning, and blockchain, to identify opportunities for innovation and differentiation.

3. Training Staff at Large

As you implement new technologies and systems, it's important to ensure that your entire team is equipped with the necessary skills and knowledge to use them effectively. Invest in ongoing training and development to help your employees stay up-to-date and adaptable.

4. Keeping Up with Innovations

The digital world is constantly evolving, and if you're not vigilant, you might find your business quickly becoming obsolete. Stay informed about the latest trends, technologies, and innovations in your industry, and be prepared to adapt your strategy and operations accordingly.

Compliance Challenges

Navigating the complex mix of tax regulations and compliance can be a significant challenge for digital businesses. Ensure that you're staying up-to-date with the latest tax laws and regulations, and consider working with a qualified accountant or tax professional to help you manage this aspect of your business.

COMPLIANCE AND REGULATIONS

Are you fully compliant with GDPR, CCPA, and other relevant regulations?

Are your employment practices optimized to reduce overhead while maintaining compliance?

1. GDPR/CCPA

Data privacy and security are of utmost importance in the digital age. Ensure that your business is compliant with the relevant data protection regulations, such as the General Data Protection Regulation (GDPR) and the California Consumer Privacy Act (CCPA), to protect your customers' personal information and avoid costly fines or legal issues.

2. Employment Overhead

As your digital business grows, you'll need to manage the various legal and administrative responsibilities associated with hiring and managing employees. This can include payroll, benefits, and compliance with labor laws and regulations. Stay on top of these requirements to ensure that your business is operating legally and ethically.

While the challenges you face as a digital business owner can seem endless and overwhelming, they're a natural part of the growth and development process. Stay proactive, adaptable, and focused on your long-term goals. Build resilient processes to overcome these obstacles. Form a strong leadership team that helps you out. Surround yourself with other executives and strong partners going through the same journey.

This is the mindset you need to develop to embrace the entrepreneurial life.

In the meantime, you need to plan the growth curve of your venture. This is contingent on working with the right team of rockstars and partnering up with consultants and providers who can help you scale further.

CHAPTER SEVENTEEN

BUILDING YOUR TEAM: OUTSOURCING VS. IN-HOUSE HIRING

The premise of growing a team can be broken down into two core considerations: hiring in-house talent or outsourcing to freelancers, vendors, agencies, contractors.

Picking the right path forward is dependent on multiple factors, including the evolution of the business, availability of talent, core roles and distributing responsibilities internally vs. externally, and how important it is to keep certain positions in-house for strategic and leadership reasons.

When it comes to growing a new startup, competing with well-founded large startups and enterprises is posing unique challenges. You are likely not going to be able to afford to pay as well, provide the same benefits, allow the same level of flexibility, company perks, additional bonuses, and more.

In-House Hiring

These are your full-time employees who work directly for your company. Building an in-house team means you have full-time resources dedicated to your business, compared to outsourcing tasks to external service providers.

For example, instead of hiring an accounting firm to handle your books, you would hire an accountant to work full-time for your company. Or instead of working with a marketing agency, you would hire a marketing manager, a social media specialist, and a graphic designer to be part of your in-house team.

THE IN-HOUSE HIRING PROCESS

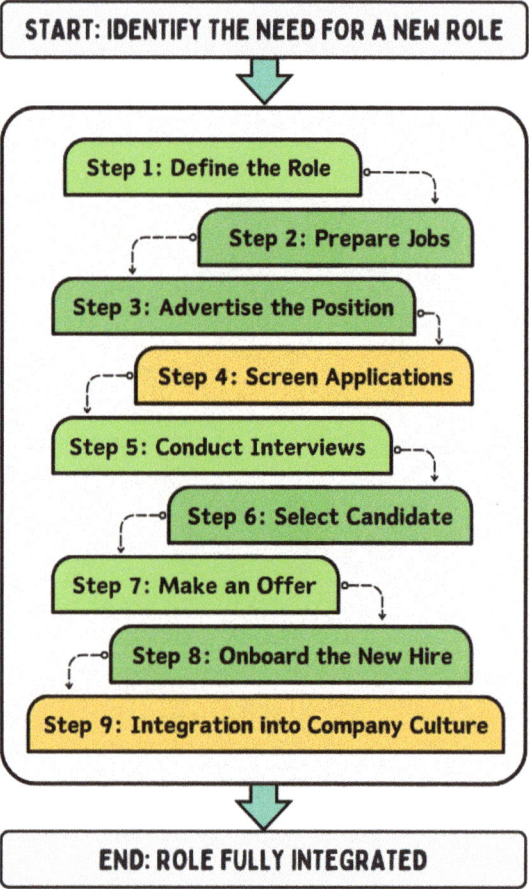

START: IDENTIFY THE NEED FOR A NEW ROLE

Step 1: Define the Role

Step 2: Prepare Jobs

Step 3: Advertise the Position

Step 4: Screen Applications

Step 5: Conduct Interviews

Step 6: Select Candidate

Step 7: Make an Offer

Step 8: Onboard the New Hire

Step 9: Integration into Company Culture

END: ROLE FULLY INTEGRATED

Advantages of In-House Hiring

1. **Specialized Expertise:** You can hire people who have very specific skills and experience that are tailored to your business needs. They can consistently deliver a higher level of expertise than you might get from an outsourced provider working on multiple projects or assigning different team members for different tasks.

2. **Strong Company Culture:** Full-time employees can help build a strong company culture where people feel invested in the success of the business.

3. **Institutional Knowledge:** Your in-house team will develop a deep understanding of your operations, customers, and industry over time, and help document and train future hires later on.

4. **Streamlined Operations:** With an in-house team, you can better coordinate and manage your core business functions for maximum efficiency.

5. **Direct Control:** When you have employees working directly for you, you have more direct control over their work and can oversee their day-to-day activities.

Disadvantages of In-House Hiring

1. **Perceived Risk for Top Talent:** Startups and small businesses may have a harder time attracting top talent, pitching them on the promise of a bright future, and pay similarly to what established corporations offer.

2. **Limited Resources:** As a growing business, you may not have the budget to hire a full executive team managing experts, forcing you to take on multiple leading roles yourself.

3. **High Overhead:** Hiring full-time employees comes with additional costs like payroll, benefits, office space, and

equipment. You also pay a full salary regardless of whether you utilize the resources or keep their workload light.

4. **Lack of Flexibility:** It's slower to scale your team up or down with in-house hiring compared to using outsourced providers.

5. **Risk of the Echo Chamber:** Relying solely on an in-house team may limit your exposure to outside perspectives and innovative ideas.

Hiring in-house talent will require you to think about the organizational chart, job descriptions, accountability, and managing different departments. As your organization grows, you will require people with different skill sets working as individual contributors or people managers with varying levels of experience in similar roles.

Leaving budget considerations aside, filling in certain roles may be harder than expected. For instance, you can't hire a regular developer for a critical project unless you can nurture them, provide a detailed software architecture, do code reviews, and ensure clear deployment protocols. Hiring a CTO directly may sound like a good idea, but most experienced CTOs manage teams of VPs and directors and don't engage in day-to-day development.

The same premise is valid for marketers or sales people. Hiring a CSO or VP of Sales won't result in calling 100 numbers a day. And hiring a sales rep will not work without effective playbooks that an experienced executive can develop and align to the market dynamics and specific considerations in your niche.

During the hiring journey, you will need to mix in different roles: startup executives (different from corporate ones managing hundreds of people), senior experts, juniors, and even interns. Small startups may prefer to teach junior people and grow them into a role as interns, and entry level hires have fewer opportunities to pick from and cost less. This still requires sufficient understanding of every department and the capabilities to train and retain people on the job.

This is one of the reasons why outsourcing is so common even among the largest enterprises out there.

Outsourcing

The act of outsourcing is delegating initiatives, projects, and types of assignments to third-party vendors: agencies, consultants, freelancers, and contractors.

This can be instrumental for new businesses and small companies because it opens up the door to specialized expertise and skills without having to hire full-time employees and take on all the costs and responsibilities that come with that.

A good portion of our portfolio of DevriX clients represent technical or marketing businesses using us as an extension to their teams simply because their engineers and marketers are focused on the core product or service or they lack niche capabilities in scaling WordPress solutions, managing HubSpot workflows, SEO, and other lines of work in our go-to-market services or experimentation suites.

When it comes to outsourcing, a general rule of thumb is to outsource business requirements that are not integral to the core of your business. The majority of the companies outsource legal services, accounting, cleaning staff for their offices, and other segments they don't want to hire full-time for. When it comes to technology or marketing, this could work both in-house, fully outsourced, or as a hybrid model.

Professional technology, creative, marketing vendors employ complete teams, including account and project managers, different types of engineers, different marketing roles, quality assurance experts, and other specialists that make a project possible. Digital CEOs and startup founders have to think twice before hiring in-house. Is it worth building a full-time team of people to manage a web project or run campaigns across multiple paid channels?

OUTSOURCING LIFECYCLE TIMELINE

01 NEEDS ASSESSMENT
Identify business needs and tasks suitable for outsourcing.

02 VENDOR SELECTION
Research and evaluate potential vendors based on expertise and reputation.

03 CONTRACTING
Negotiate and finalize terms, including scope of work and pricing.

04 ONBOARDING
Set up communication protocols and training for the outsourcing team.

05 MANAGEMENT
Monitor progress through regular meetings and KPIs.

06 EVALUATION
Assess vendor performance and provide feedback.

07 DECISION MAKING
Decide on contract renewal, expansion, or vendor transition.

08 OPTIMIZATION
Continually refine and improve outsourcing strategies.

Advantages of Outsourcing

1. **Access to Specialized Expertise:** You can work with highly skilled experts in specific domains, making sure that important areas of your business are managed by professionals.

2. **Flexibility:** As your business goes through ups and downs, you can easily scale the outsourced services without going through the full recruitment process or resorting to layoffs.

3. **Cost Savings:** On a purely hourly base, outsourcing talent costs more, but it can be more cost-effective than hiring full-time staff as you only pay for the services you need when you need them, leverage a full team of experts, don't pay recruiters, cover sick leaves or paid vacations, look for backups or hire additional people for ad-hoc tasks.

4. **Global Talent Pool:** By working with service providers around the world, you can access a much wider range of talent and expertise than you might find locally (especially valid for on-site businesses).

5. **Focus on Core Competencies:** Outsourcing allows you to focus your time and energy on the core aspects of your business that you're most skilled and passionate about and hire for very niche roles that don't make sense hiring a full-time employee to perform.

Disadvantages of Outsourcing

1. **Less Control:** When you outsource, you have less direct control over the work being done so you need to find trusted service providers and establish clear communication protocols.

2. **Security and Confidentiality Risks:** You'll be sharing sensitive information with outside parties so you need the right non-disclosure agreements in place.

3. **Onboarding and Management:** It takes time and effort to find the right outsourcing partners, onboard them, and manage the ongoing relationship.

4. **Cultural and Communication Challenges:** Language barriers and cultural differences can make effective collaboration more difficult, especially with overseas providers.
5. **Over-Reliance Risks:** Depending too heavily on outsourcing can make your business vulnerable if an outsourced provider experiences issues or fails to deliver.

Most obstacles faced with outsourcing can be overcome by working with trusted vendors with great reviews or recommendations, keeping several providers in place for scaling or backup, and building hybrid engagements combining in-house staff with external providers.

The outsourcing landscape is broad and includes agencies, contractors, consultants, advisors, freelancers. You may find yourself working with a strategic business advisor for external audits and directing your business based on best practices, turning to a freelance UX expert to polish the user experience of your product, or engaging with the leading TikTok marketing agency for the latest and most efficient strategies in the space, considering a portfolio of hundreds of other clients running campaigns and the value of their data.

Over the last 25 years, I've worked with and analyzed thousands of organizations in all industries, some reluctant to outsource and others keeping a small, lean in-house team and offloading everything else to third-parties. Both approaches are equally viable and work in different situations. The optimal approach will depend on your specific industry, your company's growth stage, your available resources, and your strategic priorities.

CHAPTER EIGHTEEN

IMPLEMENTING BULLETPROOF PROCESSES

The further your company scales and the more your headcount grows, the harder it gets to maintain the same quality of work across different departments.

Communication often falters when more and more people are added to your project management system or team collaboration messenger app. While certain conversations happen on 1:1s or during small meetings, not every detail is translated to the rest of the organization.

The power of processes refers to the ability to standardize and optimize the way your business runs, from the smallest daily tasks to the most complex workflows. Processes provide the framework for your team to work together in a non-chaotic environment, reduce mistakes, and continuously increase velocity.

The Benefits of Process Integration

Let's say you run a digital marketing agency. Without well-defined processes, your team might struggle to deliver high-quality work consistently to your clients. Each team member might follow a different, standalone process of doing competitor research, creating content, or managing campaigns. This inconsistency can lead to confusion, delays, and unhappy clients.

Professional teams develop, grow, and maintain a library of SOPs (standard operating procedures) documenting the common steps everyone has to follow whenever a specific type of activity is to be performed.

Here are the key reasons you want to start integrating processes as early as possible:

1. **Increased Efficiency:** Standardized processes help your team work more efficiently, reducing the time and effort required to complete tasks. This frees up valuable resources that can be reinvested into growth-oriented activities.

2. **Improved Consistency:** Consistent processes ensure that your products, services, and customer experiences maintain a high level of quality, no matter who is handling the work.

3. **Reduced Errors:** Well-defined processes minimize the chances of mistakes and oversights as your team follows a structured approach to their work.

4. **Enhanced Scalability:** As your business grows, scalable processes allow you to replicate your success and expand your operations without sacrificing quality or consistency.

5. **Easier Training and Onboarding:** Documented processes make it easier to train new team members and onboard them quickly, as they can follow established guidelines and best practices.

6. **Continuous Improvement:** By regularly reviewing and updating your processes, you can identify areas for improvement and implement changes that drive better results over time.

7. **Increased Profitability:** The efficiencies, consistency, and scalability achieved through the power of processes can directly

contribute to your bottom line as you reduce costs, increase productivity, and deliver more value to your customers.

Strategies for Streamlining Your Operations

As a digital business owner, there are several effective strategies you can employ to streamline your operations:

1. **Process Mapping:** Thoroughly document your key business processes, identifying the specific steps, stakeholders involved, and any potential inefficiencies or edge cases that may occur. Use specialized business process management software like Process Street or our own SaaSBPM to map core processes across the organization, including simple tasks like daily check-ins, filling timesheets, submitting expense reports, and requesting PTO.

2. **Automation:** Implement technology to automate repetitive, time-consuming tasks, such as data entry, scheduling, or customer communication. This frees up your team's time and reduces the risk of human error. The next chapter will cover common activities for digital CEOs and tools that automated recurring tasks in each category.

3. **Outsourcing:** Consider outsourcing non-core business functions like accounting, IT maintenance, or social media management to specialized service providers who can handle these tasks more efficiently than your in-house team.

4. **Continuous Improvement:** Regularly review your available SOPs, keep track of bug reports, mistakes, escalations; gather feedback from your team and customers, and make iterative

improvements to your processes over time. This ensures that your operations continue to evolve and become more efficient.

5. **Teamwork:** Involve your team in the optimization process, including staff members dealing with recurring issues on a day-to-day basis often have specific tips and ideas for improving workflows and sorting out mundane problems.

Systematizing Recurring Tasks

You know you need new processes when you are bogged down by repetitive tasks.

Sit down and revise your backlog, timesheets, team reports, and any ongoing initiatives that keep looping over the same tasks over and over again.

Recurring and repetitive tasks take a significant amount of time and are likely delivered with inconsistent quality. More people go through a similar type of task with different levels of experience and understanding of an assignment, therefore producing varying levels of results.

At scale, this pet peeve adds up with more recurring tasks in different parts of the workflow. This results in a house of cards, and it may take months to go back to the drawing board and get the processes right.

You may run an e-commerce business delivering physical products, and you need a streamlined workflow for processing customer orders. This could involve automating order confirmation emails, creating packing slips, and generating shipping labels. Systematizing these tasks ensures every order is fulfilled accurately and promptly, without your team having to manage each step manually.

E-commerce companies are a great example here because production lines and manufacturing can go wrong fast. Minor errors can lead to halting operations for hours, wasting hundreds of thousands of dollars when producing automotive equipment or other expensive hardware. Strict procedures and tight workflows are absolutely mandatory to even keep operations running. For context, Amazon employs over 1.5 million staff members. Imagine the level of chaos between manufacturing, delivery, logistics, sales and support without the continuous effort of building rock solid processes.

E-COMMERCE ORDER PROCESSING: MANUAL VS. AUTOMATED

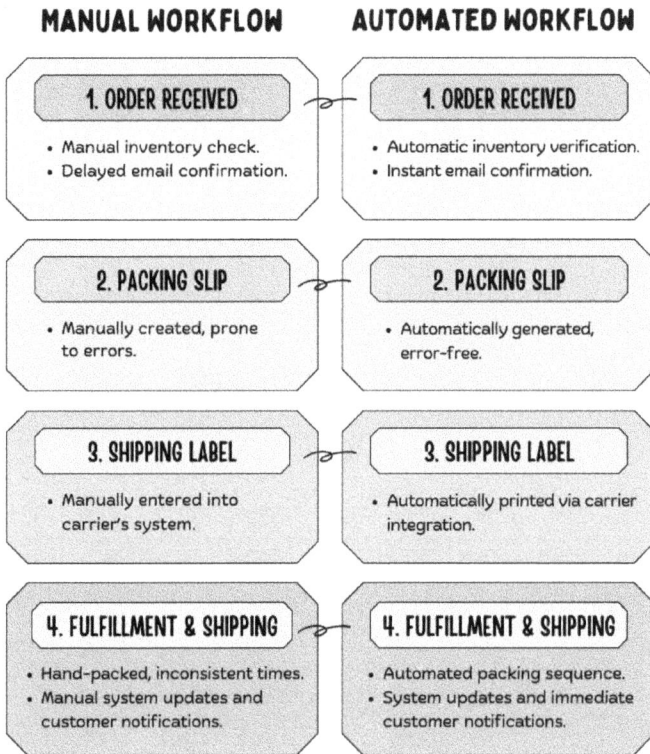

MANUAL WORKFLOW

1. ORDER RECEIVED
- Manual inventory check.
- Delayed email confirmation.

2. PACKING SLIP
- Manually created, prone to errors.

3. SHIPPING LABEL
- Manually entered into carrier's system.

4. FULFILLMENT & SHIPPING
- Hand-packed, inconsistent times.
- Manual system updates and customer notifications.

AUTOMATED WORKFLOW

1. ORDER RECEIVED
- Automatic inventory verification.
- Instant email confirmation.

2. PACKING SLIP
- Automatically generated, error-free.

3. SHIPPING LABEL
- Automatically printed via carrier integration.

4. FULFILLMENT & SHIPPING
- Automated packing sequence.
- System updates and immediate customer notifications.

Here are some ways you can effectively systematize your recurring tasks as a digital CEO:

1. **Map Out Your Key Recurring Tasks:** The first step is to identify the essential activities that you and your team perform regularly. Sit down with your leadership group or team managers and create a comprehensive list of all the repetitive tasks involved in your day-to-day operations.

2. **Create Standard Operating Procedures (SOPs):** Once you've identified your recurring tasks, the next step is to document step-by-step instructions for completing each one. SOPs can start as a simple Google Drive or a shared Dropbox folder with separate doc files that outline the specific steps, tools, and resources required to execute a task effectively.

3. **Automate Where Possible:** In the digital age, there's a good chance you can automate many of your recurring tasks using various tools and software. In software development, continuous integration and delivery tools include linters/hinters, unit and functional testing tools, and regression testing scripts. In copywriting, you can use Grammarly or proofreading APIs to minimize typos. Outline and topic cluster generation can be facilitated with tools like Semrush or Ubersuggest.

4. **Delegate and Train Your Team:** As your digital business grows, delegation will be the only way you can continue to provide quality and maintain a strategic leadership role. Assign ownership of specific initiatives and groups of tasks to individual team members and provide thorough training on established processes. In addition to distributing the workload, this also promotes accountability and consistency across your organization.

5. **Review and Refine:** Systematizing your recurring tasks is an ongoing process, not a one-time event. Regular iterations will improve efficiency and effectiveness over time. Seek feedback from your team, analyze performance metrics, and identify areas for improvement. Keep track of the holistic performance view of the organization, including net promoter score from your customers, internal employee satisfaction with feedback reviews, and churn rates.

Keeping your SOPs open across the organization can deliver a self-policing environment with moderators and team members maintaining that knowledge base internally. At DevriX, we manage our own wiki portal (like an internal Wikipedia), and team members can document and add their own processes whenever a new workflow comes up or when we integrate new tools internally.

Optimizing Efficiency With BPM Tools

In 2011, I managed a small tech startup with four employees alongside our agency (five other team members at the time). Both businesses were managed in three-team Skype groups. We worked completely asynchronously and didn't use project management systems while managing a handful of emails from clients and vendors every now and then.

While I was coming from agencies working with enterprises, utilizing professional product and project management systems and ERPs, we were nimble enough and could get along just fine.

But processes started to break soon after. Institutional knowledge was getting lost in the process, with some solved problems popping back up months later. Searching through a single channel is not the most effective way to conduct business. We were bogged by simplistic issues, and, while we wanted to avoid the overhead of introducing more software and more steps to get a problem done, it was inevitable.

We started with Asana for project management and broke down the different initiatives in separate projects. Then, we organized our Google Workspace (then G-Suite) better, with folder structure that made more sense. I documented all servers, IP addresses, tools, resources, links to licenses, and API keys. We also included separate folders and projects for marketing collateral, brand assets, designs, and fonts. Every new department was adding to this structure because it was expandable.

This worked well for project and general organization management - but one area this fell short in was the actual process management.

We had a repository of assets and licenses, and all upcoming tasks were made available in the project management system.

What about repetitive and recurring processes? They were getting lost, with multiple steps going through different people, approval requests for sick leaves, submitting expense reports, and plenty of other areas that weren't getting completed after all.

The next evolutionary layer was Business Process Management (BPM).

BPM is an enterprise concept around organizational efficiency. It is responsible for the management of internal workflows and optimization of operational processes. BPM solutions handle routine tasks better than project management apps and enable businesses to keep growing further, introduce more processes, and still maintain the same source of truth.

Policy, Process, and Procedure

POLICY VS PROCESS VS PROCEDURE

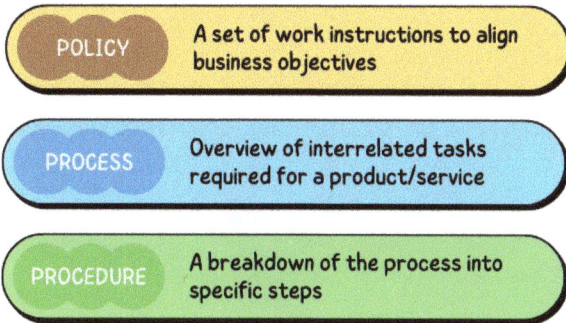

POLICY	A set of work instructions to align business objectives
PROCESS	Overview of interrelated tasks required for a product/service
PROCEDURE	A breakdown of the process into specific steps

While introducing more layers to streamline internal operations, you should be able to differentiate between policies, processes, and procedures. Here's a closer look at each one:

1. **Policies**: The high-level guiding principles around the strategic direction and general vision of the company. They set the framework within which decisions are made, ensuring consistency and compliance across the organization. Once policies are set in motion, processes build on top of them.

2. **Processes**: The sequences of activities required to accomplish specific organizational goals. Processes follow a series of steps to get from point A to point B in order to accomplish the end goal.

3. **Procedures**: Detailed, step-by-step instructions that describe exactly how every step of a process should be executed. They

ensure that tasks are performed consistently and correctly across all levels and roles in the org chart.

High-level policies may include a code of conduct, recruitment policy, email communication policy, and health and safety policy. Each of them will include a list of processes that correspond to specific needs: in the case of recruitment, specific processes may include:

- CV reviews: what to look for in specific roles, red flags, green flags
- Selection process and time frame - with all parties involved
- Expected amount of shortlisted candidates per role
- Reference check process
- Interview appointments and scheduling
- Extending a job offer
- Setting up accounts and onboarding.

Each of these processes will require a number of steps going through different people in the organization and externally. For non-apparent steps, a procedure will exist to define the specific task, additional resources, examples, links to systems in use, template emails, or anything else that would simplify the process and reduce the margin of error.

You can't manage all of that in a project management system or an endless hierarchy of doc files. With multiple parties involved, team members should interact with each other, compile resources, follow deadlines, receive notifications, and flag management for delays or blockers. Organizations not deploying a BPM would end up with team members questioning how or where to accomplish specific actions, such as asking for PTO or scheduling a 1:1 with a director in their organization. Should they browse your email archive or onboarding docs for instructions? Is this available in the project management system or the marketing automation tool?

BPMs are designed explicitly for cases like these, and the number of cases is growing every week as your business grows.

The Role of BPM Tools in Enhancing Processes

Following the previous example, BPM tools work in the following three areas:

- **Automation**: BPM software solutions automate repetitive tasks, reduce the back-and-forth between employees, HR, and managers, and minimize human error. Automation ensures that processes such as invoicing, customer onboarding, and report generation are documented and followed with triggers, reminders, automated deadlines, and predefined forms to fill out.
- **Visibility and Control**: With BPM tools, managers gain comprehensive insights into business operations. Your leadership team can monitor workflow progress and identify bottlenecks in real-time. This level of visibility supports better control over processes and helps in making informed decisions. Delayed processes or people juggling with multiple assigned tasks simultaneously may unblock the process from top to bottom thanks to transparency and real-time data.
- **Standardization**: By standardizing processes across departments, BPM tools ensure that every task is executed in

a uniform manner, improving the work quality and consistency, reducing friction for your team, and increasing productivity.

Integrating BPM Software into Existing Business Frameworks

BPM SOFTWARE CAN REDUCE COSTS:

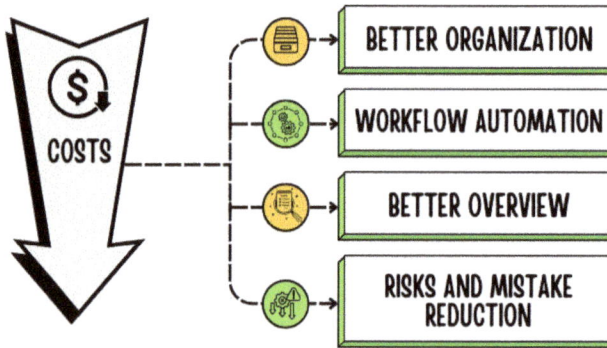

COSTS

BETTER ORGANIZATION

WORKFLOW AUTOMATION

BETTER OVERVIEW

RISKS AND MISTAKE REDUCTION

Throughout my journey as a serial founder and a business advisor, I've been involved with dozens of teams using different BPM solutions in production. Many of them were tailored to the enterprise. Large organizations cannot survive without a resilient solution in place (plus, it's a better investment for solution providers selling to high-ticket accounts).

We ended up building our own system, SaaSBPM, with my DevriX product and engineering team. It is suitable for service businesses, agencies, consultancies, lifestyle startups, HR teams, entrepreneurs in repetitive content, publishing, dropshipping, and affiliate businesses doing the same type of work over and over again.

Surprisingly, we also found great clients in our network from traditional businesses. The first two were a bar owner tracking down recurring bartender and waitress tasks and a car rental company and their sales and maintenance teams. Both businesses were in dire need of following daily, weekly, and monthly checklists for their teams, with safety checks from a secondary member, and alerts to supervisors if a step was missed.

This was the core premise that we built our system on as well.

- A list of roles based on job descriptions (engineer, marketing manager, designer) + additional set of duties (night shift, on call)
- A list of members (all employees/contractors)
- A list of processes and procedures assigned to a role or an individual
- Regularity of when a process kicks in - daily, weekly, monthly
- A set of visual views for the organization, like an org chart with all roles or team members, each with a mind map or a table of assigned roles
- Daily tasks as a checklist to tick off when a task is completed
- Management reporting system for delayed tasks and overtime.

This worked really well for our agency as job descriptions were transparent for both parties. New role requirements or expectations are integrated on the fly and visible to all team members. Escalations or reports can be filed right within the system.

One of my teams in Growth Shuttle is remote and follows a specific set of tasks every single week. As the business evolves, we drop some recurring activities and add new ones. The BPM system acts like a group mechanism to manage workload and set expectations for both parties.

Additionally, because processes are recurring, it is easy to estimate and ballpark how long each one takes. This is extremely effective for hiring and onboarding new people, assigning processes with clear time frames, and ensuring that your staff is properly utilized and not overburdened at the same time.

No matter if you start with a simple set of SOPs in a drive folder, sign up for a trial of SaaSBPM, or look up existing alternatives like Process Street or Kissflow, this book aims to provide a holistic overview of how an organization scales and obstacles that founders and executives hit on the go. You may feel comfortable with the current workload or your abilities to handle recurring tasks and manage the process yourself at the time.

Optimizing for efficiency is a never-ending process. A truly effective organization can run 3X - 5X better with limited overhead and back and forth, opening up the doors to founding other companies in parallel and instilling effective processes from the get go.

The sky is the limit.

PART IV

MASTERING THE LONG
GAME

CHAPTER NINETEEN

AUTOMATION & TECHNOLOGY

Effective organizations run fast. They employ efficient teams following well-refined processes, executing quickly on assignments and ticking boxes all the time.

This high velocity will be a constant push to deliver more results in a shorter period of time. While adding more people to fuel the system is important, there are different areas that could be optimized, automated, and structured better with established digital solutions solving these problems for millions of other businesses.

Every single day, traditional companies get disrupted by tech startups implementing a series of systems and amplifying lead generations or delivering operational results at the fraction of the time for competitive prices. Smart entrepreneurs are always on the lookout to automate tedious processes, speed up delivery times, and maximize the output delivered by the organization.

Automation and technology in digital startups strategically integrate digital tools to automate repetitive tasks, streamline workflows, and boost productivity, allowing businesses to work smarter by cutting down time-consuming manual processes. These technologies not only save time by automating mundane activities like data entry and invoicing but also enhance operational efficiency through consistent and accurate process execution, which reduces human error and increases scalability without proportional workforce increases.

Core Marketing & Operations Areas to Automate

Now that we've gone over the advantages of automation and technology for sales and marketing, let's consider solutions which we can implement to achieve these results:

1. **Automate Lead Generation:** Utilize tools like landing page builders, lead capture forms, quiz generators, and targeted advertising to automatically attract and capture new leads for your business. The end goal is to create a high-converting landing page that instantly collects contact information from interested prospects, without requiring any manual intervention on your part.

2. **Implement Marketing Automation:** Platforms like HubSpot allow you to automate your email marketing, lead nurturing, and customer engagement processes, ensuring that your leads are nurtured effectively and your customers receive timely, relevant updates. This encompasses not just the setup of automated email sequences designed to progress leads through the sales funnel, but also the orchestration of full customer journey mapping. These journeys can trigger personalized content and responses based on a customer's specific interactions with your brand, offering a cohesive and customized experience from initial contact to post-sale follow-up.

3. **Optimize Your Website:** Use tools like Google Analytics, VWO, NitroPack to continuously analyze and improve your website's user experience, content, site speed, and conversion rates. This additional layer helps you test different call-to-action buttons or headline variations, and then automatically implement the version that performs the best for higher conversion rates.

4. **Implement Sales Automation:** CRM systems, sales pipeline management tools, and automated outreach systems like Apollo can help your sales team work more efficiently and effectively or automatically engage with prospects 24/7. Live chatbots can handle simple queries and qualify site visitors on the fly before your customer support or sales team get involved.

   There are other factors one needs to address as well, such as maintaining cleanliness of your email lists and managing more complex pipelines. There are tools that tackle these issues, such as Neverbounce, which ensures that automated email campaigns reach their intended recipients by verifying emails in real-time.

   Furthermore, tools like Smartlead and Keyplay manage advanced pipelines by automating lead nurturing and helping to streamline the decision-making processes.

5. **Utilize Data Analytics:** Invest in robust data analytics tools and data warehouses that can help you track, measure, and interpret the performance of your sales and marketing efforts, allowing you to make data-driven decisions and continually improve your strategies. Business intelligence tools and personalized dashboards provide segmented reports that pinpoint which marketing campaigns are driving the most revenue so you can double down on the tactics that are working best.

6. **Integrate Your Tech Stack:** Ensure that your various sales and marketing tools are seamlessly integrated, allowing for the smooth flow of data and the elimination of manual data entry or syncing. This could involve connecting your CRM system with your email marketing platform, or your e-commerce platform with your inventory management software, to create a truly streamlined and efficient sales and marketing ecosystem.

The opportunities are endless, and every type of business has a powerful suite of tools specializing in the target market, industry, platform, or delivery segment for maximum results.

Your Automation Toolset Checklist

What works for a B2B service startup may not resonate with a dropshipping store or a real estate newsletter, but there are common types of tasks that are broadly used by the majority of the digital businesses. I will review the most common categories that utilize additional tools or automation solutions. Pick the ones that your business can benefit from and integrate them in your current stack.

1. Email Automation

Tools like Mailchimp, Beehiiv, and HubSpot allow you to automate your email communications, from sending personalized welcome messages to your new subscribers, to setting up automated email campaigns that nurture your leads and stay in touch with your customers. This can save you countless hours spent manually crafting and sending emails.

2. Social Media Scheduling

Apps like Hootsuite, Buffer, and niche tools for different networks like Taplio or Tweet Hunter enable you to plan, schedule, and manage your social media posts across multiple platforms, ensuring a consistent online presence without the need for constant manual updates. I maintain a rigorous content calendar with two weeks ahead that my team has access to for edits on the go.

3. Invoicing and Billing

Platforms like FreshBooks, Quickbooks, and Stripe streamline your invoicing, billing, and payment collection processes, making it easier to get paid and maintain accurate financial records. These tools can automatically generate and send invoices, track payments, and even send late payment reminders so you don't have to spend time on mundane administrative tasks.

4. Project Management

Tools like Asana, Trello, and Basecamp help you organize your team's tasks, deadlines, and workflows, ensuring everyone is on the same page and projects are completed efficiently. With features like task assignment, progress tracking, and real-time collaboration, these solutions will improve your team's productivity. Smaller teams may settle with Notion or even Todoist and enterprise communities often prefer Jira.

5. Customer Relationship Management (CRM)

CRM solutions allow you to centralize and automate your customer data management, lead nurturing, and sales pipeline, enabling your team to efficiently track and follow up with leads, send personalized content based on their interests, and access a comprehensive

360-degree view of your customer interactions. Here are some tailored options for different business needs:

- **HubSpot:** Ideal for businesses of all sizes, HubSpot offers a user-friendly interface with robust marketing automation, sales, and service software that helps grow your business without the complexity of traditional CRM systems.

- **Pipedrive:** Specifically designed with small businesses and entrepreneurs in mind, Pipedrive provides a straightforward and visual approach to managing your sales pipeline. It focuses on usability and simplicity, ensuring that even startups can maximize their CRM efforts without a steep learning curve.

- **Zoho CRM:** A versatile CRM that caters to businesses ranging from small to large enterprises, offering a wide range of customization and integration options to fit various business models.

- **Salesforce:** As a category leader, Salesforce offers extensive functionalities and customization options that can cater to complex business needs. However, it's important to note that its robust feature set and scalability might present a steeper learning curve for startups and small businesses, which could find the platform less user-friendly compared to other CRMs designed specifically for smaller operations.

6. Appointment Scheduling

Apps like Calendly, Acuity Scheduling, and Appointy make it easy for your customers to book appointments with you, reducing the back-and-forth of manual scheduling. Furthermore, they can integrate with your calendar, automatically block off your availability, and even send reminders to reduce no-shows. Larger CRMs often include appointment scheduling widgets and pages in their suites.

7. Bookkeeping and Accounting

Tools like Xero, doola, QuickBooks, and FreshBooks automate your bookkeeping and accounting tasks, ensuring accurate financial records and streamlining tax preparation. These solutions can automatically categorize your expenses, generate financial reports, and even handle payroll and invoicing.

8. Content Creation

Platforms like Canva, Grammarly, and Jasper AI can assist with automating various aspects of your content creation process, from designing visually appealing graphics and images to proofreading and editing your written content to even generating first drafts of articles or social media posts. This can save you countless hours spent on these time-consuming tasks. Most modern GPT bots, like ChatGPT, Gemini, and Claude, can supplement with research, outline generation, compiling statistics, proofreading content, and even generating images.

9. Lead Generation

OnePage, Instapage, Leadpages, Unbounce, OptinMonster, Hello Bar are some of the popular SaaS solutions that can help you create high-converting landing pages and lead capture forms, automating the process of generating and nurturing new leads. These tools can also integrate with your email automation and CRM systems to ensure a seamless lead management process.

10. Inventory Management

Tools like Cin7, Sumtracker, and TradeGecko enable you to automate your inventory tracking, order fulfillment, and supply chain management, ensuring you always have the right products in stock. You can leverage the core features of e-commerce platforms like Shopify and E-commerce if you end up building on the leading platforms in the space.

11. Customer Support

Chatbots, knowledge bases, and help desk solutions like Zendesk, Intercom, and HelpScout can automate your customer support, providing instant responses and streamlining your team's workflow. Aside from live chat features, they can handle common inquiries, route more complex issues to the right team members, and even provide self-service resources to your customers.

12. Task Automation

Apps like Zapier, Make, and Automate.io help you create custom integrations and workflows that automate a wide range of tasks, from data entry to document generation. Being able to automatically transfer new leads from your website to your CRM or generate invoices whenever a new order is placed in your e-commerce platform can save a significant amount of time.

13. HR and Onboarding

Tools like Deel, BambooHR, Gusto, and Zenefits can automate your HR processes, from employee onboarding to payroll and benefits management. These solutions can handle tasks like generating offer letters, setting up new hires in your systems, and even automating the distribution of employee handbooks and policy updates.

14. Document Management

Google Drive, Dropbox, and Box are some of the solutions that enable you to manage and automate document storage, sharing, and collaboration, ensuring your team has access to the information they need when they need it. These tools streamline processes like document approval workflows and version control.

15. Marketing Automation

Platforms like HubSpot, Marketo, and Pardot allow you to automate various aspects of your marketing efforts, from lead nurturing to email campaigns and analytics. The process includes automated emails that guide your leads through the sales funnel, lead scoring, form generation and placements, interactive journeys, and more.

16. Expense Tracking

Apps like Expensify, Concur, and Rydoo can automate your expense tracking and reimbursement processes, making it easier to manage your business finances and ensure compliance with company policies.

18. Form Automation

Solutions like Typeform, JotForm, and Formstack allow you to create and automate custom forms for your business, whether it's client onboarding, job applications, or customer feedback surveys. When using WordPress, you can settle with Contact Form 7 or the powerful Gravity Forms plugin with native integrations.

19. Contract and Agreement Management

Tools like DocuSign, PandaDoc, and HelloSign can automate the creation, signing, and storage of your business contracts and agreements, helping you keep track of all legal documents and even sign on the go.

20. Productivity Tracking

Apps like RescueTime, Toggl, and Time Doctor can help you track and optimize your team's productivity, identifying time-wasting activities and providing insights to improve efficiency.

There are thousands of tried-and-tested tools solving repetitive problems in each segment your business operates in. Follow the principles in chapter 18 for process evaluation and development and supplement it with additional tooling whenever possible. Tap into your internal networks or social media channels for warm referrals and recommendations, follow industry blogs and thought leaders for new additions to the list, and cross-check with Reddit, TrustPilot, and other comparison services for additional insights before onboarding in-house.

CHAPTER TWENTY

PRINCIPLES OF SUSTAINABLE GROWTH

If you followed everything to this point, finding a niche and designing a strong value proposition with a compelling offer, combined with great execution and tenacity to grow and expand, you should cross the $1M target and keep cruising from there.

I have gone through this journey with three different companies launched from zero, and the playbook is not as different whenever the formula is right: available niche, a painful problem to solve, large **TAM**, a streamlined solution, strong core team, clear go-to-market, repetition, great results, and expanding portfolio.

It took me three years on average across all companies to reach this target. Each of these milestones happened in parallel with another business growing at the time - split focus and attention while diversifying into other areas.

In all fairness, revenue doesn't mean a lot. You can sell $150K in SaaS ARR and make $135K back with automated systems and processes. Or generate $2M in affiliate or product sales and end up netting $30K at the end. I've worked with eight-figure businesses making $12M, $18M, or $23M in revenue and running in the red due to tough market dynamics, overhiring BDRs, or not tracking their COGS accurately by tapping into credit lines with high-interest rates and slow paybacks.

No matter what your number or definition for success is, most businesses end at a tipping point where the constant grind can finally end and transition to a more sustainable journey. The feast and famine turn into recurring revenue. Paid e-commerce ads for every sale turn into a portfolio of returning visitors. Publishing sites that are getting no organic traffic finally rank for SEO or grow on social media.

Processes are in place, you've hired great people or partnered up with strong agencies, and leads are coming. Business won't disappear overnight if you're not at the forefront every minute of the day.

Just like high-growth founders with successful exits find themselves in a weird situation of not knowing what to do with their lives now that it's over, sustainable business owners may end up repeating what works forever, missing the point of growing a business and managing life at the same time.

No matter if you look into a sale, launching a separate business, navigating other growth curves, or simply slowing down and taking a breath, here are 10 core principles that will help you streamline the journey and add more predictability and joy in the next phase.

1. Avoid Burnouts

Your physical and mental health are your most valuable asset. Nothing truly matters if you sacrifice your health to the extent of a complete wipeout.

While digital CEOs are more prone to keeping their physical health intact (for the most part, at least compared to construction workers or police officers), mental health takes a serious toll. This overwhelming demand to perform 24/7 did not exist prior to the Internet era. In medieval times, outside of day chores or the act of war, work was conducted during the day, with nothing much happening past the sunset.

The digital realm is consuming and demanding. You can always make more prospect calls around the globe: there's someone up and working every minute of the hour.

- Some countries, such as Israel and Saudi Arabia, officially work on Sundays.
- Social media doesn't rest.
- Email blasts never stop.
- Your content library needs to fuel the scheduled calendar to maintain cadence.
- Product selection, quality checks, taking photos, and optimizing product descriptions don't follow working hours.
- Reviewing screencasts of users browsing your site for UX issues or opportunities to increase conversions can happen at all times.

Sales, hiring, marketing, operations, quality assurance, and many areas of leadership can operate regardless of working hours. The pressure on a leader to perform at all times places a mental block on waking hours when work doesn't get done.

While going through continuous stages of hard work, late nights, long weekends is more common than not in the first months, don't let your brain shut down and remain dysfunctional for several months. Make the most out of budget and pipeline planning, find some help early on to backfill, keep your expenses low, and force yourself to get some good sleep and take some breaks.

2. Keep Innovating

The other evolutionary problem of the digital realm is the endless innovation going on around the world: new paradigms, new tools, new systems, new management frameworks, social media algorithms evolving, SEO updates kicking in, competitors launching better or cheaper products and services, supply going down.

The list is endless.

Even if you crack the code and find a successful combination, remember your competition is working hard to acquire a piece of your market, too.

Allocate strategic time every week or at least monthly to review the current state of the business and areas of improvement. Take notes of SOPs that could get better and possible integration of tools and services that save time and deliver better results. Look into new ways to package your solution, additional channels to conquer, or other markets that can benefit from your core offer.

3. Build The Leadership Team

A business that can't work without you is not a business; it's a job. This is a common fallacy for full-time freelancers who end up being "their own boss" and feeling in control for a few months until it's time for a week off and the revenue stops.

Founding CEOs are often in the same spot at first: every tough decision bubbles up to them. Any blockers from the team get elevated to the top. Angry customers find your number or reach out directly whenever a ticket gets delayed.

In a growing organization, you need a leadership team that picks up the pace, divides, and conquers its own department. Initially, this could be your very first hire who knows the process better than anyone else (except for you). Or they get promoted to team managers and get the autonomy to run their own departments as long as certain KPIs are in place.

You may decide to bring external leadership in specific seats. If you "winged" some areas like marketing and sales with your scrappy processes, you may find yourself hiring an experienced VP who gets in and introduces better playbooks and processes for your teams to follow.

But the end goal is distributing core decisions to certain individuals and extracting yourself from the day to day one department at a time.

Consider hiring a general manager, an operations manager, or a COO to take care of the day-to-day work with vendors, the team, accounting, legal, or partners. This is a common step to moving from an operational COO to a founder, board member, or another form of owner with limited operational responsibilities.

4. Grow the Brand

I am very bullish on branding and I firmly believe this is one of the best moats to develop for your business. Popular brands get special attention from virtually everywhere:

- Your existing clients feel prouder to work with you and know they made "the right choice" in the category
- Prospects trust reviews and recommendations from other people recommending the company

- Your team churns less often, refers new hires, and new people are more inclined to join vs. other companies in the market
- Mass media is more gracious with extra reviews, plugs, namedrops, press releases for your business.

Customer and employee satisfaction is higher, churn is lower, small mistakes aren't as painful, and you get more leeway as you scale the business forward. It takes less effort over time to grow the business, it's cheaper to find, close, and onboard new customers, contract sizes are often larger: it's hard to say no to branding.

Our martech agency DevriX has been working with Fortune 1000 companies, global banks and telecoms, leading consumer brands, and many B2B SaaS serving tens of millions of customers. Brand building through design, UX, SEO, funnel development, and product excellence has been an integral part of our professional collaboration with some of the best companies on the planet. Our retainer clients who closed back in 2015 and 2016 are still with us, demonstrating our commitment to long-term results.

Even if you have made sacrifices with brand development in the early stages of the business, reinvest a percentage of your revenue into brand development. Unify your messaging, look and feel, public appearance. Invest in more thought leadership and educational content that serves the broader market. Get some of your team members on podcasts or presenting at events. Provide consistent value with consistent messaging and results will follow.

5. Expand Partnerships

Jim Rohn, a motivational speaker, said, "You are the average of the five people you spend the most time with."

If you want to improve your physical health, you need to surround yourself with athletic friends who follow a strict regime, work out several times a week, and cultivate an environment of physical well-being.

If you want to read more, you join a book club with other regular readers.

Similarly, growing in a business environment solo is counterproductive. You want to build stronger bonds with strategic partners who are trying to solve the same problem of brand amplification, cross-selling, and closing larger deals together.

Look into your current partnership network and grow some of the existing ad-hoc connections. Browse your professional email for other conversations you've had with relevant executives and leaders. Find out what agencies, SaaS solutions, and products your clients use often and reach out for a formal partnership.

I have monthly 1:1s with several leaders in my industry, including direct competitors running successful WordPress agencies. With tens of thousands of vendors and hundreds of millions of websites online, there's plenty of room for collaboration, sharing industry insights, and building small circles of partners that help one another.

6. Keep NPS High

Customer satisfaction is the leading health indicator for the solutions your business provides. If clients churn more often than not and you're failing to retain clients long enough, there's an underlying problem you need to solve right away.

In down markets, your current value proposition may not be as strong as it once was. In recessionary times, corporations cut different budgets: non-essential SaaS providers, educational subscriptions that aren't widely used, external vendors that could be put on hold for six months until a better time. Your business may get impacted in the process without a clear indication why.

NPS LIFECYCLE MANAGEMENT

1. GATHERING NPS DATA

Initiate the NPS process by distributing surveys after key customer interactions, such as post-transaction or support tickets.

2. ANALYZING RESPONSES

Compile and analyze NPS responses to categorize customer sentiments and identify common trends.

3. IMPLEMENTING FEEDBACK

Act on the insights gained from NPS feedback to make necessary improvements in products, services, or customer experience.

3. IMPLEMENTING FEEDBACK

Regularly re-evaluate NPS to monitor changes over time, ensuring continuous alignment with customer expectations.

Net promoter score is one of the popular frameworks for assessing customer satisfaction for many businesses. There are various tools that support NPS surveys, including most form builders on the market. You can integrate this in your ticketing system by asking clients to leave reviews after every ticket and keep an eye on this chart. Or email clients every 3-6 months with a set of pointing questions aiming to assess the service quality and areas for improvement.

7. Develop a Strong Pipeline

During my 15+ years of managing businesses, I have faced critical issues with revenue dips that almost tanked the companies I owned for a period of time.

- Our largest client putting their 30-day notice or failing to raise another round and going out of business
- A theme marketplace rejecting two of our products and pushing back new revenue for six months
- Businesses dependent on paid ads getting banned for landing page violations or other ad accounts issues flagged by bots or competitors
- Google Ad Manager getting banned due to bot violations (resulting in no advertising revenue)
- SEO algorithm taking a turn and tanking our key transactional keywords, resulting in no inbound leads for months.

The list is endless and painful, and when it happens, it both dips into any company and personal savings of yours and immediately puts you back on the hamster wheel.

I've seen this hundreds of times both in my agency and as a business advisor for over 400 startups.

Building a strong pipeline of prospective customers through multiple channels is an integral diversification mechanism that can save a seemingly healthy business from going under in a matter of months.

8. Prioritize Diversification

Just like pipeline development is integral, so is diversification for your peace of mind, both within the business and for you as an individual.

When it comes to your startup, keep a close eye on bottlenecks that may harm your biggest source of income.

- If all of your incoming traffic comes from Facebook ads, keep testing TikTok or Instagram ads, native ads, X ads, and other tangible channels.
- If your main revenue is advertising with Google's AdX, bring in more advertising partners and focus on direct partnership deals with brands.
- Consider supplementing with monthly subscriptions, affiliate revenue, and custom services.
- Build multiple sources of revenue and pricing models to mitigate that risk.

On a personal level, you want to avoid your identity being tied to your business. Successful digital CEOs build recurring streams of income to mitigate possible risks for their main business, including:

- Starting parallel businesses
- Acquiring other companies managed as separate entities (separate P&Ls and management processes)
- Investing in the stock market or other companies as a minority shareholder
- Providing high ticket services like consulting, public speaking, training
- Developing a personal brand, including a podcast, video channel, blog (or other mediums that are monetized separately)

- Closing revenue share deals with partners to supplement revenue outside of traditional "time and material" or fixed subscription models.

I am a very, very strong proponent of diversification and cannot stress this one enough.

9. Onboard Advisors

This role may take different shapes and forms depending on your stage and needs. It might include life coaches through business advisors to niche consultants, finance advisors, fractional CFOs.

You've reached a certain point by leveraging your core skills and following the playbooks here, and that's great.

But inevitably, with every step of the process, you hit a new ceiling that requires a new set of skills. Adopting a BPM. Moving to a professional ERP. Incorporating a complex marketing automation platform. Developing thought leadership.

Digital executives wear multiple hats, and gaining expertise in all areas is mandatory, but you can't be a top 1% expert in every single department.

Even though I've been offering advisory services for over a decade, I have two advisors myself I work with and count on:

- Steve Patti, 7X CMO/VP with successful exits who launched a $20M agency with 20 people and has consulted some of the largest enterprises on the planet

- James Schramko, a veteran business mentor formerly running web and marketing agencies, now a full-time coach with a multiple 7-figure income and 7 figures in profit

I am immensely helpful for their support and guidance in the process and their balanced approach between strategic and tactical go-to-market pivots I've had to make and finding recurring, scalable, high margin execution models that fuel the system continuously. If you're looking for similar strategic support, I can absolutely recommend their services as well.

Over time, I've had other mentors, both those I met regularly and thought leaders I studied extensively for months to adopt their mindset and acquire the breadth and wealth of knowledge I deploy for our clients today (and used to author this book).

Having spent 11 years as an ambassador for global organizations myself – and working with these awesome advisors directly – I've outlined the key categories in the space in the following chart:

Brand Ambassador Types

01
BUSINESS ADVISOR

Wearing the consulting hat, external advisor in a specific role: management, ops, martech, legal, M&A. Focus on problem-solving with additional brand visibility.

02
B2B INFLUENCER

The alternative of B2C influencers: thought leaders, creators, keynote speakers, key opinion leaders. Exposure in a niche community.

03
COMMUNITY MANAGER

Advocates, evengelists, community managers working closely within a brand-driven or sponsored community, interacting day-to-day.

04
CHANNEL MANAGER

A creator responsible for launching or managing a specific channel: podcast hosts, TikTok viral experts, Influencer reel professinals, newsletter lead editors.

05
BRAND PARTNER

An independent consultant solopreneur, owner of a small shop running a consultancy/agency with a close channel partnership. Affiliate, referral-based deals, amplified collab promotion.

MARIO PESHEV

mariopeshev.com

10. Never Stop Learning

"Never Stop Learning" happens to be one of the core values of my agency DevriX.

This is deeply embodied in my philosophy and I want to be surrounded by people hungry for knowledge, eager to get better, improve their efficiency and productivity, and not settle for mediocrity.

Imagine a traditional CEO from a traditional industry like construction, healthcare, gas, energy. While they may run eight or nine figure businesses, disruptive startups and smaller organizations keep dipping into their market share by simply deploying better processes, implementing automation, and following some best practices that have been the norm over the past few years.

Once you get comfortable in the spot, close some government or enterprise contracts for years, and have a team in place in an industry with lower churn, this journey may keep going on for a while with limited risk until contract renewals come to mind. But when it does, there are suddenly dozens of other competitors who picked up the slack and gained years of additional experience, providing better solutions at better prices for shorter periods of time.

To avoid becoming a dinosaur in your own field, continuous learning is the safety net against missing the marks. Luckily, our field has been populated with wealths of knowledge available online:

- Podcasts
- Newsletters
- Video channels
- Online courses

- Thought leaders
- Social networks
- Specialized groups in Reddit/Quora/forums
- Professional Slack communities.

The greatest business leaders of our time set aside an hour a day or more for learning. If Bill Gates, Warren Buffett, or Elon Musk can do this, there's no excuse to skip this part of the process in a business that works well and has the potential to grow steadily in the future.

Or even take the exit path. There are multiple options ahead. This is what we'll cover in this last chapter.

CHAPTER TWENTY-ONE

THE EXIT PLAN

After the hardship of building a self-sustainable business venture, the future of the business can take different turns.

Some companies are built to last. Others shape into lifestyle businesses. Founders may run several companies under the same hat, either as completely separate firms or as a network of cross-functional teams isolated in different companies.

And, of course, there are multiple exit paths available.

We'll briefly review the different options once your business reaches a level of scale that makes it an attractive asset to achieving other forms of liquidity.

Considering Acquisition

One of the most common ways for digital businesses to exit is through an acquisition. Receiving an offer from a larger strategic company or an institutional investor to buy your business can be a direct way for you to cash out or move on to a new opportunity.

If this is one of the possible paths on the table, here's what you need to focus on and monitor over the next few months while preparing to speak with possible buyers or M&A advisors.

1. **Financial Performance:** Get your finance reporting in good shape, showing a clear history of generating income, plus clean

P&L breakdowns that make sense to a prospective buyer. Work with your finance team, external financial advisors, and startup and M&A specialists to gauge your current status and how lucrative of a deal it is based on financial metrics alone.

2. **Market Position:** Run a market and competitor analysis in your space and gauge the brand awareness and defensibility of your current business. Other than financial metrics, is your company a great buy? Are there organic channels generating revenue, or is it all about paid ads and cold calling? Have you developed a known and recognizable brand that speaks to consumers? This will play a role in the valuation multiples.

3. **Intellectual Property:** Protect your patents, trademarks, and other intellectual property and ensure these are transferable. Additional layers of exclusivity that slow down competitors add value to your business and make it more attractive to potential buyers. If you haven't taken this route already, work with IP and trademark experts and legal advisors to secure your market position.

4. **Relationships:** Build strong connections with industry peers, potential acquirers, and other key stakeholders. Part of your role as a digital CEO is not just sales and recruitment but making strategic relationships with influencers, journalists, investors, VC funds, high net-worth individuals, and other esteemed entrepreneurs. I have personally had dozens of serious acquisition conversations during industry events or at meetup groups, gathering the right people.

On the buy side, I've made nearly 40 acquisitions myself over the past 15 years - most of them smaller assets integrated into existing businesses, and some standalone small companies merged together.

I've made two high ticket sales for successful companies making six and seven figures in revenue, and the full process often takes months of preparing data rooms, clearing out financial gaps, and streamlining financial performance by optimizing efficiency, due diligence, compiling assets, securing transfers and onboarding of buyers, and other engagements as a part of the process.

As a Flippa ambassador, dozens of buyers and sellers reach out every month looking for a specific type of listing (affiliate site, Shopify store, content network, and mobile app) or requesting an evaluation of their current business. In this dynamic environment, some founders find themselves burned out, unable to push forward, or simply disinterested in adapting their playbooks over and over to the new models of work at the time.

In the meantime, others keep lean business models in place and keep investing in their company.

Building to Last

Many businesses are not built for sale. Generational companies can last for decades, turn into lifetime opportunities to grow a legacy, pass on a family member, or transition the ownership and still secure the future of the business with the core talent on board.

Let's go over the popular options to keep the company operational for the coming years. Creative and hybrid options are also available, including the venture path or private equity or acquisitions under specific terms, but we'll stick to the focus of securing the company's future here.

1. Bootstrapping the 10%

Some founders decide to lock in the current business terms and avoid growth at all costs. Instead, they want to retain the current state of the business, preserving their team, clients, and business model. They avoid pivoting or evolving as much as possible.

This fixed minimum growth model also overlaps with the "lifestyle business" paradigm, which is especially valid with small teams or family-style startups that seek work-life balance, covering the basics without giving in to the grind.

The 10% growth milestone is simply tied to inflation or a fixed annual expenditure of costs and payroll. As long as the 10% growth can be secured and maintained, the business can continue as-is without unnecessary risks or pivots.

2. The Cash Cow

A more aggressive version of the 10% model is squeezing a business for maximum efficiency and focusing on the gain.

The 10% model above works in more traditional businesses or moderate cost, moderate volume or a small number of transactions where the risk of churn is low and the operational overhead isn't excessive either. Cash cows can also perform similarly sometimes, but this model is often volatile and subject to change in a year or two, which is why founders can go with the flow for a while and leverage the gains until the time comes.

Think of unique video products that will be replaced by competitors or upcoming AI features, or content sites/communities running on autopilot but threatened by upcoming SEO updates or Reddit groups, or larger competitors building a similar product. Your users won't be churning soon and a massive pivot will cost a fortune. You can squeeze the gains for the next 12, 18, 24 months and restructure when sustainability is no longer secured.

3. Management Buyout

Another way to transition your digital business is to facilitate a management buyout with key employees or executives purchasing the company. This is a smart workaround to retain your core vision and culture while extracting yourself from operations.

As a founder, you can leverage the profit gains from the first two lasting models, but with some operational overhead (more or less) and limited gains. The buyout model will be an acquisition in its core, but your team is going to be in charge of the business (the people who care the most). Plus, you will receive an actual payout as a lump sum.

4. Succession Planning

This model aims to limit your operational involvement without giving up full ownership or going through a sale. This can take multiple paths:

- A generational business with family members taking on the executive seat
- Hiring a GM or external CEO with a growth structure and equity buy-ins annually
- Promoting a VP or an operations manager to an executive role

- Taking a CEO role with a COO running the day-to-day.

This level of delegation still retains the majority of the ownership stake and controlling votes, but it pulls you out of the daily duties and escalations.

5. Licensing or Franchising

One option applicable to some of the business models is licensing the technology, intellectual property, or brand to other companies for recurring revenue with high margins.

This works in defensible industries with trademarks or IP worth paying a license for, like popular brands that could serve as credibility badges or content powerhouses and other data sources that can be served to infuse other data warehouses or AI models.

Course content and other training resources can be licensed similarly. Service companies or SaaS can offload training to existing knowledge bases or use white labeled sources for onboarding resources or train new staff members internally without having to build and maintain playbooks.

6. Merger

If you want to retain the core business functions and most of the existing team but can't sustain as an individual business, mergers can form a stronger unit.

Effective mergers combine two - or sometimes three - smaller companies together into a unified brand to provide a stronger set of solutions. This could work in the same segment (several agencies, publishing sites or newsletters) or different categories (SaaS merging with a publisher or a service provider).

7. Initial Public Offering (IPO)

Traditional IPOs are slow, expensive, demanding, and controlling, which is why they are rarely applicable to small businesses. Popular stock exchanges place aggressive minimum limits to even consider listing, too (even though they have been getting more flexible to mitigate the reduced number of IPOs after 2021).

In some cases, there are two separate options that may be worth reviewing:

- Going to a small, local exchange. Smaller exchanges are less competitive, pose lower thresholds, and may include additional PR momentum for the business.
- Looking into a SPAC. SPAC is a special purpose acquisition company formed exclusively for capital raising and aiming to acquire and merge one or more companies. This workaround was very popular in the late 2010s, although many deals fell through at the end which questioned the viability of the model. As with anything else, the principles work for the right sustainable businesses.

Whatever path you decide to take, understanding all options and considerations will help you take an educated action based on viable alternatives. As with anything in entrepreneurship, hybrid options and creative structures are always possible, including strategic acquisitions of larger companies with debt, taking on VC funding to hire replacements and pull back, partnering up with private equities and others.

Studying the foundational elements can be the basis of any deal to follow, or they can allow you to stay true to growing and retaining the business yourself.

CONCLUSION

"MBA Disrupted" has been in the making for five years.

After I released my previous book, "126 Steps to Becoming a Successful Entrepreneur," I immediately felt a gap in structuring the right process when meeting early-stage entrepreneurs.

I don't have a former MBA myself. In fact, I'm a college dropout just like millions of startup founders and executives out there.

I started my semi-formal business learning journey in 2008 in the early stages of freelancing: learning the basics of budgeting and forecasting, negotiations, scope creep, project management, product planning, communication methods, lead generation, and content marketing for personal branding.

This led to years of trial and error. Despite my hard skills (professional expertise in the field), I required continuous learning, some freelancing experience on the side, and the lessons from my mother-entrepreneur with her own accounting firm where I picked up P&L management, incorporation lessons, and the core principles of the tax code.

I struggled with imposter syndrome for a decade anytime I had to break down specific principles I had applied in practice. However, whether you've completed an MBA program or not, it's probably true that you have some knowledge gaps that needs to be filled. That was my story.

I went on studying and filling in the gaps. This included:

- Diving into Ogilvy and Seth Godin for marketing principles.

- Buying textbooks from marketing specialties to catch up on the 4Ps, Ansoff's matrix, or PESTLE.
- Completing all HubSpot certificates in the process.
- Taking on Grant Cardone's sales university training programs and a handful of additional courses on cold calling and emailing, sales pitches, rebuttals, follow up, playbooks, and statistics on how to conduct and what the targets are.
- Studying management from management consulting firms and their training programs, annual reports and analyses, and dozens of other leadership and management books.
- Working with CPAs and financial advisors and following a handful of blogs and newsletters from fractional CFOs and investors on core principles and paradigms.

I applied the same ruthless and tedious process in every single vertical, week after week.

I took professional business coaching courses through Mindvalley's program, which consisted of five months of active training and practice.

The expectations to perform and stay on top of my game as an executive were endless. I couldn't just hire juniors and let them figure it out (they can't). I couldn't hire executives who don't want to be operators (and I definitely couldn't afford to hire entire teams for a starting business).

So that self-taught, grueling exercise was a long and painful journey. 15+ years later, I keep learning the ropes in certain disciplines, despite the lessons learned in the process, both in theory and practice.

I never recommend that future entrepreneurs dive right in without any practical business skills. Instead, spend several years mastering some hard skills and developing a competitive edge for your business. I stay true to this mantra.

My goal with "MBA Distributed" is simple: I want to provide a repetitive process I've followed to start, grow, and nurture multiple businesses after dozens of trials and pivots in each of the corresponding categories.

Instead of a case study for a "one overnight success story," I'm distilling the principles of work for hundreds of companies I consult or my agency manages.

This high-level overview of everything from start to finish is what I wish I had myself in 2008 when I felt lost and lacked the structure and organized insights in one place.

While the learning process will never end, and it's an aspiration for every entrepreneur, I hope that this book will help you gain the right amount of core understanding and expertise to start the right way.

More importantly, I welcome you to the book community at mbadisrupted.com, which provides what Ivy Leagues do: a networking group of like minded individuals dealing with the same challenges. They're ambitious future founders taking the hard road.

This combination of practical knowledge plus a practical community will supplement everything you need to get started. This support group I have created is designed to push entrepreneurs forward whenever ideas have merit and founders are willing to go through fire and ice to make that possible.

My continuous educational resources I publish on my blogs, in my weekly newsletters, and on social networks are the third angle you will see popping up as a constant reminder to stay on top and not give up;

the motivational nuggets, the bite-sized pieces of data and know-how, the macro strategic intelligence pointing you in the right direction.

If this book has made any impact on you or anyone around you, don't hesitate to let me know. The power of feedback cannot be understated. Neither is the power of networking, and this could be your very first practical exercise here.

In any case, here's to the next generation of experienced and creative founders, data-driven and knowledge-hungry individuals, and positive leaders eager to make a positive difference in the world and give back to the next generations.

Here's to you.

Regards, and see you online,

Mario Peshev

GLOSSARY

Core Business and Management Education

- **Master of Business Administration (MBA):** An advanced university degree in business management that prepares individuals to lead and manage businesses across various industries.
- **C-suite:** The executive-level managers within a company, typically including positions, such as CEO, CFO, CTO, etc.
- **E-myth:** A concept from Michael E. Gerber's book "The E-myth Revisited," which challenges the assumptions and misunderstandings surrounding starting and running a small business.

Investment and Finance

- **IPO (Initial Public Offering):** The process by which a private company offers its shares to the public for the first time, often to raise capital and enable easier trading of its stock.
- **Return on Investment (ROI):** A financial metric used to evaluate the efficiency of an investment, calculated as the net profit of an investment divided by its costs.
- **Cost of Inaction (COI):** A metric that evaluates the potential losses associated with not taking a particular action, used to weigh the urgency and potential impact of different strategic decisions.
- **Profit & Loss Statements (P&L Statements):** Financial statements that summarize the revenues, costs, and expenses incurred during a specific period of time, usually a fiscal quarter

or year. These are essential for monitoring the financial health of a company and making informed business decisions.

- **COGS (Cost of Goods Sold):** The direct costs attributable to the production of the goods sold by a company. This includes both direct labor costs and the cost of materials used in producing the goods.
- **Operating Expenses (OpEx):** The ongoing expenses required for running a business that are not directly associated with the production of goods or services. This includes rent, utilities, salaries of administrative staff, and marketing costs.

Entrepreneurship and Startups

- **Bootstrapping:** A method of starting a business using personal finances or operating revenues without seeking significant outside investment.
- **EOS (Entrepreneurial Operating System):** A set of simple concepts and practical tools used by businesses to define clear objectives, instill focus, discipline, and accountability throughout the organization.
- **Angel Investors:** Affluent individuals who provide capital for startups, usually in exchange for convertible debt or ownership equity, and often contribute with mentorship and advice.
- **Bootstrap Founder:** An entrepreneur who starts a company with personal finances or the operating revenues of the company itself, without external capital.
- **Minimum Viable Product (MVP):** The simplest version of a product that can be released to test a new business idea and gauge customer interest.

Corporate Structures and Legal

- **Incorporation:** The process of legally defining a company as a separate entity from its owners, providing it with its own legal rights and obligations.

- **Limited Liability Company (LLC):** A flexible business structure that offers the personal liability protection of a corporation with the tax advantages of a partnership.

- **Sole Proprietorship:** A business structure where the business and the owner are legally the same entity, meaning the owner is personally responsible for all liabilities.

- **Legal Entity:** A company or organization that has legal rights and responsibilities, including the ability to enter into contracts, sue, and be sued.

- **Partnership:** A business structure involving two or more people who share ownership, profits, losses, and liabilities.

- **Business Licenses and Permits:** Authorizations required to legally operate a business in specific industries or locations.

- **Data Protection Laws:** Regulations that set the rules for how personal information is processed and protected, such as GDPR in Europe and CCPA in California.

- **Employer Identification Number (EIN):** A unique number assigned by the IRS to businesses operating in the United States for purposes of identification.

- **Articles of Organization:** Legal documents filed with the state to formally establish the existence of a new LLC.

- **Doing Business As (DBA):** A registration by a business under a trading name that differs from its legal, registered name.

- **Tax Identification Numbers:** Numbers assigned by government agencies to track the tax responsibilities of businesses and individuals.
- **Sales Tax Permits:** Licenses required to sell goods and services subject to sales tax within a jurisdiction.

Marketing and Market Research

- **Search Engine Optimization (SEO):** The practice of increasing the quantity and quality of traffic to your website through organic search engine results.
- **Ideal Customer Profile (ICP):** A description of a company or organization that would get the most benefit from using a product or service, representing the perfect customer for a business.
- **Product-Market Fit:** The degree to which a product satisfies strong market demand, often considered essential for a startup's success.
- **Buyer Persona:** A detailed profile of a potential customer based on market research and real data about existing customers, including demographics, behavior patterns, motivations, and goals.
- **USPs (Unique Selling Points):** The factors or considerations presented by a seller as the reason that one product or service is different from and better than that of the competition.
- **Primary Research:** The process of collecting original data directly from sources through methods like surveys, interviews, and focus groups to gain specific insights into a target market.
- **Secondary Research:** The use of existing research and data sources to gather information about a market, which is

cost-effective but may not be as tailored or current as primary research.

- **Exploratory Research:** A type of research focused on exploring a problem or situation that is not well defined, often used to identify potential issues, opportunities, or the focus for more in-depth research.

- **Conclusive Research:** Research used to provide the information needed to confirm insights and which supports decision-making on specific marketing issues.

- **Focus Groups:** A qualitative research method involving guided discussions with a group of people to gather diverse perspectives about a product, service, or concept.

- **Qualitative Market Research:** Research focused on understanding the qualitative aspects of consumer behavior such as motivations, opinions, and reasons behind behaviors, often through methods like interviews or focus groups.

- **Quantitative Market Research:** Research that involves the collection and analysis of numerical data to identify trends, measure variables, and quantify attitudes or behaviors.

- **Social Media Marketing (SMM):** The use of social media platforms to connect with your audience to build your brand, increase sales, and drive website traffic.

- **Brand Ambassador:** A person who is hired by an organization to represent a brand in a positive light, thereby increasing brand awareness and sales.

Technology and Innovation

- **Blockchain:** A system in which a record of transactions made in bitcoin or another cryptocurrency is maintained across several computers that are linked in a peer-to-peer network.

- **Software as a Service (SaaS):** A software distribution model in which applications are hosted by a third-party provider and made available to customers over the internet, typically on a subscription basis.

- **A/B Testing:** A method of comparing two versions of a web page or app against each other to determine which one performs better.

- **Tech Stack:** The combination of technology services used to build and run one single application.

- **ERP (Enterprise Resource Planning):** Business process management software that allows an organization to use a system of integrated applications to manage the business and automate many back-office functions related to technology, services, and human resources.

HR and Organizational Behavior

- **Fixed Mindset:** A psychological term introduced by Carol Dweck, referring to the belief that one's abilities, intelligence, and talents are fixed traits.

- **Growth Mindset:** A psychological term also introduced by Carol Dweck, describing the belief that abilities and intelligence can be developed through dedication, hard work, and resilience.

- **The Great Resignation:** A phenomenon characterized by a significant number of workers voluntarily leaving their jobs, especially noticeable following the COVID-19 pandemic.
- **Standard Operating Procedures (SOPs):** Documented procedures meant to standardize how specific tasks or operations are executed within a company.
- **Business Process Management (BPM):** A discipline involving any combination of modeling, automation, execution, control, measurement, and optimization of business activity flows, in support of enterprise goals, spanning systems, employees, customers, and partners within and beyond the enterprise boundaries.

Business Strategy and Development

- **Mergers and Acquisitions (M&A):** The area of corporate strategy, corporate finance, and management dealing with the buying, selling, dividing, and combining of different companies that can help an enterprise grow rapidly in its sector or location of origin, or a new field or new location, without creating a subsidiary, other child entity or using a joint venture.
- **Management Buyout (MBO):** A form of acquisition where a company's existing managers acquire a large part or all of the company from either the parent company or from the private owners.
- **Go-To-Market (GTM) Strategy:** The action plan that specifies how a company will reach target customers and achieve competitive advantage. It includes all aspects of introducing the product to the market, from marketing and distribution to pricing and customer support.

- **Key Performance Indicators (KPIs):** A set of quantifiable measurements used to gauge a company's overall long-term performance.
- **Objectives and Key Results (OKRs):** A framework for setting goals in business by establishing clearly defined objectives and measurable key results that aim to achieve strategic outcomes.
- **Net Promoter Score (NPS):** A management tool used to gauge the loyalty of a firm's customer relationships. It serves as an alternative to traditional customer satisfaction research.
- **Total Addressable Market (TAM):** The total market demand for a product or service, calculated as the entire revenue opportunity available for a product or service if 100% market share was achieved.
- **Business Model Canvas:** A strategic management tool that provides a graphical representation of various elements of a business model, helping companies to visualize, design, and reinvent their business strategies.

Market Dynamics and Trends

- **Fortune 500:** An annual list compiled and published by Fortune magazine that ranks 500 of the largest United States corporations by total revenue for their respective fiscal years.
- **Liquidation:** The process of winding up a company's financial affairs by selling off assets to pay creditors and distribute any remaining assets to shareholders.
- **Metaverse:** A collective virtual shared space, created by the convergence of virtually enhanced physical and digital reality.

Product Development and Customer Interaction

- **Affiliate Marketing:** A performance-based marketing strategy where a business rewards one or more affiliates for each visitor or customer brought by the affiliate's own marketing efforts.
- **Dropshipping:** An e-commerce fulfillment method where a store doesn't keep the products it sells in stock but instead purchases the item from a third party and has it shipped directly to the customer.
- **Freemium Model:** A pricing strategy where a product or service is provided free of charge, but money is charged for additional features, services, or virtual goods.
- **CRM Systems (Customer Relationship Management):** Technology for managing all your company's relationships and interactions with customers and potential customers.

Communication and Collaboration Platforms

- **Slack:** A communication platform that allows for the creation of private and public channels for community interaction, ideal for real-time communication and integration with various tools.
- **Discord:** Originally popular with gamers, this platform supports extensive community engagement through text, voice, and video chats, and customizable roles within communities.
- **Skool:** A community platform focused on collaborative learning, enabling users to create groups, host live sessions, and engage in topic-based discussions.

- **Circle:** A versatile community platform that supports creating spaces for discussions, integrating with other tools, and managing memberships.

Research and Development

- **Firmographics:** Business demographic information, such as industry, company size, and revenue, which can be used to segment markets.
- **1:1 Sourcing:** Direct engagement with individuals who interact with content to gain detailed insights into their preferences and perceptions, enhancing content relevance and engagement.

Miscellaneous

- **Ikigai:** A Japanese concept meaning "a reason for being," which helps individuals find personal satisfaction and meaning in life through a balance of their passions, skills, societal needs, and economic opportunities.
- **Thought Leadership:** Content that taps into the talent, experience, and passion inside your business, or your community, to answer the biggest questions on the minds of your target audience on particular topics.

www.ingramcontent.com/pod-product-compliance
Lightning Source LLC
Chambersburg PA
CBHW041207220326
41597CB00030BA/5072